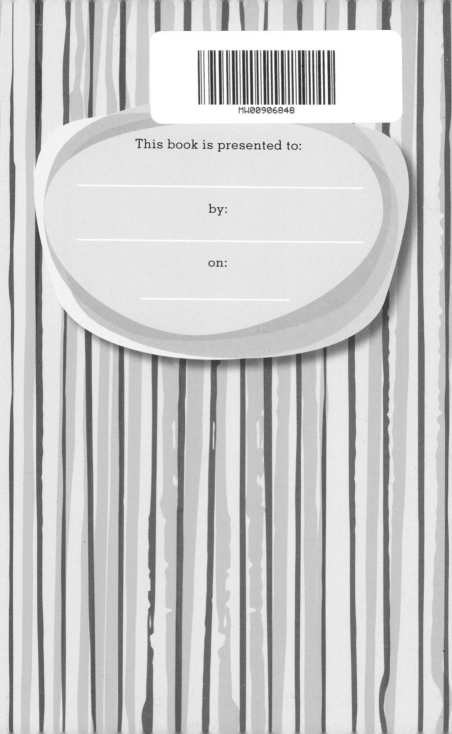

MW00906848

This book is presented to:

_____

by:

_____

on:

_____

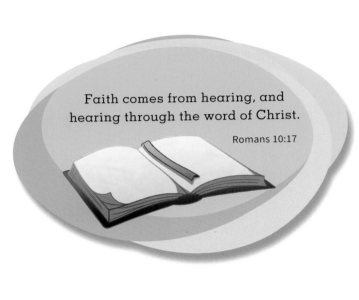

Faith comes from hearing, and hearing through the word of Christ.

Romans 10:17

Portals of Prayer for Kids

DAILY DEVOTIONS

Läna Schurb, Editor ✱ Jeremy Provost, Illustrator

CONCORDIA PUBLISHING HOUSE • SAINT LOUIS

Dear Parent,

Today's busy families are pressed to make time in their lives for all the necessary activities, let alone time for devotions and prayer together. Yet the practice of regular devotion time is an excellent way to strengthen the family bond and to lead children to Christ.

As the child's first faith teachers, parents are tasked with teaching faith principles, laying a foundation for faith, and instilling the habit of dedicated time in the study of God's Word and in prayer. This collection of devotions is offered as an easy-to-use resource families can utilize to achieve that task. It was written by pastors, teachers, parents, and others who call on their own experience and education to aid parents in involving their children, sparking conversation, and sowing seeds of faith.

May all who use it grow stronger in their faith and be blessed as the Holy Spirit works through these words.

To God be the glory.

Copyright © 2017 Concordia Publishing House

3558 S. Jefferson Avenue, St. Louis, MO 63118-3968

1-800-325-3040 • cph.org

Versions of these devotions originally appeared in various volumes of the magazine My Devotions.

Manufactured in Penang, Malaysia/055760/416399

2 3 4 5 6 7 8 9 10 11   31 30 29 28 27 26 25 24 23 22

All Aboard!

Today begins a new journey. Once again, the earth will travel around the sun. Since we live on the earth, we'll be going along. Are you ready? It's a long journey, but we'll be traveling at a good rate of speed. We'll be moving 365 days, 24 hours a day. The trip will take 8,760 hours.

Who knows what will occur in the weeks ahead? We don't know what might happen to our families or friends. Whatever happens, there is no need for God's children to worry.

Today's Bible verse praises the Lord, saying, "Your eyes saw my unformed substance; in Your book were written, every one of them, the days that were formed for me, when as yet there was none of them" (v. 16). Before you were born, your heavenly Father knew exactly what you would experience every day of your life.

We have an all-powerful and all-knowing God. We also have a loving God, who sent His Son to die for our sins. He can take care of big problems like sin, death, and the devil. He can also take care of all our little problems. One day, He will care for us in His absolutely perfect heavenly home.

As you begin this new year, remember that the God who created the universe and knew you before you were formed will be with you each day. He will be your God during each test, practice, and doctor visit, during time with friends and family, and in every hour of the new year.

Journal: List three examples of God's love and care that you have already experienced on the first day of this new year's journey.

Pray: Father, I thank You for giving me a new year to serve in Your kingdom. Help me to trust Your guidance through each day of the journey. In the name of Jesus I pray. Amen. H. W.

Made with Love

I have a blue blanket that's really important to me. It's made of simple cotton fabric. It's getting old, and there are a couple of tears in it and it is getting thin. But a little tag in one corner makes it valuable. The tag says: "Made with love by Grandma."

The blanket's value for me doesn't come from its fabric, color, or age. Instead, the blanket is valuable to me because my grandma made it. She has made a blanket like this for each of her twenty-three grandchildren. And because Grandma made it, it's precious to me.

Psalm 139 says that you were knitted together (v. 13) by God in your mother's womb. God created you carefully and beautifully, the same way my grandma sewed my blanket. And God is a master craftsman. So the psalm writer says you are "wonderfully made" (v. 14).

Sometimes, I don't feel valuable. Sometimes, I feel like I can never be smart enough or talented enough or good enough. Do you ever feel like that?

The next time you don't feel worth very much, remember that you are "Made with love by God." In fact, you are so precious to God that He sent Jesus to save you when you were lost to sin and death. My blanket is precious because my grandma made it. Think about how much more precious you are because God Himself made you. Wonderful are His works indeed!

Journal: Draw a tag that says "Made with love by God." Remember that a tag like this could be attached to you!

Pray: Dear God, thank You for making me. Help me remember that anything You make is wonderful. When I feel worthless, remind me that I have great value because I am Yours. Amen. E. B.

Oops! It Slipped Out Again!

Your best friend tells you the big news, and it slips out. You find out Mr. Hartman, the "drill sergeant," is going to be your gym teacher, and it slips out. Your little sister colored all over your new book, and it slips out.

On TV, in the movies, on the radio, it is repeated. It's such a common expression that there's even an abbreviation for it: OMG! Are these words a harmless exclamation or something more serious?

The Second Commandment says, "You shall not misuse the name of the Lord your God." In the Small Catechism, Luther writes that this commandment teaches us to call upon God's name "in every trouble, pray, praise, and give thanks."

God's name is holy, and His holy name should be honored among us. In Old Testament times, God's people refused to utter God's name for fear of misusing it.

Today, we often throw God's name around without giving it a second thought. In so doing, we misuse the precious name of our loving Creator, Savior, and Comforter.

God *wants* us to use His name rightly. He's a Father longing for His children to come to Him in our need. So God's name should be on our tongues often—in prayer, in trouble, in praise, in thanks.

God forgives sinners. Christ's death on the cross paid for all of our sins, including sins against God's name. As God's love richly dwells in us, words sprinkled with grace will come from us too.

Journal: Think up some new expressions or exclamations that do not misuse God's name, but rather are as unique and original as you are. A fun one might be "Jumpin' monkeys!"

Pray: Dear God, Your name is holy. Guide me to call on You in every situation. Forgive my thoughtless and sinful use of Your name. Instead, lead me to use it in ways that honor You. Amen. J. S.

Time to Pray

Shelby stumbled into the house. Just inside the door she dropped her book bag, her sports bag, her clarinet, and herself.

"You look loaded down," her mom noticed.

"Volleyball practice ran late because we have a tournament on Saturday. My science project is due Friday, and my original story is due Thursday. My social studies test is Wednesday, and I have a whole page of math homework for tomorrow," Shelby complained.

"That's a lot," Mom sympathized.

"And," Shelby continued, "my band concert is Sunday, and Kelsey's birthday party is after the tournament on Saturday."

"Wow," said Mom, "sounds as if you need some quiet time."

"I don't have time for quiet time," Shelby moaned.

"The Bible shows us that whenever Jesus had a difficult job facing Him, He first went to a quiet place to pray."

"Really?"

"Yes. He prayed before choosing the twelve disciples. He prayed before feeding the five thousand. He prayed in the Garden of Gethsemane before He was arrested and crucified. The Bible tells us to pray too."

"Then I'm going to pray too," said Shelby.

God commands and invites believers in Jesus Christ to pray. He promises to hear our prayers. You may pray for your own welfare and also for your neighbors' welfare. You can also praise and thank God for who He is and what He has done. So, fold your hands. Bow your head. He's listening.

Journal: Luke mentions prayer often in his Gospel. Look up these verses and write when or where Jesus prayed: 3:21–22; 6:12–16; 9:28–29; 22:40–42.

Pray: Dear Jesus, sometimes there's just too much to do. Thank You for showing me how to commit my tasks to prayer. Thank You for the peace that is mine because of Your death and resurrection for me. Amen. V. S.

He Is for All

The Bible tells us that there was nothing special about Jesus' appearance (Isaiah 53:2). So when He was young, He probably looked like other infants—no surprise there. But something made Him unique, something surprising and startling. Early in His life, He had some amazing visitors who were led to Him by a bright star.

Matthew records this visit of the Wise Men. The account begins with the word *behold,* which grabs our attention. As we read the story, we behold the events. A bright star shone above the house where Jesus and His mother were staying! A toddler was called the King of the Jews! Travelers from the East fell down in worship before Him. They offered this Child gifts of gold, frankincense, and myrrh.

In the Old Testament, God chose one people, the children of Israel, to receive His covenant. They were the *only* ones who could enter the inner courts of the temple and worship God. The Gentiles were outsiders. But when the Wise Men, who were Gentiles, came to worship Jesus, God showed that all people have access to Him because Jesus is God in the flesh.

Behold! Tomorrow, Epiphany, we celebrate that Jesus is the promised Savior for all. This little boy we read about in Matthew 2 has come to be one of us, to bear our sin. God has revealed this to us. Seeing this child as our Savior is an "aha" moment, an epiphany, for us. We, too, bow down and worship Him.

Journal: Draw a star in your journal. Tell how God has led you to know that Jesus is your Savior from sin, death, and the devil.

Pray: Heavenly Father, there are so many wrong ideas in this world about how a person can be saved. Thank You for guiding me to believe that Jesus is Your Son and my Savior. In His name I pray. Amen. H. W.

JANUARY 6

Isaiah 60:1–6

Happy Epiphany

Epiphany is the day we remember that God led the Wise Men to see Jesus. You know the story of how they traveled many miles, stopped off to chat with King Herod and *his* wise men, and then continued to follow the star to the young Savior and King. When they saw Jesus, they honored Him with expensive gifts of gold, frankincense, and myrrh.

Even if you forgot about Epiphany until you read this devotion, you can still do what God says in today's Bible reading. You can "arise" and "shine"—even if you don't feel like it—because the glory of the Lord is also shining on you. Even though you are a sinner, you have good reason to rejoice: Jesus is your Savior!

Who led you to Jesus? Perhaps your parents wanted you to be baptized. Maybe you first heard about Jesus from a teacher at Vacation Bible School or Sunday School. Thank God for that person. But to really see who Jesus is, the Holy Spirit gets involved. He works through God's Word and Sacraments. He shines on Jesus, pointing out that He is God's Son, our Lord and Savior.

Yes, when the Wise Men went home, they were different. They had survived a dangerous mission in foreign lands. They had knelt down before the King of all people. What a story to tell!

God's people continue to spread the Good News that Jesus is the Savior of all people. So, arise! Shine! Happy Epiphany!

Journal: Draw a "Happy Epiphany" card, and show it to a friend.

Pray: Thank You, dear God, for leading me to Jesus in Baptism. As I journey through life, give me ways to show love to others and tell them that Jesus was born to be their Savior King. In His name I pray. Amen. E. G.

A Refuge

After the flood in the aftermath of Hurricane Katrina in 2005, thousands of people left New Orleans, Louisiana. They had no fresh water, food, or electricity. So they left. They became refugees.

A refugee is someone who has to flee in search of refuge. Sometimes, refugees leave their homes because of war. Sometimes, it's because of a natural disaster.

Churches, relief groups, and government agencies in the surrounding area hosted these people. They gave these refugees places to stay as well as food, water, and medicine.

Jesus was a refugee. Sometime after Jesus' birth, King Herod heard from the Wise Men that Jesus would be a future King. King Herod didn't like the sound of that, so he tried to kill Jesus. Miraculously, an angel came to Joseph in a dream and told Joseph to flee with Mary and Jesus.

And flee they did. Mary, Joseph, and Jesus traveled from Bethlehem to Egypt. Scripture does not reveal much about this period in Jesus' life. We simply know that He was safe there, away from Herod.

Victims of the flood in New Orleans found one kind of refuge in Louisiana, Texas, and other places all across the country. We might hope that they also found another kind of refuge—one from sin's flood, death's waters, and the devil's destruction.

God is our refuge from evil. In His name, we have been baptized. By His power, we are forgiven. In Him, we are safe in life or death, even in hurricanes.

Journal: Describe a time in your life when you were traveling away from home or when you were a refugee. How can God's presence in His Word reassure us?

Pray: Lord, thank You for the many blessings in my life. Thank You for being my refuge. Please help me to reach out to others in their need. In Jesus' name I pray. Amen. J. S.

JANUARY 8

2 Peter 1:19–21

The Prophetic Word

The weather forecasters started talking about snow. As the days went on, the predictions got stronger and people began to prepare. Everyone stocked up on bread and milk. They bought snow shovels and ice melt. Kids were thinking about snow forts and snowmen, while grown-ups were thinking about batteries and flashlights.

Finally, the blizzard arrived. The storm began very early that Sunday morning. By the time the snow finally stopped a few days later, there were more than twenty-six inches on the ground! What a blessing those weather forecasters were! Without them, people would not have been prepared.

Many years before Jesus was born, prophets declared that the Messiah was coming. Micah forecast that He would be born in Bethlehem. Isaiah prophesied that Jesus would be born of a virgin and be called Immanuel. Samuel announced that the Savior would come from the house of David. Hosea wrote that the Christ Child would spend time in Egypt.

With all of those forecasts, everyone should have been prepared to recognize Jesus as the Savior, but that wasn't true. As Isaiah also prophesied, many people rejected Him. How sad! But for Christians, the words of the prophets and the words of Jesus Himself are a true blessing, for in those words, we have eternal life! Thanks be to God!

Journal: Isaiah wrote more about the coming Messiah than any other prophet. Write one of his prophecies in your journal.

Pray: Lord, thank You for Your words of eternal life. Amen. N. D.

How Long Is Forever?

Peter's mother had a flat tire on the way to pick him up from basketball practice. When she finally pulled into the parking lot, Peter asked, "Where have you been? I've been waiting here forever."

Jasmine and Rachel have been in the same class at school for six years. They both play basketball, play the flute, and like to read. Under her picture in Rachel's yearbook, Jasmine wrote, "Best Friends Forever!"

For his birthday, Ryan received a new watch. A note on the packaging read, "Powered by Super Life—guaranteed to run forever without replacing the battery."

Avery's dad got married again. His dad and new stepmom promised to love each other until death parted them. Is that love forever?

Exactly how long is forever? Ten years? A hundred years? Forever is without end. That's a long time. No one can make a promise that will last forever. Right?

God can! In Psalm 136, what does the psalmist say will last forever? Right, God's love. We know that God loves us because He sent His only Son to die for us. In addition to loving us right now, God promises that He will always love us.

He will love us longer than Jasmine and Rachel will be friends. He will love us longer than Avery's dad will love his bride. He will love us longer than the life of Ryan's watch battery. The love He poured out for us on the cross will continue even after we leave this life. His love endures forever!

Journal: How has God shown His love to you through His Son? How does God show His love to you through other people?

Pray: Lord God, thank You for creating me and loving me. Give me faith to trust in You all the days of my life. In Jesus' name I pray. Amen. S. S.

Dressed Right

Philip liked to play in the snow. But when he was invited to go skiing with Blake, he was worried. He had no skis or proper clothing.

"No problem," said Blake's father. "We have skis and clothes you can borrow."

Philip got a head-to-toe outfit with wrist and ankle wraps. These wraps went over the tops of the gloves and boots. Now Philip could fall down in the snow and stay dry. Because he stayed dry, he stayed warm. It didn't matter that he fell down often. He had fun because his clothing protected him.

Just as Philip's ski clothing protected him in the snow, spiritual armor protects us in our spiritual life. If we don't dress properly, temptations get to us and we give in. We sin.

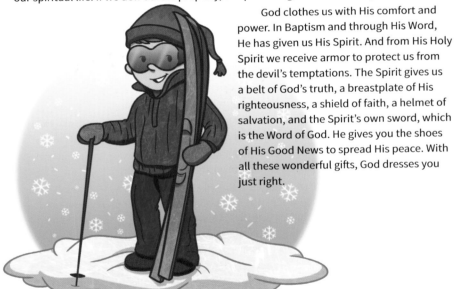

God clothes us with His comfort and power. In Baptism and through His Word, He has given us His Spirit. And from His Holy Spirit we receive armor to protect us from the devil's temptations. The Spirit gives us a belt of God's truth, a breastplate of His righteousness, a shield of faith, a helmet of salvation, and the Spirit's own sword, which is the Word of God. He gives you the shoes of His Good News to spread His peace. With all these wonderful gifts, God dresses you just right.

Journal: Draw and label a few pieces of God's armor.

Pray: Dear God, thank You for the armor Your Spirit gives to me to fight against the temptations of the devil. In Jesus' name I pray. Amen. P. L.

Lots of Love

"What's for dinner?" Mario asked his mother.

"Tamales."

"Yes!" Mario called out as he punched his fist in the air. "They're my favorite. I love tamales!"

His sister, Patti, asked, "Mario, do you really love tamales?"

"Yep," Mario answered, "I sure do."

Patti giggled. "Then why don't you marry them?"

Have you ever heard that joke? It's silly to think that someone would love food enough to marry it!

We use the word *love* in many ways. There's the love you have for your parents and siblings. There's the love your mother and father have for each other. And sometimes, like Mario, we say we love something when we just mean that we like it very much.

When you love someone, you put his or her interests in front of your own. You respect the other person's wishes. It's easy to love someone who loves you, but it is not so easy to love those who don't love you.

God did that hard thing. He loved us while we were yet sinners. He showed us that love in an important way, "that God sent His only Son into the world, so that we might live through Him" (v. 9). He sent Jesus to be our Savior.

Each day, in the little things we do, we have opportunities to show love to one another. We can never love perfectly as God does, so He sends us His Holy Spirit. With His help, we have lots of love to share with others!

Journal: What are some ways God has shown His love to you today?

Pray: Dear Father, thank You for the love You've shown me. May Your love shine through me today. Amen. J. A.

JANUARY 12

Ephesians 4:32

Everyone Smells

Even before you were born, bacteria could have been on your body. Then, each person who touches you—from your parents to your doctor to the kid who bumped into you yesterday—adds a little bit more bacteria. This bacteria stays with us for the rest of our lives, giving each of us our own special smell.

Similarly, from the moment we are baptized or hear the Word of God, our faith is being shaped by the people in our lives. Some of us have parents who take us to church. Others have teachers who lead us in daily devotions. Many have loving friends. The Holy Spirit touches our lives through the Christian people who surround us as they share God's Word, strengthening our faith in unique and life-changing ways.

What about someone who is bullied? What about somebody who doesn't have any friends? Or what if someone is surrounded by people who aren't looking to Jesus?

Jesus loves and offers to hear people who have felt pain and rejection, who have been struck by disappointment and hatefulness. The Holy Spirit uses us to embrace those who are hurting. God has placed people such as our parents, grandparents, godparents, teachers, and friends in our lives to remind us of the forgiveness we have because of Jesus' death and resurrection. We have the opportunity to share that forgiveness with those who don't know Him. *That* touch is one that will certainly stay with them (and *you)* for the rest of their lives.

Journal: Who are some people in your life who encourage and forgive you?

Pray: Dear Lord, thank You for those who encourage me in my faith. Strengthen me to tell others about Your saving love. Amen. L. E.

Wake Up!

How do you wake up in the morning?

A. An alarm clock rings.

B. Someone calls your name.

C. Someone calls your name many times.

D. Someone flips on the light in your room.

Different people wake up different ways. Some of us just need a quick buzz of the alarm clock, while others may need a combination of things from the list above!

Today's Bible passage tells us to arise, or to get up. It is a call for people to pay attention to God's Word and to hear His promises for them. It is a reminder that God's promises are for all nations.

Many people across the world have never heard God's wake-up call. They live under the weight of their sin each day. They do not yet know Jesus' forgiveness.

Our churches have missionaries across the globe working in many ways to share the love of Jesus. They translate the Bible into new languages and train new Christians to set up congregations of their own.

Epiphany is a time when we especially remember Christ coming to save all nations. Use the prayer guide below. Each day, choose a continent. Pray for the people of that continent. Pray that more and more people will be able to wake up each morning knowing that Jesus is their Savior too.

Journal: Write a day of the week next to each continent.

Africa _____

Asia _____

Australia_____

Europe _____

North America _____

South America_____

Pray: Pray that God's Word will be clearly spoken by our missionaries. Use the seventh day of the week to pray for the missionaries themselves. Ask God to make them strong and wise. L. H.

Light!

"Mommy! I'm scared!" cried Alexis.

Mom came in and turned on the lamp by Alexis's bed. "We can leave the lamp on while you sleep, if you like," she said soothingly.

"Okay. The dark scares me," said Alexis.

"Then we'll leave the light on while you sleep. And remember, you can always have the light with you, no matter what."

"What do you mean?" Alexis asked, puzzled.

"Well, it always helps me in the dark to remember Jesus," Mom said. "Jesus tells us 'I am the light of the world. Whoever follows Me will not walk in darkness, but will have the light of life' (John 8:12). That's the very best light. Jesus promises to shine in our hearts to overcome darkness, even the darkness that comes from Satan. Do you remember what Jesus did so we could have His light in our hearts?"

"Yes, my Sunday School teacher told us how Jesus was born. Then He died on the cross for our sins and rose on Easter."

"That's right. Now you can sleep peacefully, knowing Jesus is with you, and His light will defeat all darkness."

"Does everyone know about the light of Jesus?" Alexis asked.

"No, they don't. That's why Jesus turns us into light bulbs."

"What?"

Mom replied, "Jesus tells us, 'You are the light of the world' (Matthew 5:14). Jesus wants us to let our light shine so others can know about the love, joy, and peace He brings to our lives."

"I get it. Like the song says, 'This little light of mine, I'm going to let it shine.' "

Journal: How do you let the light of Jesus shine in your life?

Pray: Dear Jesus, thank You for being the light of my life and showing me the way to heaven. Help my light shine so others can see You in my life. Amen. P. L.

Jude's Safety Plan

Do you have a safety plan in case a fire breaks out in your house? Do you know what to do if bad weather blows your way? What would you do if a stranger invited you into his car?

Safety plans are important! Do you have a safety plan for when your faith in Jesus is attacked by others? Today's Bible verses from Jude give you a three-part plan.

Part 1: Build up your faith. But how? The Holy Spirit brought faith into your soul. You believe that Jesus is your Savior. But a time might come when you have trouble believing this. Your safety plan will help you. The best way to implement part 1 is to read the Bible. Read it now, read it when you're in high school, and read it all of your life.

Part 2: Pray. Talk to Jesus every day. He listens. He knows your challenges. He knows what you need. Thank Him for loving you, for taking away your sins. Ask the Holy Spirit to protect your faith.

Part 3: Remember God's love. The devil and your own sinfulness will tempt you to forget how much God loves you. Jude's safety plan will remind you that you belong to God. You belong to Him forever.

As God keeps you strong, you help others with Jude's safety plan. How do you do that? You are kind, good, and forgiving. You show others what Jesus did for you.

Journal: Draw a three-panel cartoon that shows Jude's safety plan.

Pray: Heavenly Father, I need Your help. Keep me safe from the devil and my own temptation, so that I'm always faithful to You. In Jesus' name I pray. Amen. E. G.

Whom Did God Pick?

God's people, Israel, needed a new king. God sent the prophet Samuel to find a new king from among Jesse's sons. Whom should he pick? Someone strong? handsome? old enough? Jesse's oldest son was tall and strong. Samuel thought, *This must be the one.*

But God often picks people that you or I wouldn't pick. God told Samuel, "He's not the one. Man looks at outward appearance, but the Lord looks on the heart."

Jesse's seven older, stronger sons passed by Samuel, yet the Lord didn't choose any of them. Instead, God picked David, the youngest, smallest son in that family, and he became Israel's greatest king.

But David was sinful; he failed too. So God picked another king. Once again, He chose someone unexpected. This king came from a small town in the middle of nowhere, from a poor family. No one knew who He was. But you do. It was Jesus!

Even though God picked Jesus to be our King, sinful people rejected Him. Because they didn't want Him to be King, they killed Him. But He was the right King, and God raised Him from the dead. Jesus is alive, and He is still the King.

Even today, many people do not believe in Jesus. They don't trust Him as their Savior and King. But because God picked Jesus to be our loving King, we know He's the only true King—now and always.

Journal: Think about whom God chose—Jesus. Draw a crown in your journal to remind you of your eternal King.

Pray: Father, thank You for choosing Jesus to be my King so I can live with You forever. Amen. R. G.

Surprise! God Picked You!

Who is "popular" in your class or neighborhood? What makes someone popular? Does it depend on appearance, grades, or being good at sports? Do we look at cool stuff like electronics or new clothes? Because we are sinful, we think someone is important because of outward things like this. The prophet Samuel made the same mistake when picking a king.

Fortunately, God sees people differently! Jesus says, "I pick you! I baptize you! You are Mine." He chooses us! But why? Is it because of something we've done? No way! It doesn't depend on our being cool or smart. We may seem good on the outside, but inside all of us are dark and sinful. We certainly don't deserve to be picked by God.

Thank God for Jesus! Jesus makes us important, even though we're not the most popular or the prettiest. He makes us Christians, and that's the most important thing in the world.

When we look at people, we can see them the way God does—through Jesus. It doesn't matter how they look on the outside or how they act. Maybe you know some folks who get picked on instead of being picked. What can we do? We can be friends with them. We can help people or even defend them when others aren't so nice to them. We can pick them and love them, just as God picked us and loved us.

Journal: Try to think about people the way God does. Who will you pick or be kind to the next time?

Pray: Father, thank You for picking me to be Your child. Help me to see other people as You do and to love them as You do. Amen. R. G.

What Peter Confessed

Today we celebrate what Peter, one of Jesus' twelve apostles, confessed and believed. Jesus asked His disciples, "Who do people say that I am?"

You might wonder why Jesus even asked. Didn't He know what people were saying about Him? Of course! Jesus knows everything, so why ask? It could be that Jesus wanted Peter to give a confession. He wanted Peter to say with his mouth what he believed in his heart.

In church, we use our ears. We listen to Bible readings and to the sermon. We listen to prayers and pray along. During the confession of the Creed, we use our mouths. It is our opportunity to say, "Yes, I believe this."

Who do you say God is? God is the Father Almighty, maker of heaven and earth. Jesus is His only Son, our Lord. The Holy Spirit is the Lord and giver of life, who proceeds from the Father and the Son. The Holy Spirit puts these words on your lips and in your heart. He creates the faith in you to believe in God.

During the church service, we make another confession. We acknowledge that we have sinned and that we need God's forgiveness, which He freely grants to us in His Son, Jesus Christ. What we believe about God changes how we view ourselves. We know we are sinners and in need of God's love, so we confess our sins and gladly receive God's forgiveness. Knowing we have received so much from God, we freely give to others.

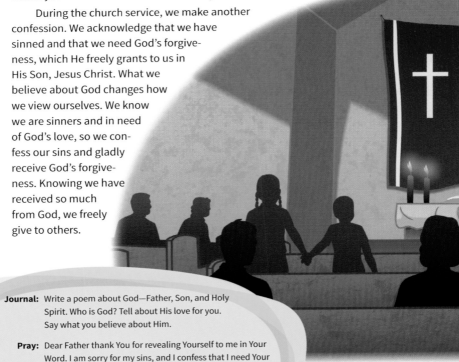

Journal: Write a poem about God—Father, Son, and Holy Spirit. Who is God? Tell about His love for you. Say what you believe about Him.

Pray: Dear Father thank You for revealing Yourself to me in Your Word. I am sorry for my sins, and I confess that I need Your forgiveness. Thank You for giving me faith in You. Help me always to trust in You to bring me to everlasting life. Through Jesus Christ I pray. Amen. J. S.

The Truth

Mr. Turner's Sunday School class was on a search for truth. How long did each day of creation last? Nyadach thought maybe each day of creation had lasted millions of years. Jeremy thought that maybe each day of creation lasted just long enough for God to say the words, "Let there be . . ." Brayden didn't know what to think.

Mr. Turner's class knew where to turn. They reread Genesis 1. Over and over again, the chapter says, "There was evening and there was morning, the first (second, third . . .) day." Mr. Turner explained that the Hebrew word for "day" in Genesis 1 means a twenty-four-hour day. Each day of creation was just like our days today.

How thankful we are that God has given us the Holy Bible! God's Word has the answers we need. As today's reading says, it makes us "wise unto salvation through faith in Christ Jesus" (v. 15). Does it matter whether we believe each day of creation was twenty-four hours or millions of years or a blink of an eye? Yes, because *all* of God's Word is truth. Genesis 1 is truth. John 3:16 is truth. Jesus is the truth. And the truth says that God has loved His people from the very beginning—from the first day of creation—and He will continue to love us throughout eternity.

Journal: Copy John 3:16 into your journal.

Pray: Dear Lord, thank You that Your Word is truth. Help me trust Your Word. In Jesus' name I pray. Amen. S. S.

How Do You Know?

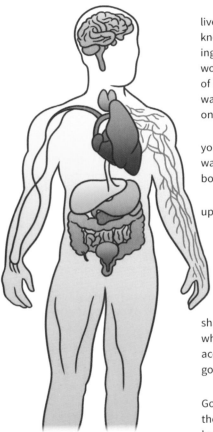

You breathe. You eat. You sleep. That is how you live. It doesn't sound hard. It sounds boring, but you know better. What happens while you're breathing, eating, and even sleeping is exciting. You are one of God's wonders! Just think: inside that skin of yours are miles of blood vessels, zillions of cells, muscles stretching this way and that, and nerves firing electrical messages to one another. Is all this really true? How do you know?

Scientists have proved many things about how your body works. You can't see your body working this way, but you believe scientists who have studied the body.

Doctors have never seen a soul. It doesn't show up on x-rays or scans, but the Bible says we each have one. God gave them to us. He knows they are inside of us. We also have the gift of faith in Jesus. It is a precious gift from God. Jesus paid for this gift with His life on the cross. The Holy Spirit placed faith inside you. He makes it work.

Today's Bible verses tell us that "the righteous shall live by faith" (v. 17). Righteous people are those who know they are right with God—they are people God accepts into His family. Righteous people know that good news because Jesus told them.

Righteous people know they once were wrong—God couldn't accept them into His family because of their sins. Good thing Jesus took our sins away! We know that because Jesus told us.

Journal: List some of the things that faithful people might do to show thankfulness for their faith.

Pray: Dear God, thank You for giving me faith to know that Jesus is my Savior. Amen. E. G.

Out of Control!

It was a bright wintry day, a perfect day for taking a ride in the country. Mr. and Mrs. Miller were enjoying the scenery when Mrs. Miller said, "Oh, look at the beautiful deer!"

The very next second, the car lurched and left the road. Mr. Miller shouted, "Hang on!"

Mrs. Miller's injuries were minor, but Mr. Miller was seriously injured with a broken back. They had gone from a great country ride to what looked like a battlefield. They were very scared and prayed to God for help.

God was already helping even before they prayed. An emergency room nurse driving by saw the crash and immediately knew what to do. Six men who'd been hunting came running over, and one was a paramedic. Another man called for an ambulance on his cell phone. God saw the Millers on that lonely country road and sent people to help.

Mr. Miller had surgery and went through months of pain and rehabilitation. All that time, God was always with him—loving, caring, and comforting.

God is never out of control. He made the world and everything in it. God loves and cares for this world. God loves us so much that He sent His Son, Jesus, to take away the sins of all people. Every day, He richly blesses us with mercy and grace. When we die, we will go to heaven to live forever with the Lord.

It's wonderful to know that God is always in control no matter what!

Journal: Think of times when you were scared or worried. How did God help you? How did you know God was in control?

Pray: God, thank You for always being in control. Help us not to worry but always to trust in Your love and care. Amen. J. D.

JANUARY 22

Matthew 5:13–16

Make a Difference

Salt is such a common thing, and we probably don't think much about it. We might notice if there is too much salt or not enough salt in our food. Otherwise, we pretty much ignore it.

No one knows who first discovered that salt could preserve food. But using salt to preserve fish and meat was already widespread in ancient times. Salt was even used as money in ancient Ethiopia and China. Roman soldiers were given a ration of salt as part of their pay.

During the time Jesus lived on earth, salt was valuable. In Matthew 5:13, Jesus tells His followers and us, "You are the salt of the earth." Jesus was saying that we are important and valuable.

Salt makes a difference in the food it seasons. It makes food taste better or keeps it from spoiling. Like salt, we can make a difference too. We can make a difference in the lives of the people around us. The way we serve and talk sprinkles God's love—in a good way.

We can tell others of God's love and care. And we can spread the Good News of Jesus' death and resurrection. With the faith God gives us, our Savior preserves us from the evils in the world. When we die, we will live forever in heaven. And heaven is a million times more valuable than all the salt in the world!

Journal: Jesus also called us "the light of the world" (v. 14). Where can you be "the salt of the earth" and "the light of the world"? Write down those places in your journal.

Pray: Father, thank You that because of Jesus' work on the cross, I am free to be a salty servant. Please show me who to help by what I say and do. In Jesus' name I pray. Amen. J. D.

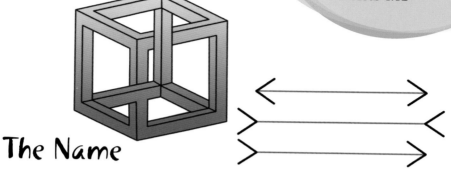

The Name

Do you like optical illusions—like a picture where one person might see a tree, while another person looking at the same picture sees a horse? Or how about the illusion where one line looks longer than the other, but they are really the same? Then there is the one with the steps—are they going up or down?

Different people see the same thing in different ways. This can be fun when looking at optical illusions, but when speaking about our faith, different views can be a matter of life and death.

In our society, the word *god* has become very popular. We hear government officers, movie stars, and people in our communities speak about a god. You may hear your friends talk about their god. You may even know that their family attends church.

Are you wondering why the word isn't capitalized here? It's not a mistake. It's not an optical illusion. It is not capitalized because many people use the word *god*, yet they are not talking about our God, the triune God—Father, Son, and Holy Spirit.

Just because people talk about god doesn't mean they believe in Jesus. They may be thinking about things very differently than you are. Ask them what they mean. Ask them what they believe. If their answers don't include news about our Savior, then the Holy Spirit might use you to lead them to church or Sunday School, where they can hear about Jesus, God's Son, their only Savior.

Journal: Write down two or three sentences you often say about God. Now, if needed, rewrite them so that they include exact information about Jesus as your Savior.

Pray: Jesus, You alone can save from sin and death. Use me to invite others to hear Your message proclaimed and taught, that they may believe Your love for them. Amen. L. H.

JANUARY 24

Isaiah 43:16–21

The Way in the Desert

The saguaro cactus grows in the Sonoran Desert of Arizona and California. Fully grown, it can be almost fifty feet tall and weigh as much as five cars! Notice the arms stretching out with pleated spines. The pleats expand like an accordion when it rains so that the cactus can store water. God created the saguaro cactus so it could thrive in the desert.

The Bible talks a lot about survival in the desert. In today's reading from Isaiah, God said He would provide water in the desert for His people. He would make a way for His people to walk through the desert. God kept His promise. He provided springs of water. He helped His people out of the sand and heat of the desert.

Living with sin and our sinful condition are like the struggles of a thirsty person in the desert. Can anyone survive the sinful desert of life? Yes, with God's help. God promised to make "a way" for us to survive (v. 19). He did that by sending His own dear Son to the cross. He refreshes us with the living water of His Word and Sacraments. When we hear the pastor, in Jesus' name, forgive our sins or read God's word of love and forgiveness, it's like getting a drink of cool water in the hot desert.

Imagine Jesus with His arms stretched out wide, dying for your sins. He's making the way for you. Hear Him say, "I love you so much."

Journal: Draw a cactus. Around the picture, write words from the Bible reading that give you hope.

Pray: Dear Jesus, thank You for giving me a way to be with You forever. Thank You for the refreshing waters of Your Word and Sacraments. Amen. C. E.

Where the Gifts Are

Lexi's family needed God's love and forgiveness, but they were all so busy. Lexi was a gifted volleyball player. Lexi's brother was good at baseball and tennis. Lexi's father frequently traveled for his job. Lexi's mother was constantly juggling her roles as wife, mother, and accountant. Yes, Lexi's family needed God's love, forgiveness, and strength, but her family was busy!

There were the Sunday morning volleyball tournaments and baseball practices. Lexi and her brother were strong players. Their teams needed them. They could always go to church next week. God would understand.

But when next week came, Lexi's family felt they needed to spend Sunday morning sleeping in and catching up on chores. Somehow, the extra rest and catching up left everyone sort of grumpy and depressed. But with their schedule, God would understand.

Little by little, Lexi's family cut themselves off from God's gifts. Lexi's family was successful, but they had needs that couldn't be met at the ball field, with extra sleep, or even by fun and entertainment. There wasn't much joy or peace or strength in Lexi's family anymore. Her family desperately needed God's gifts of forgiveness, love, and salvation.

God has promised to deliver His gifts through His Word and Sacraments. In His Word, we hear the beautiful message that our sins are forgiven because of Jesus' perfect life, death, and resurrection for us. In His Word and Sacraments, God gives us peace and joy and strength. He changes us to live for Him.

Journal: Are there activities in your life that keep you from the gifts God gives in the church service and through the study of His Word? Write about them.

Pray: Dear Lord, forgive me for the times I have cut myself off from Your gifts. Keep me always close to You. Amen. S. S.

Like Monkeys?

"Jason, are we like monkeys?" Brad asked.

"No, of course not," his older brother answered. "Why?"

"My teacher said so. He said we're 98 percent like apes and gorillas and monkeys. So doesn't that make us just like big monkeys?" Brad was confused.

Jason said, "What if I say, 'My shirt is yellow' and 'My shirt is not yellow.' Aren't those sentences almost alike?"

"I guess so," Brad said.

"Would you say they're about 98 percent alike?" Jason asked, arching an eyebrow.

"Oh!" Brad said, his eyes lighting up. "You're saying that things can be a lot alike and still be very different?"

"Yep," Jason said. "Just because we're like monkeys in some ways doesn't mean we're apes without all the fur. Humans are God's special creation."

Jason has it right. But some scientists compare monkeys and human beings, saying we are so similar to monkeys that we must have come from the same ancestors. But does this make sense?

The Bible makes it clear that humans and monkeys and all animals are God's creation. It also tells us that humans are very different from the animals God made. God formed human creatures, breathed into us His breath of life, and gave us dominion over all animals.

We humans are made in the image of God. We humans think differently. We also read, write, make art and music, and worship our Creator.

And that Creator sent Jesus to die for the sins of all people. And because we have a Savior, through faith we are 100 percent forgiven!

Journal: Write a poem to thank God, your Creator, for making you special.

Pray: Dear Creator, thank You for making me in Your image and, through the work of Jesus, saving me from all my sins. Amen. J. S.

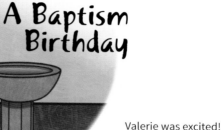

A Baptism Birthday

Valerie was excited! Today was her Baptism birthday, and her mom always made it a special time for her. The table was set, and her favorite meal was waiting for her. After they ate, her dad would have a special prayer for her. She loved looking at the pictures taken on her Baptism day. A Baptism banner hanging in her room reminded her that she was God's child. She felt special and knew she was loved.

The Bible readings tell us about Baptism. Paul tells Titus that Baptism is the washing of regeneration that gives us the hope of eternal life. Paul tells the Corinthians that baptized people have been anointed. God has put His seal on them. The Holy Spirit lives in their hearts as a guarantee.

Just what do those words mean? They mean that in the waters of Holy Baptism, we become God's children. God's Word combined with the water washes us clean by forgiving our sins. The pastor makes the sign of the cross, God's seal, upon the forehead and upon the heart. Some pastors also anoint the child's head with oil.

In Baptism, the Holy Spirit is given to each of us. The Holy Spirit creates and nourishes our faith. The Spirit helps us hear the Word and believe it. And faith in Christ as our Savior is our guarantee of eternal life. A guarantee means it is good; it will happen. That's good news and a reason to celebrate on your Baptism birthday and every day!

Journal: When is your Baptism birthday? Do you celebrate it each year? What is another way to remember your Baptism every day of the year?

Pray: Heavenly Father, thank You for giving me Your Holy Spirit in Baptism. Thank You for claiming me as Your own. Help me to hear Your Word and believe it. In Jesus' name I pray. Amen. B. S.

A Day That Will Live

Many people can remember exactly where they were and what they were doing when they heard about a terrible tragedy. After the bombing of the naval base in Pearl Harbor, President Roosevelt called December 7, 1941, a "date which will live in infamy." That means it will be remembered for the bad things that happened. September 11 is a date like that, and, for many school children who are now grown-ups, so is today.

On January 28, 1986, the Space Shuttle *Challenger* launched from the Kennedy Space Center in Florida. Just seventy-three seconds after lift-off, the shuttle disintegrated. All seven astronauts died. Everyone was shocked and horrified. It was a day that will live in infamy.

Perhaps that's how Jesus' followers felt on the day Jesus died. One disciple said, "We had hoped that He was the one to redeem Israel" (Luke 24:21). That Friday seemed to be a bad day to remember. But just three days later, the disciples discovered that their bad day was really a *Good* Friday. Because on Easter, Jesus rose from the dead! Jesus is the Redeemer of the entire world! And because He lives, we will live also! For everyone who believes in Jesus, one day there will be no more days of infamy; there will only be days of everlasting righteousness, innocence, and blessedness. God "will wipe away every tear from their eyes, and death shall be no more." What a glorious day that will be—a day that will last forever! Praise the Lord!

Journal: How can God's love for us make us feel better when sad things happen?

Pray: Jesus, You always know when I am sad or hurting. Thank You for holding me in Your arms and comforting me with Your everlasting love. Amen. N. D.

Winner or Loser

It was election day at school. For weeks, everyone had been reading the campaign signs posted on bulletin boards. Today, each student would vote for the new class officers. At the end of the day, everyone would know the results.

As soon as Kellan walked into the kitchen, Mom knew the results. Kellan walked in with his head down. "I'm a loser," he said.

"Just because you didn't get the most votes doesn't mean you're a loser," his mom said.

"You're wrong, Mom," Kellan said. "I tried my hardest. I asked everyone to vote for me, and I told them why they should elect me. And still, I didn't win."

"You did try your hardest," Mom replied, giving him a big hug. "That's all anyone could do. There could be only one winner. You knew that when you decided to run for class president."

Do you think Kellan was a loser?

When God looks at us, His children, He sees winners. Maybe the election didn't turn out as Kellan would have liked, but God doesn't look at our accomplishments. God looks at our hearts. When we are baptized, Jesus comes to live in us. He makes our hearts clean and pure.

Would Jesus have come only for the people the world sees as winners? Absolutely not. Jesus came for everyone, young and old, short and tall, class officers and class members. As Christians, we are all the winners of forgiveness and eternal life, regardless of how many votes we get in any elections.

Journal: Write about a time when you felt like you were a loser. What made you realize you were a winner in God's eyes?

Pray: Dear God, thank You for Jesus' death and resurrection, which makes sinners like me winners in Christ. Amen. P. L.

Seasons and Time

- Curtis Wyatt Fuller would be baptized tomorrow.
- ✓ Sammy was learning to walk.
- Megan was successful in tying her shoes.
- ✓ Catherine was trying to learn long division.
- Finally, Anne finished the bibliography for her term paper.
- ✓ Alex was memorizing symbols for his chemistry test.
- Ian was taking the ACT college-entrance test again.
- ✓ John asked Sarah to marry him.
- The doctor told Scott he needed knee-replacement surgery.
- ✓ Jean's mother died after a long illness.
- Debby moved her parents to the nursing home.
- ✓ Chris ordered his garden seeds.

So many events in our lives! Today's Scripture says there is "a season, and a time for every matter under heaven." In this life, we live in time—years, months, days, hours—and we see changes. We are born, grow older, and experience different events. In time, there is sin, sickness, and death as well as God's gifts of healing, laughing, and dancing.

God made sure we would live in time and forever with Him. God sent Jesus into this world of time to help us. Jesus lived for about thirty-three years before He died on the cross for the sins of all people. After Jesus rose from the dead, He ascended into heaven, where time will never end.

When this lifetime—the good and the sad—ends for you, you will live forever in endless joy as a child of heaven. Jesus made it all possible.

Journal: What are the events of your life today? How is God at work?

Pray: Dear Jesus, be with me through all the joys and sorrows of today—this day in my life. Thank You for making me Your child so that I can live forever and ever with You. Amen. B. S.

Filling Bread

Did you know that pancakes have been around for at least six hundred years? In the thirteenth century, the Romans had a fried cake called *Alita Docia,* which means "another sweet." These cakes often had honey and nuts in them or even meat and cheese. Native Americans had their own version of pancakes, and they may have been the first to eat them with maple syrup. Some people put whipped cream, jam, or fruit on their pancakes. Others eat them for dinner or even for dessert. But no matter when or how pancakes are eaten, most people would agree that they are delicious!

One day, Jesus said to the crowd, "I am the bread of life." Then He told them that anyone who believes in Him will never be hungry or thirsty. Did Jesus mean that we would feel full, like we do when we eat a stack of pancakes? No. Jesus wants us to remember that when He gave His body and shed His blood on the cross, He died for the life of the world. Jesus said, "Everyone who looks on the Son and believes in Him should have eternal life, and I will raise him up on the last day" (John 6:40).

When we believe in Jesus, we are filled with His Spirit. And when we die, Jesus will take us to heaven. Never again will we be sick or tired, sad or hungry, or even thirsty! We will be full forever!

Journal: After Jesus said this, many people stopped following Jesus. Read John 6:66–69. What did Peter say? What do you say?

Pray: Jesus, bread of life, thank You for coming down from heaven to give me eternal life. Amen. N. D.

FEBRUARY 1

Are You Sure?

"Where's Raul?" asked James as he scanned the locker room. "He's never late for practice."

"I heard Raul is in big trouble," Anton said. "He might even get kicked off the team! Frank saw him in the principal's office!"

Chad and James looked at each other. Raul was the star on their basketball team. What would they do without him?

Just then Raul rushed into the locker room. "Sorry I'm late," he said. "Principal Wilson saw me in the hall. He wanted to know how my brother Ramon is doing in college. I told him Ramon is playing on the basketball team. Just like me."

James and Chad high-fived Raul as the three of them hurried to the gym. Anton trailed behind his teammates. Next time, he would get the facts before he opened his mouth.

In Ecclesiastes 7:21, we are told, "Do not take to heart all the things that people say." We can't believe everything we hear or read. Many times people say what they believe is true, when it may not be true at all. Spreading rumors or gossiping can hurt people. Maybe someone has said something untrue about you. Then you know how bad it can make you feel.

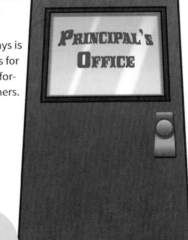

There is only one place where we can get the whole truth. That is in the Bible. Everything God says is true. There we can read that God offers forgiveness for people who spread rumors and gossip. God offers forgiveness because His only Son, Jesus, died for sinners. Those are the facts!

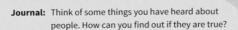

Journal: Think of some things you have heard about people. How can you find out if they are true?

Pray: Lord, help me to avoid gossip and the hurt it brings to others. For Jesus' sake, please forgive me when I don't. Help me to speak the truth. Amen. J. D.

The Light in the Darkness

Early this morning in Punxsutawney, Pennsylvania, lots of people stood outside to watch a groundhog named Phil come out of his burrow.

Can groundhogs really predict the weather? Of course not! But it's a fun story that goes back to the Early Christian Church and a festival called Candlemas. On that day, priests would bless and give out candles to the people to use for the winter. In Germany, the people would say this poem: "For as the sun shines on Candlemas Day, So far will the snow swirl until the May." They noticed that hedgehogs were coming out of their burrows that time of the year. The legend became that if a hedgehog saw its shadow on Candlemas, there would be a long winter. Years later, when German immigrants settled in Pennsylvania, there weren't any hedgehogs, but there were plenty of groundhogs!

Whether the sun is shining today or not, we know Phil doesn't really predict how long winter will last. But we do know about a "light" that shines day or night, snow or rain, winter or spring. In the Book of John, we read that in Jesus is life, and that life is the light of all. John wrote, "The light shines in the darkness, and the darkness has not overcome it" (John 1:5). Jesus is the light of the world. With Him, we never walk in spiritual darkness (John 8:12). Jesus has paid for our sins. He forgives our sins and gives us eternal life. And that is the brightest part of any day!

Journal: Read Matthew 5:14–16. According to Jesus, what are we? What does He want us to do?

Pray: Jesus, You are the light of the world. Help me reflect Your light to others so they will see You as their Lord and Savior. Amen. N. D.

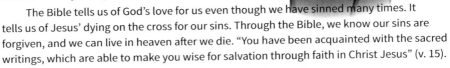

The B-I-B-L-E

"The B-I-B-L-E, Yes, that's the book for me;
I stand alone on the Word of God: the B-I-B-L-E."

That song was a favorite each day in preschool. The little kids didn't understand some of the words, but they knew the Bible was God's Word. We talked about how all the words in the Bible are true. Together, the children and I learned some of the Bible verses.

Even though it's been years since you were three years old, this song is for you too. It's even for me, and I have had many, many birthdays since I was three!

The Bible tells us of God's love for us even though we have sinned many times. It tells us of Jesus' dying on the cross for our sins. Through the Bible, we know our sins are forgiven, and we can live in heaven after we die. "You have been acquainted with the sacred writings, which are able to make you wise for salvation through faith in Christ Jesus" (v. 15).

Look up these verses to find other names for the B-I-B-L-E.

Joshua 23:6 _____

Psalm 119:105 (2) _____

_____

Luke 11:28_____

Romans 1:16 _____

2 Timothy 3:16 _____

Hebrews 10:7 _____

Journal: How is the Bible important in your life? Think of how you "stand alone on the Word of God."

Pray: Almighty God, thank You for telling me the truth about Your love and forgiveness in the Bible. Help me to stand on the Word of God. In Jesus' name I pray. Amen. J. D.

Answers: Book of the Law, lamp, light, word of God, gospel, Scripture, scroll of the book.

What Are You Thinking?

"How was the sleepover?" Dad asked Alex.

"Great," Alex said, dropping his sleeping bag on the floor. He slumped down on the sofa next to his dad. "We had a lot of fun."

"You must have stayed up all night. Your eyes look droopy."

Alex shrugged. "Nah, we didn't stay up that late. I just couldn't sleep."

"Really? Why's that?" Dad asked, surprised.

Alex hesitated, but then he started talking. "We really did have a great time. But Dwayne's got this video game called 'House of the Dead.' It's kinda creepy—you've got to kill these zombies."

Dad nodded. "Sounds like you didn't like it."

"I didn't. But the other guys thought it was cool, so I played it too. Then I couldn't fall asleep. I couldn't stop thinking about it."

"In a way, I'm glad that disturbed you." Alex gave a puzzled look. Dad continued, "When we see things like that, God's Spirit in us reacts, and our conscience is bothered. This is one way God guards our hearts and minds that were claimed in Baptism."

Alex looked up at him. "It does?"

"Yes, it sure does. Jesus is the resurrection and the life. He helps us focus on the things we have heard, received, and learned from Him. He can replace the bad things with good and pure things instead. Let's ask Him to do that, okay?"

"Okay," Alex answered with a smile, "and then I'm going to take a long nap!"

Journal: Read Philippians 4:8 again. What things have you heard today that are worthy of praise?

Pray: Dear heavenly Father, You want what is best for me, but I am often tempted to say, think, and do things that are not good for me. Forgive my sins and strengthen my conscience. Help me think on things that are true, honorable, just, pure, and pleasing to You. Amen. J. A.

One Step at a Time

Makayla was staring at the science project sheet, trying unsuccessfully to hold back her tears. Her mom came over to the table and asked what was wrong.

"I don't know," Makayla replied. "It is just so much. I don't know if I can do it all."

"So you're feeling a little overwhelmed?"

Makayla nodded.

"You are right," Mom said, and Makayla looked a little surprised. Mom continued, "You probably can't do this all . . . today. You need to break the project down into steps and work on it one step at a time. If you keep at it, you'll get it done."

There are many things in life that seem so overwhelming that it is hard to realize they can be overcome. When life seems like too much, remember that the Lord is always by your side. He gives us other people to help us as well.

Remember, too, to take things one step at a time. The Bible reading for the day says, "Commit your work to the LORD, and your plans will be established" (v. 3). You may not be able to see the whole journey, but God shows you the way for the part you are on right now.

The next time you are facing a difficult project or a difficult time in life, try not to be overwhelmed. Remember that you are not alone. Then, take it one step at a time.

Journal: Write a favorite Bible verse in your journal today.

Pray: Lord, life can be really difficult sometimes. Thank You for always being with me and showing me the way I should go. Amen. M. W.

King of Kings

What do you want to be when you grow up? An oceanographer? A paramedic? A teacher?

For most of us, as long as we have the ability, we can become anything we want to be. If you're talented in art, you could become a designer, a cartoonist, or a graphic artist. If you're good at science, you could be a researcher, a pharmacist, or a meteorologist. If you like to help people, you could be a police officer, a firefighter, or a soldier. There are so many choices!

But for an English girl nicknamed Lilibet, the job she would have was chosen for her when her dad became king. As a young girl, Lilibet started learning about her job. She continued to train for it when she was a teenager and young adult. Then on February 6, 1952, Lilibet's father, King George VI of Great Britain and Northern Ireland, died, and her job began. At the age of 25, Lilibet became Queen Elizabeth II!

When Jesus was born, He also knew what He would do when He grew up. Jesus, Lord of lords and King of kings, knew He would lay down His crown to suffer and die for His people. But when He defeated the devil and rose from the dead, Jesus took up His crown again, ascended into heaven, and is seated now at the right hand of God. Jesus has prepared a place for us with Him in His heavenly kingdom, where we will praise Him forever!

Journal: What do you want to be when you grow up? How can you serve God in your vocation (job/career)?

Pray: Dear Jesus, thank You for saving me from my sins and bringing me into Your kingdom. I love You, Lord! Amen. N. D.

Fan the Flames

Around 11:00 a.m. on February 7, 1904, a fire broke out in a downtown business in Baltimore, Maryland. It was a windy day, and the small fire soon became an uncontrollable blaze! Embers landed everywhere until eighty blocks were in flames. For two days, Baltimore firefighters fought side by side with units from Washington DC; Philadelphia; Wilmington, Delaware; and New York City. By 3:00 p.m. on the second day, the Great Baltimore Fire was under control, but it would smolder for weeks. In the end, 1,500 buildings were destroyed and another thousand were damaged, but not one citizen or firefighter died.

The winds in Baltimore fanned the flames and created a destructive fire. But in the time of the apostles, fire had a much different effect. The Holy Spirit fanned the flames of the Gospel into a "fire of faith" that spread throughout the world! When the Holy Spirit came in fire and wind at Pentecost, the disciples began to preach the Good News of Jesus to everyone who was in Jerusalem (Acts 2). Soon, thousands of people became Christians. This upset Jewish leaders, who threatened the disciples with destruction, so they left Jerusalem and spread out into Africa, Europe, and Asia, preaching the Good News. As the Pentecost flames were fanned, people from all nations became believers.

Today, God uses pastors, teachers, and missionaries to keep the fire burning for Jesus until the day when "every tongue [will] confess that Jesus Christ is Lord" (Philippians 2:11).

Journal: How can you fan the flames of the Gospel today?

Pray: Dear God, thank You for Your Spirit, who empowers people to tell others about Jesus. Bless their words and actions for Jesus' sake. Amen. N. D.

A Terrible Time

Margot heard the door open and buried her face in her pillow. Her mom came in and sat down on her bed, smoothing Margot's hair with her hand.

"Honey, are you okay?"

Margot sat up and her mother put her arms around her. "Did Daddy really do the things they said he did?"

Her mother wiped away tears of her own. "I don't know, sweetheart. I don't think so, but we're going to have to find a lawyer and get Dad out of jail before the trial."

"But why, Mom?" Margot asked. "How could God let Daddy get arrested? What's going to happen to all of us?"

"I don't know," her mother answered. "But whatever happens, God will help us. Jesus knows what it's like."

Margot's attention was caught. "What do you mean, He knows what it's like?"

"His cousin John got arrested too," said her mother. "And Jesus was very sad and upset about that. But it didn't stop Him from doing what God wanted Him to do. And Jesus will help us now."

Margot was struck by a thought. "And Jesus got arrested too," she said.

"Yes, He did. And He suffered and died and came back to life again—for all of us—you, me, and Daddy too. He did all of that so we could be God's children. If He loved us that much, you know He isn't going to leave us alone now."

Journal: When did Jesus help you when you were scared or sad?

Pray: Dear Lord, thank You that You never leave me alone. You always take care of me. Amen. K. V.

Upside Right

When ice is cold enough and thick enough, you can walk and skate on it. People in Alaska, Minnesota, and other northern states drive their trucks out onto the middle of a frozen lake. Then they cut a hole in the ice, set their line, and sit on a comfy seat. They sip hot chocolate or coffee while they fish.

Ice *should* sink to the bottom of the lake. But God turns ice upside right. He made an exception to the laws of nature with water and ice. If ice did sink, then the whole pond or lake would freeze solid from the bottom up and all the fish would die. Instead, God made ice expand. He made it get lighter than water. Ice floats to the top, and fish and other lake creatures can still live in the water under the ice.

Ice isn't the only thing God turns upside right. He does it for us. We are sinners, and God's Law says sin must be punished. Our sins are so great and so heavy that on our own we sink under their weight.

But God sent His Son, Jesus, to make things right. Jesus kept God's Law—every single bit. Then He took all the weight of our sins on Himself, died to pay the punishment for those sins, and rose victorious from the grave. Now through faith, Jesus takes away our sin and gives us His victory. Jesus turns our lives upside right, and now we live forever!

Journal: Write about an experience that you had with ice, ice-skating, or ice fishing. Think how God has turned your life upside right.

Pray: Dear God, thank You for sending Jesus to turn my sinful life upside right. Thank You for taking away my sins and giving me a new life in the waters of Baptism. In Jesus' name I pray. Amen. P. L.

Word Power

Words are very powerful—in a bad or good way. Nasty, mean words hurt people's feelings and make them feel like losers. But uplifting words such as "Way to go!" or "Thanks!" can make someone feel loved and appreciated. Those words are encouraging and caring.

Our words can also be used to tell others of God's love. We can tell them the Good News that Jesus died for our sins. Now we are forgiven, and someday we will live in heaven forever with Him. What wonderful words to hear!

To find a Bible verse about words, carefully follow these eight directions:
Cross out the last letter of each line. **Cross out** all numbers except 1, 2, and 5. **Cross out** the As and Zs in line 2. **Cross out** animal names in line 1. **Cross out** vegetables in lines 4 and 6. **Cross out** the Bs and Vs in line 3. **Cross out** every other letter in line 5. **Circle** the leftover letters and write the words in your journal.

B	I	R	D	A	6	W	O	R	D	3	C	A	L	F	Y
7	3	F	A	Z	I	T	Z	9	L	A	4	Y	Z	6	R
S	B	V	4	P	O	V	K	E	B	N	I	V	S	7	M
P	E	A	S	L	I	T	O	M	A	T	O	8	K	E	T
A	L	P	Z	P	E	L	R	E	O	S	R	O	T	F	G
B	E	E	T	S	G	O	L	D	C	A	R	R	O	T	L
P	R	O	7	9	V	E	6	R	B	S	2	5	1	1	S

Journal: Who needs sweet words? What will you say? Pray for that person, and encourage him or her with your words.

Pray: Lord, I ask that Your love guide me so my words encourage others and show them I care. In Your name I pray. Amen. J. D.

Answer: "A word fitly spoken is like apples of gold." Proverbs 25:11

Who Is Welcome at Your Table?

Today's Bible reading says that Jesus "receives sinners and eats with them" (v. 2). All people were welcome at Jesus' table. Was Jesus praised and commended for this?

Absolutely not! The scribes and Pharisees, important leaders of Jesus' day, grumbled about Jesus. You can almost hear the sneer in their voices, "This man receives sinners and eats with them."

Maybe you've heard that same sneer in your voice. Maybe there is a girl in your class who is not welcome at your lunch table. Maybe you don't stick up for the boy whom everyone teases. Maybe you have a friend you only acknowledge when nobody else is around. We have all sinned because we want to be popular and fit in.

However, maybe you are the child who has been rejected—you were told to take your tray and eat elsewhere. Maybe you're the one who feels friendless and alone. Maybe you have sinned in your loneliness by hating or mistreating those who mistreated you. Thankfully, there is good news for us sinners—the best news. "Jesus receives sinners and eats with them."

Whether we are the sinners who have rejected others or the sinners who have been rejected, Jesus welcomes us. He is not ashamed to call us His friends. He died on the cross to pay for our sins of rejecting and hating others. His death and resurrection guarantee that we are forever welcome at His heavenly banquet table.

Journal: Is there someone in your class who needs the welcome you can give?

Pray: Dear Jesus, thank You for welcoming me and being my Savior. Please give me the strength and courage to be a friend to others—popular or unpopular, rich or poor, beautiful or not-so-beautiful. Amen. S. S.

Spared

Samantha loved candles. One evening, she lit a lilac-scented candle. She started reading and fell asleep while the candle was burning. All night while she slept, that candle kept burning. When Samantha woke up, she couldn't believe she had forgotten to blow it out before she fell asleep. Quickly, she blew out the candle.

She was thankful that nothing bad had happened. The candle didn't tip over and catch the carpet on fire. It didn't send a spark onto her desk and catch papers on fire. Samantha knew that God had kept her and her family safe in spite of her carelessness.

Each day in many ways, God saves us. Not only from sin, death, and the devil, but from other careless or foolish things we do. We deserve more punishment than we ever get, but we don't experience it all because God is compassionate.

Sometimes, our actions have earthly results. We cheat on a test, so we fail. We leave a bike outside, and it gets stolen. But sometimes, we get away with our sins. That doesn't mean that we're any less guilty; it's just that no one noticed.

It's a similar situation with Samantha and her candle. She did something that endangered herself and her family. But our God is full of mercy; He is tenderhearted toward us at all times. He leads us to repent and ask for mercy, which He freely gives us because of our Savior's sacrifice for us.

Journal: Can you think of a time when God has spared you from a punishment you deserved? Write a prayer of thanksgiving to God.

Pray: Dear Father, thank You that You are slow to anger and abounding in compassion. I am thankful for Your kindness to me, though I don't deserve it. In Jesus' name I pray. Amen. J. S.

The Greatest Discovery

On February 13, 1955, Israel bought four of the Dead Sea Scrolls. These scrolls were discovered in high caves near the Dead Sea. It was a great discovery because they contained some of the oldest copies of the biblical text. An even greater discovery is when a person discovers that the Bible is the Word of God.

The greatest discovery of all comes through faith. But we don't have to go searching for this discovery. When we were baptized, God made that "greatest discovery" for us. That's when God made us His dear children. He washed away our sins and gave us His Holy Spirit. He put faith in our hearts to believe that Jesus Christ is the Savior. God loves each one of us as His special child, and He calls each one of us by name.

The Bible tells us that when Andrew discovered that Jesus was the promised Savior, he didn't keep that great discovery to himself. The first thing he did was go and tell his brother Simon about Jesus. Andrew said, "We have found the Messiah" (v. 41).

That's the greatest discovery—one worth sharing!

Journal: What is something that you have discovered lately? How has the greatest discovery, knowing Jesus as your Savior, made a difference in your life?

Pray: Dear God, thank You for showing me through Jesus that You love me. Thank You for the Bible, where I discover more about You. Help me remember all You did to save me. Amen. L. E.

Love Is . . .

Today is Valentine's Day. According to one legend, a man named Valentine grew flowers and gave them to children. Then Valentine was put in prison, and the children missed him. They tied notes to flowers and tossed them through the prison window. After Valentine died, people began sending loving messages to their friends on the anniversary of his death, February 14.

Valentines are messages of friendship and love. But people have all kinds of meanings for "love." We say we love our parents or our dog or basketball. Maybe we love pizza or sleeping late on Saturday.

God describes love too. There is a whole chapter in the Bible that tells what true love is. Read 1 Corinthians 13:4–7 to unscramble these words describing love. "Love is tenpait and dnki; love does not ynev or sobta; it is not rtaargon or dure. It does not ssntii on its own way; it is not batliirre or luftenser; it does not ijreoec at wrongdoing, but ijceoers with the rutth. Love serba all things, livebese all things, shope all things, rudenes all things."

You may get valentines today. But the best valentine you can ever receive or will ever receive is God's valentine—His very own Son, Jesus! God loves you so much that He sent Jesus to die for your sins. Now you are forgiven, and you will live forever with Him in heaven someday. God's valentine is given to you every day of your life.

Journal: Think of God's "valentine" to you. Write a letter to God thanking Him for His special love.

Pray: Loving God, thank You for Your special valentine of love and forgiveness. Help me to show love to my family and friends today and every day. Amen. J. D.

FEBRUARY 15

1 John 4:1–3

A Short Test

Today's devotion is a test. (No groaning, please.) Answer these questions true or false.

1. Jesus suffered and died to take away your sins.
2. Buddha and Muhammad died to take away your sins too.
3. You can live such a good life that God will take you to heaven.
4. Jesus did not do enough to save you, so now you must do many good deeds if you want to join Him in heaven.
5. Jesus did everything needed to save you from your sins and make you His own.

Numbers 1 and 5 are true. Never believe 2, 3, or 4.

If you had a perfect score, thank God. He gave you faith to believe that Jesus is your Savior. God also gave you today's Bible verses. They teach how you can be sure that you believe in the only true God—God the Father, Son (Jesus Christ), and Holy Spirit.

Sadly, many people do not believe the truth about God. They may think that believing in others who are called gods will help and save them. Other people think they do not need God. They think that being kind and good will get them to heaven. How wrong!

The Bible tells you exactly what you need to know. The Bible says that Jesus is our only Savior. Study the Bible. At just the right times, it will help you to be strong for any test.

Journal: In your journal, write a text message that tells a friend about Jesus.

Pray: Thank You, dear God, for preparing me to spot wrong teachings about You by giving me faith in the one and only Savior. Amen. E. G.

Night Vision

Cats are amazing animals. They are light on their feet and can creep up on you, making hardly a sound. They are incredible jumpers; even if they accidentally fall from something, they almost always land on their feet. And they seem to be able to see in the dark.

Cats can't see in total darkness, but they only need about one-sixth the amount of light a human does in order to see clearly. Their pupils react to a change of light by changing size, the same way our pupils do. The difference is that cats have a special layer of cells behind their retinas that act like a mirror. The light bounces off these cells, making it easy for a cat to see.

It's hard to see the consequences of what we are doing in this dark world of temptations. We live in a sinful world, and wrong actions can be tempting. We might lie or cheat or steal to get something we want. Then sin darkens our hearts. But God's grace sees through the darkness of sin, death, and the devil. In Baptism, God grants us forgiveness and a new life. Though we sin, the Holy Spirit leads us to repentance. The Holy Spirit renews us daily and helps us to resist temptation.

Because of Jesus' sacrifice, we are saved from eternal darkness. Thanks to God's grace, we are assured that the darkness of sin will never overtake us. What a wonderful thing to know!

Journal: What are some temptations that are common to children your age? How can God help you to overcome them?

Pray: Dear Lord Jesus, thank You for saving me from the darkness of my sin. Help me to remember that You are with me when times are difficult and the road ahead looks dark. Amen. J. A.

Hidden Sweets

Hidden below are names of four delicious desserts. See if you can find them. They can be forward, backward, across, or down.

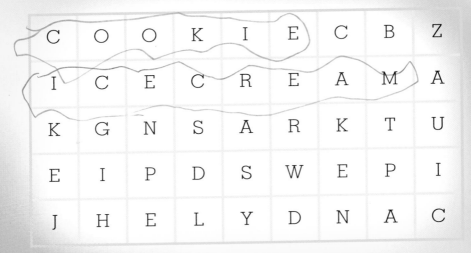

C	O	O	K	I	E	C	B	Z
I	C	E	C	R	E	A	M	A
K	G	N	S	A	R	K	T	U
E	I	P	D	S	W	E	P	I
J	H	E	L	Y	D	N	A	C

So . . . which one is your favorite? Have you ever eaten a lot of it? Have you ever eaten too much of it? Eating too many sweets isn't good for anyone. In fact, after eating one too many cookies or pieces of candy, dessert doesn't even sound good anymore.

However, there is one "sweet" you can enjoy over and over. You will never get tired of eating it. It is always okay to ask for more. It is sweeter than honey, yet it won't decay your teeth. You can "eat" it lots of times each day. What is it? God's Word!

How do we "eat" God's Word? We read it or hear it read or preached and think about it. As God's children, we are hungry for it. God's Word is a Means of Grace. Through it, God Himself comes to us.

Cookie jars and cake pans will become empty, but God's Word is always full of sweet promises. Help yourself to a giant helping of God's Word today. Read all of Psalm 19, another favorite psalm, or a verse from last week's devotions. The next time you are hungry for a snack, remind yourself that you are hungry for God's Word too!

Journal: Write down a verse from Psalm 19 that you would like to memorize. Then you have a sweet treat to take with you wherever you go!

Pray: Dear Father, Your Holy Word is rich and sweet. Lead me to read, study, and share it with others. In Jesus' name I pray. Amen. L. H.

Not Everything Changes

Take a minute to think about things that change. First, think about your favorite things. Do you have the same favorite book you had last year? Do you have a new favorite cartoon character? How many different favorite shirts have you had?

Usually, people choose new favorites because they get tired of the old ones. We tire of hearing the same song. Clothing styles change, and we get tired of wearing some outfits. "Change is good," we are told.

Today is a special day. It is a day to commemorate—or honor—Dr. Martin Luther. As you probably know, Martin Luther was a man God used in a powerful way. Luther taught others the truths of God's Word. He wrote many books and preached hundreds of sermons. He helped people remember that God and His Word do not change.

That all happened almost five hundred years ago! Since that time, our Lutheran Church has carefully continued the work of Martin Luther. It still clearly teaches that the Bible is true and inspired, that faith is a gift from God, and that we are forgiven *only* through faith in Jesus.

Styles, songs, and movies will come and go. We will get tired of them and look for something new. But God's Word never goes out of style. It will never seem old-fashioned, and its message of salvation will always be the same.

Journal: Many hymns are at least five hundred years old! Some were written by Dr. Luther. The next time you sing a hymn, look for three things: (1) the year it was written; (2) who wrote it; (3) the rich truths of God's Word. Enjoy praising God with songs that never go out of style!

Pray: God, so many things change. It seems there is always something new. Thank You that Your Word will always be the same, telling me that I am forgiven because of Jesus. Amen. L. H.

FEBRUARY 19

Psalm 25:4–7

Forgive and Forget

Dylan's dad listened as Dylan prayed. "And forgive me for lying today, and thank You for sending Your Son, Jesus. In His name I pray. Amen." Dylan unfolded his hands and slipped under the covers.

"Did you ever lie to your dad?" he asked as Dad tucked him in.

"Well, I'm sure I did, but I can't say that I remember it."

"Do you think when I'm older, I'll remember lying to you today?" Dylan asked.

"You might remember it for a while, but I hope that what you remember is that you have been forgiven for lying to me today," Dad said as he smiled and kissed Dylan on the forehead. "I've forgiven you, and so has God. To Him, your sin is already forgotten."

Have you ever thought about how a perfect God, who knows everything and is all-powerful, could forget the bad things we do? Sometimes, we have trouble forgiving and forgetting, but God doesn't. Because of Jesus' death on the cross, God always remembers His mercy and always forgives and forgets our sin.

Forgetting our sins is a way for God to emphasize to us that His forgiveness is forever. God will never hold our sins against us. Jesus has already paid for every one of them.

For us, remembering our own sin can help us to serve God better by learning from our mistakes. For God, there is no reason to remember our sin, because He already sees us as holy and blameless because of Jesus.

Journal: Write about a time when you were forgiven and a time when you forgave someone else. How did it feel to forgive and be forgiven?

Pray: Lord God, thank You for forgiving and forgetting my sins. Through the power of Your Holy Spirit, give me strength to forgive others who sin against me. In Jesus' name I pray. Amen. S. S.

Leader among Leaders

He was the only president who didn't live in Washington DC. He was the only one of the founding fathers to free his slaves. His second inaugural address was only 135 words.

Who is he? George Washington, the first president of the United States. We celebrate his birthday on Presidents' Day, the third Monday of February.

Americans honor George Washington for many reasons. He was the first commander in chief of the Continental Army, leading the new country to victory in the Revolutionary War over two hundred years ago. He presided over the convention that produced the Constitution by which the United States operates today. Washington's character, the standards he set, and his service are models for presidents and other leaders today.

Some may think such an outstanding person would easily be admitted to heaven for all his accomplishments and sacrifices. But Washington, like all of us, was a sinner.

Today's reading reminds us "all have sinned and fall short of the glory of God." But there is Good News too! We "are justified by His grace as a gift, through the redemption that is in Christ Jesus." We are all unworthy of forgiveness but, because of Jesus, God forgives us and welcomes believers to eternal life with Him. We are free to serve Him joyfully wherever He places us to be His children in His world.

Journal: Read 1 Peter 2:16. In what ways might heeding this advice help to explain George Washington's success?

Pray: Father, bless our leaders so that their work might be pleasing to You. In Jesus' name I pray. Amen. H. W.

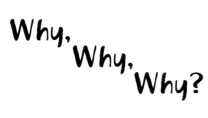

Why, Why, Why?

Why are we having meatloaf for dinner *again*? Why do I have *so* much homework? Why do we have another spelling test? Why do I have to shovel the driveway? Why are little sisters so annoying? Why won't my mom buy me what everyone else has?

Do any of these questions sound familiar? Maybe you can think of more "why" questions. Are you ever guilty of whining or grumbling? Maybe someone in your family tends to grumble. Perhaps it's your brother. He's the one who *really* complains a lot.

And yet, Philippians 2 says, "Do *all* things without grumbling or disputing" (v. 14). This way we will stand out and "shine as lights in the world" (v. 15). God's love shines through us, and other people can see that.

Sometimes, grumbling and complaining feel good. We don't want to stop. Sometimes, we don't want to shine. We would rather keep grumbling.

But God knows that. He knows that a lot of times we don't want to do what's right. So God sent Jesus to live perfectly for us. He lived without ever grumbling or whining—not even once. Then He died and came back to life to pay for all our sins of complaining. And Philippians says that now God "works in you, both to will and to work for His good pleasure" (v. 13). God promises to help you *want* to do His will. For Jesus' sake, He promises to give you the strength to do it.

Journal: Make a list of the five things you complain about most. Then cross them out and write down five things you are thankful for.

Pray: Dear God, please forgive me for whining and complaining. Thank You for sending Jesus to forgive these sins. Help me do all things without grumbling so others can see I'm Your child and give You glory. Amen. E. B.

Outcasts

"Mom," Alex asked, "can I shave my head?"

"That's a wonderful idea!" she replied enthusiastically.

"Willis's mom is a barber, and she said she'd do all of us tomorrow after school. She just wants to be sure I have your permission."

"Well, of course you do! I'll call Willis's mom to tell her. Alex, I'm really proud of you!"

What's going on here? Why is Alex's mom so happy that Alex wants to shave his head? It's because Alex's classmate Ethan has cancer. The treatments for cancer are making Ethan lose his hair. Ethan feels embarrassed about being bald. He thinks the other kids will laugh at him. So a group of his friends decided to be "outcasts" with him. They decided to shave their heads so they would be bald too.

In Jesus' time, if you had a skin disease, you were an outcast. You couldn't come close to other people, and no one would want to touch you. But Jesus let the sick man come close to Him. Jesus touched him and healed him.

He did that for all of us. He came to earth. He lived in our world of sin and died the death of an outcast on the cross. In doing that, He healed us of the sickness of our sin. In Baptism, He touches us through the water and His Word. God's power creates faith. Our sins are forgiven, and we are healed. Each day, God creates a new person through His healing power.

Journal: Have you ever felt like an outcast? What are some ways Jesus was an outcast?

Pray: Dear Jesus, thank You for being an outcast for me and healing my sin-sickness through Your power. Amen. E. G.

FEBRUARY 23

Psalm 91:14–15

Answered Prayers

"God didn't answer my prayer," Jacob said. "I prayed that w would win the game. But we didn't."

"God didn't answer my prayer," Kelsee said. "I prayed for Grandma to get better, but she didn't."

"God didn't answer my prayer," Kim said. "I prayed that I would get an A on my spelling test. I didn't study because I was busy. God let me down."

Jacob, Kelsee, and Kim need to learn more about God and about prayer. God answers all of our prayers. Sometimes, He says yes; sometimes, He says no; sometimes, He says wait. The fact that we don't get the answer we want doesn't mean He didn't listen or answer.

One part of the Lord's Prayer says, "Thy will be done on earth as it is in heaven." When we pray these words, we ask that God's good and gracious will be done in our lives. God's will includes breaking and hindering the plans of the devil, the world, and our own sinful nature. What a God we have!

Did God answer the prayers of Jacob, Kelsee, and Kim? Yes, He did, but not in the way they wanted or understood.

Journal: Do you remember how God answered some of your prayers? Think back. Remember what you have prayed for in the past.

Pray: Dear God, remind me when I pray that Your answer—yes, no, or wait—is always best for me. Thank You for promising to hear my prayers for Jesus' sake. In His name I pray. Amen. P. L.

The next time you pray, remember that God hears and answers your prayers in His own way and at His own time. He answers them as you pray in Jesus' name, with confidence, and according to God's will. God answers them because He loves you!

I Am . . .

Carmen sat at the kitchen table, chewing on the end of her pencil. She was thinking so hard that she was twisting her mouth.

Peter looked at her and asked, "Hey, little sis, what are you writing? The way you look, you must be using every part of your brain."

Carmen answered, "Mr. Bailey gave us an assignment for Sunday School. We have to write all the things about ourselves that can come after 'I am.' I have written down six, but I want a really *long* list."

Peter looked at Carmen's list. "You're doing well. But you forgot some of the most important ones."

"What?" asked Carmen. "I said I am a girl, and I am ten . . ."

"How about 'I am a Christian,' 'I am forgiven,' 'I am going to heaven,' " said Peter. "Those are more important than anything."

In the Bible, we can read about times when Jesus said "I am" to describe Himself. He said, "I am the light of the world" to show people the way to heaven (John 8:12). He also said, "I am the vine; you are the branches," because when we are connected to Jesus we have life and can bear fruit (John 15:5). Look up these verses and make an "I am" list for Jesus.

Jesus said, "I am . . ." _____

John 6:35 _____

John 10:7–9 _____

John 10:11–14 _____

John 11:25 _____

John 14:6 _____

_____

_____

_____

Journal: List words or groups of words about you that can finish the sentence "I am . . ."

Pray: Dear Jesus, sometimes I forget how special it is to be Your child. Thank You for calling me through Baptism, forgiving my sins, and giving me life forever with You. Amen. J. D.

Fight for Me!

Junia threw her book bag on the kitchen floor. "Mom!" she called. "Mom! Guess what I found out in school today?"

Laughing, her mom gave her a hug. "What news has you all excited?" she asked.

"My old babysitter joined the army!" exclaimed Junia.

"Wow! That is pretty exciting news. How do you feel about that?" asked her mom.

"Well, I'm going to miss seeing her, but I think it's neat that she'll be fighting for me instead," replied Junia.

"Are you afraid for her?" her mom asked.

"A little, but I'll be praying for her. I know she'll be well trained. God can take care of her no matter what happens or where she goes," answered Junia.

"That's true. God's children have someone very powerful fighting for them. It's Jesus. He defeated sin, death, and the devil. But we still sin and need help. The Bible tells us that we have an advocate."

"What is that, Mom?" asked Junia.

"An advocate is someone on your side. Jesus is our advocate. He pleads for us before our heavenly Father. God listens to Jesus and declares us sinless!" declared Mom.

"Wow, Mom! That's one great advocate. I'm glad He's on my side," smiled Junia.

Journal: Do you know any people in the military? Write their names in your journal and remember to pray for them.

Pray: Dear Jesus, thank You for dying for my sins. Thank You for fighting for me. Because of what You've done, I am declared sinless. Help me always to trust in You. Amen. B. S.

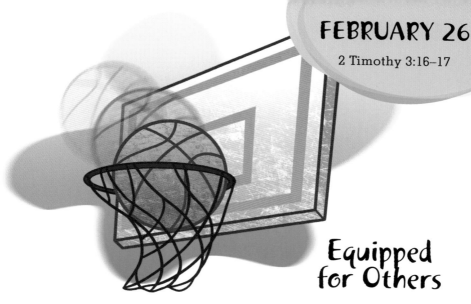

Equipped for Others

It was a close game. The teams were evenly matched; the score was tied. Joshua was nervous. He thought, *What if the ball comes to me? What will I do?*

Then, it happened. The ball came to Joshua. He wanted to call a time-out, but he couldn't. The team had no time-outs left, so Joshua acted quickly. Thanks to his coach, he was equipped. He *did* know what to do. He had done the drill many times. Joshua threw the ball inside to Zack as Zack broke for the basket. Swish. Score. Victory.

Joshua and Zack had a good coach who knew the game and equipped them for every situation. The boys knew the "right way" to run the out-of-bounds play and how to work the zone. They knew how to make a wall-on defense with arms up and out. They knew when to use the bounce pass.

In our Bible reading, Paul was a good coach for young Timothy. Paul taught Timothy how to use what he had learned and believed about God's Word. Paul told Timothy to use God's Word "for reproof, for correction, and for training in righteousness" (v. 16). For this young pastor, the Word of God was essential.

God's Word is essential to know so we can live as God's children in a sinful world. Our pastors help us read it, understand it, and find personal ways to use it. We can be ready to live and share God's love: Jesus' death, Jesus' resurrection, Jesus' victory.

Journal: Who has helped you know and understand God's Word? Who has equipped you?

Pray: Lord, You have given me Your Word. Continue to train me so I can show Your love and care to others. In Jesus' name. Amen. T. S.

2 Corinthians 11:24–27

Again?

Matthew was sitting at the breakfast table still in his pajamas, eating in slow motion. He didn't like getting up early and leaving home every day.

"Matthew, get dressed," Dad said. "It's almost time to leave."

"Again?" Matthew asked. "How many days do I have to go to school?"

Connor, a second grader, laughed. "A million!" he said.

We all feel like Matthew at times. We get tired of doing the same thing over and over. But probably none of us will have as much trouble doing our jobs as Paul had doing his.

Paul was the first missionary. He traveled all over the world telling others that Jesus had suffered and died for their sins. Sometimes, people didn't want to hear God's Good News. So Paul's work was difficult and dangerous. To find out how difficult, look at 2 Corinthians 11:24–25 and fill in the missing numbers.

"_____ times I received at the hands of the Jews the _____ lashes less _____. _____ times I was beaten with rods. _____ I was stoned. _____ times I was shipwrecked."

God kept Paul going even when he was tired, beaten, and shipwrecked. God wants all people to hear His message of salvation. Your parents may share with you night after night that message of Jesus Christ. It's the message your pastor proclaims every Sunday, week after week, year after year. Thank God that He provides messengers and missionaries who bring His Good News again and again.

Journal: What do you get tired of doing over and over? Talk to God about it. He will help you find a way to make those things easier.

Pray: Dear God, sometimes I don't feel like doing the same thing. Help me remember that You love and forgive me over and over. Amen. J. D.

Answers: 5, 40, 1, 3, Once, 3.

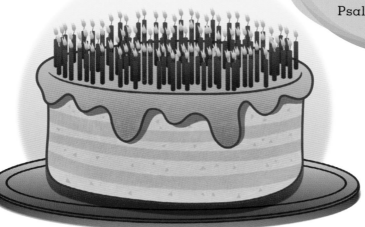

One Hundred Candles

On the front of the invitation was a birthday cake ablaze with candles. It read, "Please come and help Grandpa Joe blow out one hundred candles."

Grandpa Joe was Juanita's great-grandpa. He lived in a nursing home. "Mom, do I have to go to the party?" Juanita asked. "I could make a card, and you could take it to him."

Mom said, "A card is a good idea. You can give it to him at the party."

Juanita asked, "But what will I say to him? Grandpa Joe is ten times older than me."

"Grandpa can't see well and walks with a cane, but his brain is fine," Mom said. "Why don't you ask him questions about when he was a kid? Find out some of the things he did."

At the party, Juanita enjoyed a lively conversation with her great-grandpa. They talked about games he played when he was young and about what school was like for him.

"There have been lots and lots of changes in the one hundred years that I've lived," said Grandpa Joe. "But one thing has never changed. God has loved me and taken care of me from before I was even born. God never changed. He sent Jesus to die for my sins. All my one hundred years' worth of sins are forgiven. When I die, I will go to heaven. I'm looking forward to that big celebration with Jesus and all believers."

Journal: Interview an older person. Write about changes the person has seen.

Pray: Lord, thank You that You never change. Thank You for loving me, watching over me, and forgiving me each year You give me. Amen. J. D.

FEBRUARY 29

Psalm 127:1

Strong Foundations

In 1173, builders of Italy's Tower of Pisa laid its foundation. Five years after construction began, the weight of the tower caused it to sink it on the soft side. The dense clay mixture under the tower could not support its weight.

From 1990 to 2001, more than eight hundred years after the tower was first begun, engineers worked to reduce the tilt. Today, the tower is sturdy and safe. But the tower that was intended to be straight still leans twelve feet. What a difference it would have made if the builders had taken time to build on a stronger foundation.

Today's Bible reading reminds us the key to success in everything is God. Unless He is involved, the work is in vain. God wants to be involved in building Christian homes. In those families, members read God's Word, go to church and Sunday School, and pray with and for one another.

But even with a strong foundation in God, Christian families go through difficult times. We have problems and heartaches. We sin against one another. The devil tries to turn us away from God, but God's Word has power to help. God's Word reminds us to seek forgiveness from God as well as from one another. And just as God forgives our sins for Jesus' sake, God's Word reminds us to forgive others who sin against us.

Our lives are built on Christ. Through His death on the cross, He has secured for us a solid foundation. Through Him, we have forgiveness, life, and salvation.

Journal: Draw a house on a firm foundation. Write Jesus' name at the bottom and the names of the people in your family above the foundation.

Pray: Heavenly Father, build my family together on You so that we love and forgive one another. Help us serve others. I pray in Jesus' name. Amen. H. W.

Perfect Timing

Hannah and Manuel stood just behind the stage curtain. They helped the actors with their entrances, exits, and lines. They wanted the class play to be a success.

"I knew I could catch you in the act!" Alan cried as he crashed onto the stage. Hannah and Manuel gasped. The actors on stage didn't know what to do. Alan was not supposed to enter yet!

Jasmine recovered and said, "You haven't caught us at anything. Why don't you go back where you came from?"

After the play, Hannah and Manuel held a meeting. Everyone glared at Alan. When they told him he made a mistake, he said, "I thought it was more dramatic my way."

"It may have been more dramatic to you," Manuel said, "but not to us. You need to come in at the right time—the way it is written."

Jesus knew a lot about timing. He came into the world according to God's script, at just the right time and place. He lived perfectly and died for the sins of all people. He willingly took the world's sins to the grave to give us eternal life.

Sometimes we are afraid when unexpected things happen: our team loses, our family moves, our dog dies. But we can trust God's timing. He is the Author and Creator of all things, including time. He knows what is best for us. And because He loves us, He will take us to be with Him in heaven at just the right time.

Journal: List some times you have been impatient. What can you do to become more patient?

Pray: Dear God, thank You for sending Jesus to be my Savior at just the right time. Forgive me when I worry about the timing of things in my life, and give me a faith that trusts You. In Jesus' name I pray. Amen. J. H.

MARCH 2

John 12:23–30

Days of Thunder

Many years ago, the people of northern Europe named a day of the week after their god Thor. They believed that Thor sent rain and created thunder by beating his hammer against an anvil. Eventually, Thor's Day became known as Thursday.

It's easy to imagine thunder sounding like a hammer. Does thunder ever sound like God's voice? One day, a crowd listened to Jesus explain that soon He would die. Jesus wanted to give glory to God by doing what the Father wanted, so He said, "Father, glorify Your name" (v. 28).

God spoke from heaven, "I have glorified it, and I will glorify it again" (v. 28).

Many people in the crowd thought the voice from heaven was only thunder. The people weren't willing to listen to God and understand His will.

Jesus heard God's voice. He knew God wanted Him to die and rise again for us. And it's very Good News for us that Jesus did this—He gained our salvation!

Do you ever hear God speaking? Perhaps you wonder whether to go outside and play ball or stay inside and help your brother or sister with homework. Suddenly, it starts to rain, and that could be God's answer. God can also speak through Christian friends, parents, pastors, and teachers when we need advice.

But there's no more certain way to hear God's voice than to read the Bible. There, in His Word, we find God's message of eternal life through faith in Jesus.

Journal: Think of an important decision you might need to make. What word from God might help you?

Pray: Dear Jesus, give me ears to hear Your voice in Your Word and, through Your Spirit, work in my life to do Your will. Amen. D. S.

March Madness

Dad noticed that Sam seemed sad. "What's up, Sammy?" asked Dad.

"I didn't understand what Coach said tonight," said Sam. "He said that basketball players get mad when they play basketball in March. But I'm not mad. I love basketball!"

Dad laughed. "Don't worry, Sam," he said. "That's not what Coach meant. He was talking about March Madness. That's when college basketball teams play their tournaments," Dad explained. "The best sixty-eight teams go on to play in a championship tournament. The games are very exciting, and the fans cheer like crazy. That's why it's called madness."

"Oh, so they cheer like you and Mom do when I make a basket?"

"Yes, Sam, but Mom and I cheer for you even when you don't make a basket. You're always a winner to us. That's not the way it is in March Madness. When the tournament is over, only one team will take home the winner's trophy. In March Madness, there can be only one champion, and it might not be your team. But you do have a champion that has won everything for you, Sam."

"I know who it is, Dad! Jesus defeated sin, death, and the devil. He won eternal life for me, didn't He?"

"That's right! Jesus won the victory for us when He died on the cross and rose again. He is the ultimate champion!"

"With Jesus, we're always winners!"

Journal: What would you shout if you were a cheerleader for God?

Pray: Dear Jesus, thank You for being my Savior and Champion. Forgive me when I treat others like losers. Help me instead to be kind. Amen. N. D.

Growing in God

Was Jesus ever a toddler? teenager? young man? Sure, He was. Our Lord Jesus was a baby, a child, a teenager, a young adult, and a man. He went through growth stages too. He lost His baby teeth. His voice changed. Perhaps He even felt clumsy as His body grew faster than His motor skills.

The Bible doesn't tell us much about Jesus as He was growing up. From Luke 2:41–52, we know that when Jesus was twelve years old, He sat in the temple, listening and talking to the teachers. He enjoyed being in His Father's house.

Jesus can relate to the physical changes you go through. He also understands your spiritual growth. You may have questions about the Bible. You may become more curious to learn about God's Word than when you were younger.

For Jesus, the temple was a wonderful place to listen, learn, and respond. You will also find that your church is a wonderful place to listen and respond to God and His Word. Through His Word, you will grow in your understanding of who God is and what Jesus did while He was on earth. Through God's help, your spiritual muscles will be strengthened and grow.

God loves you and wants your body, mind, and heart to be healthy. Through His Word and the living power of Baptism, God is making sure that you grow in wisdom, and He helps your body mature. He helps you relate with God and with other people.

Journal: Where or when do you learn about God? Think of something that God taught you about Himself this week.

Pray: Dear Lord Jesus, I pray that You would help me see how I am growing in wisdom, how my body is maturing, and how I can be more like You. Thank You for caring about the way I grow up. Amen. C. R.

Dear Dad

"Who will close our class with prayer?" Mrs. Mack, the Sunday School teacher, asked.

"I don't know about others," Michael said, "but I don't volunteer because I don't know what to say in a prayer or how to say it."

Mrs. Mack decided that she would teach the class a little more about prayer.

She started the next week with a silly example. "Imagine saying to your dad, 'My dearest and most wonderful Father, please allow your humble child to be seated near you at your dinner table to eat this wonderfully delicious food, which my noble mother hath prepared for me, your hungry child.'"

The children laughed. "My dad would wonder about me!" said Kendall.

"I'd just say, 'Dad, is it time to eat yet? I'm hungry,'" offered Amy.

Mrs. Mack explained. "God wants you to talk to Him as easily as you talk to your own parents. You are God's child, His very own son or daughter."

We who believe Jesus paid for our sin can talk to God as if He were our dad, because He is. We don't have to talk to our heavenly Dad formally. Our prayers do not need to be long or difficult. We don't have to be afraid that God will think our prayer is not good enough. Prayers can be one sentence or many. Any prayer expressed through faith in Jesus is good and acceptable to our heavenly Dad.

Journal: What are your favorite prayers?

Pray: This time, pray your own prayer. C. R.

MARCH 6

God Knows the Answers

Imagine sailing with Christopher Columbus on his most famous voyage. Feel the *Santa Maria*, the ship Columbus captained, rocking up and down on the ocean's waters. Think about seemingly endless days when water and sky are all you see. Feel the surprise and joy when someone calls, "Land ahead!"

The sailors weren't sure where they were. It was land, all right, but *what* land was it? Since there were no modern charts or tools, we aren't sure where Columbus landed. No one, not even historians or mathematicians, can prove for certain where Columbus sailed or landed.

Do you think God knows where Columbus landed? Sure, He does. After all, God has been keeping track of His world since the beginning of time. He even knows the future of this earth. Jesus said, "Heaven and earth will pass away, but My words will not pass away" (Mark 13:31).

Jesus lived on earth too. Even then, He knew what was going on in far-off places. He also knew His own history would include His death and crucifixion.

If Jesus knew that He would be nailed to a cross, why did He allow it to happen? He did it willingly. He loves His children. If Jesus hadn't died for our sins, we and all other people would have no way to reach heaven. We would be like a ship rocking up and down on the water without reaching land.

Jesus wouldn't allow that to happen. He loves us and wants us to live with Him in heaven. Our Lord needs no charts, maps, or apps. He knows how to bring us safely through the rough waters of this life to Himself in heaven.

Journal: Write about two great things God has done.

Pray: Dear Lord, thank You for watching over all people. Give me trust in You throughout my entire life, until I safely reach home. Amen. K. M.

Scrubbing Out the Dirt

When Sean's family bought their new house, it was a mess. Some windows were broken, a sink leaked, the walls were covered with handprints. The people who lived there before them didn't keep things very clean, so Sean and his family had a lot of work to do.

Every evening, Sean and his family worked on the house. Soon their long hours of hard work made a difference. When the house was clean, Sean's family moved in. What a tough job it had been, but it was worth it. "I bet there's not a single speck of dirt in our house now," Mrs. Lindsay said.

When we were born, there was a kind of dirt in us called original sin. There was no way we could scrub ourselves clean of this sin. That's why we needed Baptism. Through Baptism, God washed us clean. He did the work we couldn't do. Now when God looks at us, He sees His children, cleansed by Jesus' blood.

Did Sean's house always stay clean? No, of course not. Sometimes the floors needed vacuuming and the furniture needed dusting.

In Baptism, we are always God's children, loved and forgiven by God because of Jesus. Do our lives stay free from sin because we were baptized? No, of course not. Every day we sin. When we ask God to forgive our sins, He always says yes. He knows that Jesus suffered and died for those sins, and He always forgives them. Then we are clean again.

Journal: Why didn't Sean's house stay clean all the time? Why can't we stay clean from sin?

Pray: I don't want to have sin in me, dear Lord. I want to be clean. But, Lord, I was born a sinner, and I sin daily. Remind me of my Baptism and how You scrubbed me clean. Then give me peace in knowing I am forgiven. In Jesus' name I pray. Amen. P. L.

From Death to Life

Mr. and Mrs. Buchman are an older couple at my church. Mr. Buchman had a stroke, and he moves slowly with a walker. He needs help with even simple things. Mrs. Buchman is in better health. She does for him many of the things he cannot do for himself.

When I see them, I think about two things. First, I am sad because nothing in life lasts. Mr. Buchman was once an officer in the United States Army. He was a strong leader of soldiers. Now, he needs help. Because of sin in the world, we will all die. For those who live to be old, bodies and minds often become frail and weak.

The second thing I think about is God's faithfulness. That fills me with joy. Mrs. Buchman is a wonderful example of faithfulness. Surely, she must tire of doing so much. Yet she never leaves his side and she always smiles.

Our heavenly Father is even more patient and faithful with us. He gave us eternal life when He sent His Son to the cross. He never stops loving and forgiving us, even when we sin and disappoint Him. He never leaves us, even if we forget He is by our side. Someday, we will live with Him in heaven, where there will be no more suffering and tears.

We remember the sad and deadly price of our sins. We also rejoice in the forgiveness and eternal life in Jesus, who paid that price for us.

Journal: Memorize this verse: "For the wages of sin is death, but the free gift of God is eternal life in Christ Jesus our Lord" (Romans 6:23). How are both sin and eternal life part of your life?

Pray: Faithful God, thank You for eternal life! Amen. D. N.

You Are Beautiful!

What does it mean to be beautiful? Well, it depends on whom you ask. If you watch TV, read magazines, or listen to what the world says, the list might look like this: *clear skin *thin *muscular *shiny hair *fashionably dressed *perfect teeth *manicured fingernails.

If you listen to what God says through His Word, you see a completely different picture of beauty. His list might look like this: *a gentle, quiet spirit *fears the Lord *wise *generous *hardworking *faithful *worships Jesus.

If you asked, "How can I be beautiful?" you would also receive two different answers. The world's answers: *use the right skin and hair products *buy expensive clothing *lift weights *go to the beauty salon.

God tells us differently. He says: *listen to My Word *forgive as I forgive you *be humble *trust in Me *believe in Jesus as your Savior.

There is nothing wrong with looking nice. God wants us to care for our bodies. But He tells us true beauty is on the inside. This beauty far outshines any outward makeover we could have. Inner beauty that comes from the Lord lasts forever. It is pleasing and of great worth. This beauty was given to you in Baptism. There, God gave you faith, a faith that shines through you in service.

You know this "faith beauty" when you see it. It might be a smile, words of encouragement or forgiveness, a hymn of thanks and praise, generosity, or the words "Jesus loves you!"

Journal: What has God done in your life to make you beautiful? How can you show this beauty to others?

Pray: Dear Jesus, thank You for making me beautiful through Your precious gifts to me, through Your death and resurrection. Amen. C. K.

Forever Forgiven

Mrs. Fielding sat down, bending her head into her hands. She sniffed. "Help me, Lord," she whispered. "Forgive me for being impatient and unkind."

Her daughter peeked inside the door with concern. "Mom? What are you doing?"

"I'm praying, Audrey. I am asking God to forgive me and help me do better."

"But you're a mom. You're the one who teaches us to ask for forgiveness and to forgive others."

"True," Mom agreed, "and I am a sinner too. I need God to forgive me."

Audrey left the room thinking, *I guess I won't ever be perfect. Even when I'm all grown up, I'll still sin. And just like I'm forgiven now, I'll be forgiven then too. I will still be a child to my heavenly Father, and He will always hear my prayers and take away my sin.*

Mrs. Fielding emerged with a crumpled tissue and a peaceful look on her face.

"Thanks, sweetie, for caring about me. I feel better now. Do you know why?"

Audrey nodded. She did know why!

Together they recited, "If we confess our sins, He is faithful and just to forgive us our sins and to cleanse us from all unrighteousness."

Journal: Write about a time when you found it difficult to pray. How does God encourage us to come to Him with all our needs?

Pray: I'm not perfect, Lord. Thank You for forgiving me as often as I sin. Amen. R. A.

Jesus Says, "Come"

Do you know what the main worship area of a church is called? It's the nave, which comes from a Latin word meaning "ship."

The next time you're in church, imagine you're in a boat. Pretend it's Peter's fishing boat. According to Matthew 14, you might hear the disciples saying something like this: "Who's walking on the water toward us? . . . Come back, Peter! You can't walk on that rough water!"

Peter went anyway because Jesus told him, "Come." If Jesus would say to you, "Come," would you be afraid? Would you go?

We learn from Peter's experience that when we're with Jesus, we don't have to be afraid. Of course, you're not really in a rocking boat on a lake. You're in your church nave. Yet Jesus still invites you to come into the "boat" of faith, where you receive forgiveness.

When you leave your church boat, where is Jesus? He wants to go with you to your home or school. In those places, you could experience some stormy things. Just think of the problems in schools and families. We could easily be afraid.

Psalm 73:26 says, "God is the strength of my heart and my portion forever." The Holy Spirit gives you courage so you can think more about Jesus and His wonderful love than about your own worries. That's what it means to keep your eyes on the Lord, just as Peter first did. Jesus will not fail you. He is your hope, your Savior from sin.

Journal: How can leaving church be like Peter getting out of his boat?

Pray: Dear Jesus, thank You for Your Word and Sacraments. They strengthen me while I rest in Your boat, the Church. Through Your mercy and grace, stay with me when I leave that place. Fix my eyes on You. Amen. K. M.

The Alabaster Jar

The woman in Mark 14 brought an alabaster jar with her to Jesus a few days before He died. She broke the jar, and out flowed expensive ointment. She poured the ointment over Jesus' head.

Does that seem like a weird thing to do? Maybe so, but in Jesus' time, this was a way to show honor to a guest.

This jar and contents were so valuable they might have cost the woman her entire life's savings. But that didn't stop her. Neither did the criticism of the other guests in Simon's home, who fussed about what the woman did. They said she could have sold the ointment and given the money to the poor. Giving money to the poor is a good thing, but these men didn't understand what was happening before their eyes. They didn't see the "beautiful thing" (v. 6) this woman in faith had done to honor Jesus.

But Jesus saw it. He understood. He said, "She has anointed My body beforehand for burial" (v. 8). Jesus was about to give His life for all people on the cross.

The alabaster jar can remind us of Jesus' extravagant love. We can think about how His body was broken for us. His blood was poured out for us. His riches were given to us. The jar also reminds us that through the power of the Holy Spirit, we can love Jesus and confess that faith through beautiful actions, even actions that other people think are foolish or weird.

Journal: Write about some extravagant ways others have shown love to you.

Pray: Dear Jesus, help me to see who You are and what You have done for me. Then through Your Holy Spirit, continue to do "beautiful things" through me so I can show my love to You and others. Amen. E. G.

The Towel and Basin

Do you ever feel too proud to do certain tasks? Do you like cleaning up messes you didn't make? Are you *always* eager to help at school or happy to do chores? You probably won't get an award for doing jobs no one likes. You might not even get noticed. Instead, you may be bothered by a "naggy" voice inside that tries to convince you it's not necessary to help others.

To help us live by faith, Jesus showed us what true love is like. It is humble service. It is caring for our brothers, sisters, or parents through small tasks. It is doing little things on the bus or in the school hallway that no one may notice. The small deeds are really big deeds in God's eyes.

On the day after Jesus used the towel and basin to wash His disciples dirty feet, He did His most humble, lowly work. Do you know what He did? He died on the cross to pay for our sins. His death was shameful and lowly. But Jesus wasn't too proud to die for us.

We are thankful He did. Jesus' love is perfect and ours isn't. He kept God's Law and we can't. Jesus served as our perfect sacrifice, our Savior. He did it for us.

Now, through the power of His love, the Holy Spirit changes us from the inside out. He helps us pick up the towel and serve others.

Journal: What is your favorite way to serve others in Jesus' name?

Pray: Dear Jesus, thank You for serving me by dying on the cross. Help me to love others in Your name and for Your sake. Amen. E. G.

The Rooster

When Jesus told His disciples He was about to be arrested, they boasted that they would be brave and loyal. They said they would die with Him. Peter especially thought he would be brave. But Jesus warned him that before the rooster crowed, Peter would deny he knew Jesus three times! Jesus knew Peter would get scared and He warned Peter because He knew he would need to learn to trust in Him.

Sure enough, Peter denied Jesus three times that night. He was afraid he might be arrested too. Maybe he would be whipped or even killed! No, he'd better say he had nothing to do with Jesus. But then the rooster reminded him of his words and of Jesus' warning. Peter was so ashamed that he cried.

That's not the end of the story. Jesus died for Peter, but He didn't stay dead! Jesus rose from the grave on Easter, and He went on loving Peter. He forgave Peter. Peter learned to be a brave witness for Jesus because he had the power of Jesus' forgiveness and the joy of knowing that Jesus was alive to help him.

We may be like Peter, trusting our own power, yet denying Jesus by our words or actions. Afterward, we may also feel guilty and sad. At those times, we take comfort in believing that Jesus died for us. He is ready to forgive us just as He forgave Peter. We can trust that He is alive to go on forgiving us and helping us, no matter what!

Journal: How might someone your age deny knowing Jesus? Where can you find strength to live as God's child?

Pray: Dear Jesus, when I am tempted to deny You, give me Your power to resist evil. As You restored Peter by Your grace, please forgive and restore me. Amen. E. G.

The Dice

In Jesus' time, people played with something like dice, perhaps made of bone, to "cast lots" to make decisions. While Jesus was dying on the cross, the soldiers cast lots to decide who would get Jesus' tunic.

Can you imagine? While Jesus was suffering on the cross, the soldiers nearby were laughing and gambling for His clothes! For them, executions were everyday work, no big deal.

Jesus might have gotten upset with the soldiers and others who had put Him on the cross, but He didn't. The Bible tells us that He prayed for them. Luke 23:34 includes His beautiful prayer for them: "Father, forgive them, for they know not what they do."

We might think of the soldiers who crucified Jesus as super-bad guys. They were the ones who pounded the nails into His hands and feet. But Jesus was their Savior too. He died for their sins and pleaded that God would forgive their cruelty.

That's good to remember. Sometimes we can also be cruel. We might laugh at others, say unkind words, or exclude them. Sometimes we don't realize how much we are hurting them. But Jesus is ready to forgive our cruelty. He helps us become kind and caring.

Sometimes people are cruel to us too, and it's hard to forgive them. That's when we pray to our Father in heaven. The strength to forgive others comes from the Holy Spirit through God's Word and Sacraments. Look there.

Journal: Write Jesus' words in Luke 23:34 in your journal.

Pray: Dear Jesus, forgive me when I am cruel to others. Thank You for suffering cruelty for me and offering me Your love and forgiveness. Amen. E. G.

MARCH 16

John 19:28–29

The Sponge

As Jesus hung on the cross, He said "I thirst." He was probably dehydrated. In response, the soldiers dipped a sponge in a jug of sour wine and offered it to Jesus. John tells us that Jesus "received the sour wine" (John 19:30).

How strange, if you think about it! Jesus was God's Son. As God, He didn't need water or anything else to live. As God, He could have made water appear for Himself out of nowhere. Instead, Jesus the man let Himself depend on others for a drink.

The sponge reminds us that Jesus, even though He was God, became a human for us. He let Himself be weak and in need. Sometimes He was hungry, thirsty, tired, and in pain. He knows what it's like when we feel these things. Isn't that a great comfort? We can tell Him our troubles and know that He understands.

Jesus didn't become human just so He could understand our problems. Jesus became a man so that He could take our place. He suffered the punishment for sin that we deserve. He had to be a man to do that. He had to be a human being to die on the cross for us.

When we see a sponge, we can think of how Jesus became a human being for us and suffered because of it. We can remember how He saved us from the penalty of our sins. He took care of it all on the cross. For us!

Journal: What are some ways you can provide "drinks" for others who thirst?

Pray: Dear Jesus, thank You for taking my place and becoming human to live and die for me. Amen. E. G.

The Curtain

The people of Israel worshiped God in His temple. The room in the center of the temple was reserved for the ark of the covenant. This was a box that held the tablets on which God had written the Ten Commandments. A long purple curtain hung from the ceiling, hiding the ark from view. The room was called the Most Holy Place. No one could go there except the high priest. Once each year, the high priest went there to offer a sacrifice for his sins and for the people's sins.

The Most Holy Place was where God was located. No one could come before God then, because He is holy and people are sinners. Just as the curtain separated this place, the sins of the people separated them from God.

When Jesus died on the cross, He became the perfect and final sacrifice. When God ripped the temple curtain from top to bottom on the first Good Friday, He showed that Jesus' sacrifice was complete. Jesus' death covers the sins of all people everywhere! Priests no longer need to make sacrifices and present them at the temple. Now people come to God through Jesus.

The Bible doesn't tell us what happened to the curtain. But we can tell the story of the torn curtain. We can say that Jesus opened the way to God. We can say that His death and resurrection saved us from sin, death, and the devil. We tell of Jesus' love.

Journal: Think about a time some sin made you feel separated from God. How can remembering what Jesus did on the cross help?

Pray: Dear Jesus, thank You for Your sacrificial love, which opened the way for me to be with You forever. Amen. E. G.

The Stone

After Jesus died, a man who loved Him took down His body from the cross, wrapped it in cloths, and laid it in a grave. Then a big stone was rolled in front of the grave's opening.

When people die, we bury them and try to go on with our life as best we can. Death makes us sad because we miss the dead person, and we think about the fact that someday we will die too.

But even though it looked like it, the grave was not the end of Jesus' story. Three days later, someone else pushed away that big stone. You know who it was. An angel rolled the stone away, and Jesus came out of that grave.

This is good news. Our Lord is not dead. He is alive right now, and He hears our prayers. He sends us help. He forgives our sins and gives us victory over death. Although we are sad when someone we love dies, if that person believed in Jesus, we know we will see him or her again. And we don't have to be afraid to die, because Jesus will take us to heaven.

Many things are reminders of Jesus' pain, sadness, and death, but the stone is different. It rolled away all that sadness. That rolling stone reminds us that Jesus' death and resurrection brought joy and victory in the end! May Jesus' victory roll away your sadness too.

Journal: If you made a Lent display, what items would you put in it? Write about how those things would be reminders. If you can, collect and display your pieces. Then tell your story.

Pray: Dear Jesus, thank You for rolling away my fears about sin and death. Thank You for winning a victory over sin, death, and the devil for me! Amen. E. G.

MARCH 19

Luke 23:44–46

Lent and Love

Have you seen a lot of purple at church recently? That color goes along with Lent, the forty days from Ash Wednesday to Holy Saturday. During these days, we "think purple," we confess our sin, and we read again about the high price Jesus paid for our redemption. LENT shows us God's LOVE through Jesus' sacrifice.

Let's think about Lent and Love in acrostics. An acrostic is a kind of poem. The first letter of each line spells out a word. The words in the lines tell something about the main word.

L ove
E ternal
N ullifies our
T respasses

God's love is eternal. His love caused Him to send His only Son to suffer for our trespasses. Trespasses are the things we do wrong against Him and others. No matter how hard we try, we can't get rid of trespasses by ourselves.

God knew we couldn't. He knew we were helpless. So to cancel the debt we owed Him, God sent Jesus to nullify the cost of our sin and to defeat the devil.

During Lent, we hear again about Jesus' Passion. We learn of His love for us on a cross and His victory over all evil.

L earn of the Lord's
O verwhelming
V ictory over all
E vil

Journal: Write your own acrostic poem about Jesus or God's love.

Pray: Thank You, Jesus, for all You did for me on the cross. Amen. J. L.

We Are Winners

"And the winners are . . ."

Maybe you have heard someone say those words at the end of the school science fair or an art show. You've probably heard those words on TV when an announcer gives the winning numbers for a game of chance. Perhaps you've even dreamed of winning such a game yourself. Everyone loves to be a winner.

But do you realize that you already are a winner? Because you believe in Jesus Christ as your Savior, you have what you need to come through this life victorious. Jesus made us winners forever when He died on the cross and rose again. He took the punishment for our sins. He beat death and the devil for us by rising again on Easter morning. That makes everyone who believes in Jesus a member of His eternal kingdom.

Even if we won a million dollars, someday it would be spent, wasted, or perhaps stolen. But the prize of life in heaven with Jesus is for keeps. No one can destroy it. No one can take it away from us. As long as we trust in Jesus as our Savior, we have the greatest treasure—an eternal home in heaven with our Lord. We are winners!

Journal: What does it mean to "lay up for yourselves treasures on earth" (v. 19)? What does it mean to "lay up for yourselves treasures in heaven" (v. 20)?

Pray: Lord Jesus, when I am tempted to think that I am a loser, remind me through Your Word that You have made me a winner through Your death and resurrection. Amen. J. D.

Our Circle of Defense

Sara looked out the open sides of the tram at the lush grasslands that had been created to look like the Serengeti Plain in Africa. Zebras ran races, and a baby giraffe stood on wobbly legs by its mother.

Every year, the fifth graders looked forward to their trip to Wild Animal Park in San Diego. It meant having to write a report on your favorite animal, of course, but it also meant a bus ride and seeing beautiful African animals in a natural setting.

The guide asked everyone to look at a hillside on the right. There, in the shade of some trees, lay a circle of delicate gazelles. "Look at how the gazelles have made their circle," the guide said. "It's called a circle of defense. They can see an enemy coming from any direction."

Interesting, thought Sara. The gazelles weren't looking inward. Each gazelle looked outward in a different direction.

Fortunately, we don't have to live our lives carefully huddled in a circle of defense. We can remember that we have a sure defense. Jesus died for our sins. He took the punishment that was ours, and that brings us peace. We can live safely in His care.

That means that each Sunday we celebrate the Easter victory of Jesus. Satan may sneak up and try to tempt us, but God saw him coming and took care of him.

Journal: Write down some temptations you face. Remember that God is your defense. Draw a circle around the words you wrote.

Pray: Dear God and Defender, thank You for keeping me safe from danger and from sin and from Satan. I pray in Jesus' name. Amen. R. G.

Our Good Shepherd

Brooke and Cole couldn't wait to tell about the special guest they had in Sunday School. It was Hannah's Uncle Tom, who was visiting from Texas.

"It was so awesome," said Brooke. "Uncle Tom works on a sheep ranch. He showed us pictures of how he cares for his flock."

Cole said, "He cares for hundreds of sheep."

Brooke continued: "Tom explained that there are two types of shepherds. The first type herds the sheep from behind. He uses horses, dogs, and even Jeeps to move the sheep along."

Dad asked, "What's the other type?"

"That's the kind that Tom is," Cole answered. "Instead of herding from behind, Tom calls to them from the front. The sheep recognize his voice, and they follow him!"

Brooke nodded her head and added, "Tom guides his sheep to the greenest pastures and the freshest water. And in the evening, he leads them into the sheep pen where they are safe."

"But that's not even the best part," said Cole. "Tom told us that there are only two places in the world where shepherds lead their flocks. One is the American Southwest, where Tom works. The other is Palestine, where Jesus lived. When Jesus said that He is the Good Shepherd, people understood that He was calling and leading them. They knew that a good shepherd would risk his own life to save one of his sheep. And that's exactly what Jesus did; He gave His life for each one of us. That's the best part!"

Journal: You are Jesus' little lamb. Read Psalm 23. How does your Good Shepherd care for you?

Pray: Jesus, loving Shepherd, thank You for calling me by name and making me Your little lamb. Amen. N. D.

The Fight

As Mark got close to home, he heard shouting. Again. It seemed to him like his parents were always fighting. He was tired of seeing Mom's puffy red eyes and Dad slumped in his chair, talking to no one. When Mark's parents fought, the whole house felt different—unsettled and angry. Mark worried. Would his parents get a divorce? Mark stopped outside his front door and sat down on the porch. He hoped the anger would blow over soon.

Have you ever felt like Mark? While it's perfectly normal for people to argue, it doesn't make it any easier to live with. Sometimes, fighting can lead to more problems. But sometimes, talking helps bring feelings and thoughts to the surface to be dealt with.

Sin leads to brokenness even in families. Joseph in the Old Testament went through trouble after trouble, but finally, he was able to see God's amazing plan at work in his life and in the life of his family members.

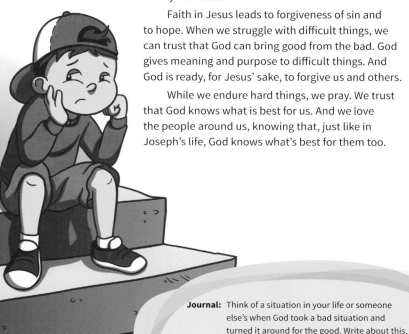

Faith in Jesus leads to forgiveness of sin and to hope. When we struggle with difficult things, we can trust that God can bring good from the bad. God gives meaning and purpose to difficult things. And God is ready, for Jesus' sake, to forgive us and others.

While we endure hard things, we pray. We trust that God knows what is best for us. And we love the people around us, knowing that, just like in Joseph's life, God knows what's best for them too.

Journal: Think of a situation in your life or someone else's when God took a bad situation and turned it around for the good. Write about this.

Pray: Dear Lord, thank You for giving me strength when difficult things happen in my life. Help me to trust that You will bring good from the bad and care for me along the way. Amen. J. S.

MARCH 24

Psalm 56:3

The Comforter

Maria sat up in bed. She shivered. It had been a scary dream, full of hungry, fire-breathing dinosaurs chasing her.

She pulled her blankets up to her chin and tried to breathe deeply and go back to sleep. It didn't work. Maria flung back the blankets and went into her mom's bedroom.

"Bad dream?" Mom asked. Maria nodded. Mom opened her arms, and Maria crawled into bed with her mother and fell asleep instantly.

The next morning at breakfast, Maria said, "Why do I have bad dreams, Mom?"

Mom smiled. "You're not the only one! I have bad dreams too."

"What do you dream about?" Maria asked.

"I forget them."

"How do you forget? If I close my eyes, I still see the dinosaurs."

"I pray," Mom said. "That's what my mom told me to do when I was a girl, and we know God always hears our prayers."

"What do you say when you pray?"

Mom put her arm around Maria. "I tell God what I dreamed about, and I ask Him to wrap His arms around me and help me sleep. Then, I take some deep breaths and list all the blessings God gives me. I usually fall asleep while I'm counting."

"And it works?"

Mom nodded. "God longs to comfort us, Maria. He loves us so much! So next time you have a bad dream, remember to pray about it. God is always with us to give us His love and His comfort."

Journal: Describe a bad dream you've had. How does God bring you comfort?

Pray: Dear God, thank You for comforting me when I am afraid. Remind me of all the blessings You've given me. In Jesus' name I pray. Amen. K. G.

A Puzzle for You

Solve the puzzle that follows to find out why God sent His Son to die for you. Cross out the letters X, B, and Z.

X	B	F	O	R	B	X	G	O	D
X	Z	S	O	L	B	O	Z	V	E
Z	D	X	B	Y	O	U	X	T	H
A	T	X	B	H	E	X	B	D	I
E	D	Z	Z	X	F	B	O	X	R
X	X	Y	O	U	X	Z	B	X	Z

Did you find out why God sent His Son? Because God loved you!

An important church leader named Nicodemus was puzzled by Jesus' actions and teachings, so he came one night to chat with Jesus. Nicodemus and Jesus talked about how a person becomes part of God's kingdom and how someone old can be born again.

You know how it happens, right? It happens through the power of Baptism. Through Baptism, a person of any age is born again through water and the Spirit. There, a baby, toddler, tween, teen, or adult becomes a child in the kingdom of God.

Someday, some puzzled person may ask you, "What do I have to do to be born again?" You know the answer: you don't do anything. God does it all. In love, He sent His Son, Jesus, to die for your sins. In love, He gives you faith. In love, He forgives your sins and gives you eternal life. Now the puzzle is what would you like to do?

Journal: If you, like Nicodemus, could sit down and chat with Jesus, what would you ask Him?

Pray: Dear Jesus, thank You for loving me so much that You came down to earth to be human like me in order to save me! Help me to share this great news with others. Amen. P. L.

No Favorites

"Let's invite Jen to Bible study," said Naomi.

"I don't think she will come," said Mariann. "She doesn't go to church. Sometimes she says mean things about other people. She doesn't seem like she would be interested in learning about God. I don't think we should invite her."

Still, Naomi invited Jen to join them and she accepted. In the weeks that followed, Jen never missed a meeting. The girls got to know her better. They helped her learn about God's loving grace and mercy. She asked a lot of questions about how Jesus had come to be her Savior and take away her sins. She volunteered to pray at the end of each class. That summer, Jen was baptized.

In the years that followed, Jen continued to read and study God's Word, and she attended church and youth group. When she went to college, she started a Bible study in her dorm. Eventually, Jen became a missionary.

Imagine how differently things might have been if Naomi had not invited Jen to that first Bible study!

How wonderful that God does not look at people like we do. His Word tells us that He has no favorites. He does not judge people as we do. No sin is too big for God to forgive. No life is too bad for God to change. His Holy Spirit can bring faith to even the hardest heart. Our amazing God wants all people to find salvation through Christ.

Journal: Draw a cross in the center of a circle. Add spokes coming out of the circle. At the end of each spoke, write the name of someone who needs to know about Jesus. Leave some spokes blank and fill them in later.

Pray: Dear Lord, open my eyes to the people around me who need to know about Jesus. Help me to pray for them, invite them to church, and speak Your truth in love to all. In Jesus' name I pray. Amen. D. N.

The Boat, the Bedroom

The fierce storm frightened Heather. As Mom tucked her into bed, she said, "Remember, Jesus has power over everything. He will be with us tonight even if the wind and rain are really bad."

During the night, a loud crash woke Heather's family. A tree had fallen on the corner of the house where Heather's bedroom was. But when the tree fell, Heather wasn't in her room. She was in the bathroom. God had spared her life.

The next day, after the family had temporarily fixed the damage, Heather and her mom talked again about the Bible story they had read the day before. It was a storm story.

Jesus was in a boat with His disciples. A storm had come up on the open sea. They woke Jesus so that He would help. In a miraculous way, Jesus calmed the wind and the sea. He said, "'Peace! Be still!' And the wind ceased, and there was a great calm" (v. 39).

"Heather," said her mom, "God has power over storms and falling trees. He has power over our worst enemies—sin, death, and the devil.

"I'm thankful He used His power to watch over you. And I'm thankful that He continues to watch over us all our days."

Since that night, Heather and her parents have had many opportunities to tell others how God took care of Heather that night. And that story gives them a chance to tell another story—about Jesus, their Lord and Savior.

Journal: How has God helped you through tough times?

Pray: Dear Jesus, forgive me when I doubt Your care. When I am afraid, remind me of Your watchful eye and love. Lead me to trust in You. Amen. D. G.

MARCH 28

Matthew 14:22–33

A Music Duet

Jacob and Mark were going to play a duet on their recorders for the school's spring concert. Mark was just beginning to learn to play, but Jacob had been playing for several years. Mark was nervous. What if he messed up in front of the entire school and all the parents? When the time came to play, Jacob played the piece without a single mistake. Mark, however, made several mistakes.

When their duet was finished, everyone applauded. Were they just being nice? Several people even told them how good they sounded. "Didn't you hear my mistakes?" Mark asked. To his surprise, nobody had heard them. Jacob's perfect performance had covered up Mark's mistakes.

In our Bible reading, Peter wanted to walk to Jesus on the water. He began boldly looking at Jesus, but then he got scared. He wasn't able to walk on the water. As Peter sank, Jesus caught him. Jesus rescued Peter.

When we look at the world's troubles and our mistakes, we are scared too. But God is rich in mercy and grace and catches us. Jesus reaches out and rescues us. Through the power of Baptism and His Word, Jesus holds us up. He saves us from the power of Satan, the punishment of sin, and eternal separation from Him through death.

Our life song is a duet. God is the perfect musician. He is with us, working in and through us to serve others in His kingdom. With our eyes on Him, we confidently play on.

Journal: Write about a time when Jesus held you up.

Pray: Dear Jesus, through Your perfection, death, and resurrection, cover up my sin and doubt. Hold me up forever with Your strong hands. Amen. E. G.

Again and Again

Dad pulled out the family Bible and called the crew to attention. Rob groaned on the inside but didn't dare let on. One of his little brothers wasn't so smart though.

"Not again! We do this every night. I think we've heard all this stuff a million times by now."

Rob winced. This would not go over well.

Dad said, "Well, son, thanks for telling me what we need to hear. You make it easy!"

He turned to Deuteronomy 6 and raised his voice a bit when he got to verse 7. Finishing the passage, he looked at his children.

"There's not going to be a time when we don't read God's Word. By it, we are kept firm in the faith. We are forgiven. We are taught. We are guided along life's way. We don't get tired of hearing and learning it, because this 'stuff' is so important. It's the truth that we are sinners and the promise that we are saved by Jesus. Isn't it great that we get to hear that again and again?"

Rob and his siblings looked at their dad. They nodded in both shame and relief. "Let's pray, kids," Dad said.

Journal: What are some creative ways you could memorize portions of Scripture?

Pray: Thank You for Your Word, Lord. Through it, You love me. I love You too. Amen. R. A.

Deluxe Cleaning

Taylor vacuumed the carpet, walked the dog, set the table, and loaded the dishwasher. He even helped wash the windows.

All this cleaning was for Grandma, who was coming to visit! The house had to look spotless, with each window sparkling. Grandma only visited three or four times a year because she lived so far away. Still it seemed funny to make a big deal just for Grandma.

Long ago, the Israelites made a big deal out of meeting with God and asking Him for forgiveness. They knew that God was holy and that they deserved only punishment from Him. So they stopped what they were doing in order to get ready for worship. They skipped meals. They washed their clothes and put on clean ones to show God they wanted Him to wash away their sins and make them clean again.

It may seem unnecessary to make a big deal out of Lent. We may think we don't need to focus on Jesus' sacrifice or ask God for forgiveness.

But Lent, with its special services and rituals, helps us concentrate on how much we need Jesus as our Savior. We see Him as the only one who can make our hearts clean again. Lent is an opportunity to develop a closer friendship with Jesus, our Savior. As God's Spirit works in us, we are well-prepared to receive the Easter gift of freedom, the victory Jesus won over death and the devil.

Journal: What are some special things you are doing to observe Lent? Write about them in your journal.

Pray: Lord Jesus, take away the dirty clothes of my sin and replace them with the clean robe of Your holiness. Amen.
J. H.

Where I Fit In

Romans 12:1–3

Emma watched her little brother pick up a square peg. He hammered it, trying to force it into a round hole.

As Emma watched, she thought she often felt like that square peg.

"Hi, kids!" their mom called. She hugged Eli and looked at Emma. "You look thoughtful." She set Eli down. "What's on your mind?"

Emma pointed to Eli's toys. "Sometimes I don't fit in anywhere—like a square peg in a round hole."

"That feels lonely, doesn't it?" Mom said. "Maybe your latest Sunday School memory verse will help."

Emma paused and recited. " 'Do not be conformed to this world, but be transformed by the renewal of your mind' (Romans 12:2). My teacher said God transforms us and makes us new."

"Yes, transformation begins when God makes us His own in Baptism," Mom said. "The Holy Spirit guides us throughout our lives. Our transformation is complete in heaven. Right now, though, think about the first part of that verse."

"Do not conform." Emma paused. "That means 'Don't be like everyone else.' "

"Right. God made you unique, Emma. He loves you so much that He sent Jesus to die for your sins."

Emma smiled. "I'm supposed to feel out of place!"

Just then Eli clapped. He found the right peg for the hole. Emma clapped too. She found where she fit in. She was a child of God.

Journal: Draw a picture of a place where you fit in.

Pray: God, thanks for making me Your unique child. Through the Holy Spirit, continue to transform me. In Jesus' name I pray. Amen. J. H.

APRIL 1

1 Corinthians 1:22–25

The Foolishness of God

Today did you tie someone's shoelaces together? Did you put salt in the sugar bowl? Did you put a sign on someone's back that said "Kiss me"?

On April 1, practical jokes and hoaxes can be fun to do, but tomorrow, we might fuss at someone who tries to fool us and say, "April Fools' Day is past, and you're the biggest fool at last."

Foolishness can also be sinful. Destroying property is wrong. Sending mean text messages or posting lies on a computer is wrong. Taking things that don't belong to us is wrong.

Can a wise teaching be foolish to some people? The Bible says, "The foolishness of God is wiser than men, and the weakness of God is stronger than men" (v. 25). God's foolish truth is this: Jesus Christ died for sinners. If someone is looking to be saved by his or her good deeds, the idea of salvation only through Jesus' deeds is foolish. Is someone expecting Jesus to do miracles before he or she believes in Him? Well, that's foolishness too.

Nothing we do saves us from sin, death, and the devil. God does it all. He saves us. He sent His only Son to take the punishment we deserve. Jesus took our sins to the cross. There, He paid for them.

No joke.

Jesus is the wisdom and power of God. No kidding. God's Word gives us Jesus. There is no other way. Jesus gives us salvation.

Journal: Draw a picture to show your thanks for Jesus' sacrifice. Share the drawing with a friend or family member. Tell that person why you are so thankful.

Pray: Dear heavenly Father, thanks for sacrificing Your Son so I can receive salvation. In His name I pray. Amen. J. L.

Countdown

10 . . . 9 . . . 8 . . . 7 . . .

What do you think about when you hear a countdown? Do you imagine a rocket launch? a New Year's Eve party? the last few moments before summer break?

When you think about it, the Bible is a little like a giant countdown. From the time Adam and Eve sinned, people looked forward to the promise God gave in the Garden of Eden: a Savior would come to restore God's relationship with us. Ten . . . nine . . .

Abraham led his family to the land God promised and became a father to Isaac and eventually to nations—including the Messiah. Eight . . . seven . . .

Moses led God's people out of slavery and into the Promised Land, reminding us of our Deliverer. Six . . . five . . .

Esther pleaded for the life of the Jews—the people who would give the world the Redeemer. Four . . . three . . .

John the Baptist preached repentance and pointed to the coming Christ. Two . . . one . . .

As you look forward to Easter, remember that this was the point in history where God showed the world His salvation for all—through Jesus' death and resurrection.

We also remember that Jesus has promised to come again to bring all believers to Him forever. We start a new countdown—the countdown to the day when sin and death are no more!

Journal: Do you like waiting for things? What do you think it will be like when Jesus returns?

Pray: God, thank You for keeping Your promise to save us through Jesus. Help me tell others this Good News of salvation as I wait for Jesus to come again. Amen. L. C.

Future Shock

Anna two-stepped up the stairs and through the door. Soccer practice had gone longer than expected. All she could think of was how good dinner would taste, but once she heard hushed talking, thoughts of food left her mind. Her mother was talking about test results and medical bills. Later, with tears in her eyes, Anna asked her father about the conversation.

"I heard Mom talking. It sounded serious."

Her father asked her to sit down so he could explain. Anna learned that her mother had been talking about the test results for their cat, Honey. Anna felt embarrassed but relieved that her mom was fine.

Have you ever heard bad news and assumed the worst? Martin Luther said that fearing the loss of God's love and care for our daily lives is a tool of the devil. He uses it to make us doubt God's love.

Our heavenly Father knows all of our needs. He provided for our greatest need when He sent His only Son, Jesus Christ, to suffer, die on the cross, and rise again for our salvation. God does not want us to doubt His unconditional love for us.

The next time you hear bad news, remember God's power and love. He is in control. Jesus said to His disciples: "Therefore I tell you, do not be anxious about your life, what you will eat, nor about your body, what you will put on." That's good news. The Holy Spirit replaces worry about our future with faith.

Journal: Write about a time that you overheard bad news and feared the worst would happen. Did the worst thing happen?

Pray: Dear Lord, when I hear bad news, remind me of Your love. Through Your Word, send Your Holy Spirit so that I may trust Your plan for my life. In Jesus' name I pray. Amen. J. H.

Dishwasher for the Lord

Have the words "Time to do your homework" or "Time to go to bed" or maybe "Please take out the trash" ever put you in a bad mood? For Sarah, the words "It's your turn to wash the dishes" gave her a stomachache!

One Sunday, a Bible reading caught her attention. She felt as though God were speaking to her through this verse: "Whatever you do, work heartily, as for the Lord and not for men" (v. 23). Whatever I do, Sarah wondered, even washing dishes? She prayed, "God, I haven't been able to change my feelings on my own. Help me to think about Jesus the next time I'm asked to do the dishes, and help me to do them without making a fuss."

The next time Sarah was asked to do the dishes, she still got a stomachache. But she prayed for God's help and repeated the Bible verse to herself. And she did the dishes without any tears! It took several dish-washings before she thought, This isn't such a bad job. I like using the time to pray.

Sarah's story can help us understand what it means to do all things "for the Lord." We don't work to make God happy so He will like us or save us. God already loves us because He made us and saves us through Jesus, who truly did everything "for the Lord." Now, because of Jesus, God works in our lives as He worked in Sarah's.

Journal: Consider a specific chore you have. Would you perform the chore differently if you thought you were doing it for the Lord?

Pray: Dear God, thank You for Your Holy Spirit, who works in my life. Help me remember that everything I do flows from my love for You. In Jesus' name I pray. Amen. C. R.

Passing the Test

David hated this time of the year. This was the week his school took achievement tests. He knew he would have to spend hours hunched over his desk trying to figure out what exactly the questions were asking and what exactly the answers could be.

If he did well, his teacher and parents would be happy. He would be relieved. If he messed up, everyone would be upset, and he might not pass into the next grade. Who knows? He might not even get into the right classes in high school. He might not get into the college he hoped to attend. He might be a failure all of his life. All because of a test he didn't want to take in the first place.

Do you ever worry about tests? Many people feel pressure when they are asked to show what they know and then are judged by the results.

The good news is that God does not require you to pass a test to qualify for His love or forgiveness. He offers it freely. It is Jesus who has earned the A that God has placed beside your name in His record book.

You do not need to worry about passing God's test. He does not ask, "How did you do?" He only asks, "Who is your Savior?" And the Holy Spirit has given you the answer to that question. It is Jesus.

Journal: What is your favorite subject in school? Thank God for the things you are learning. What do you want to learn more about in the future?

Pray: Dear Lord, thank You for teaching me about Your world. Help me remember that Jesus has given me all I need to succeed in this life and to live with You forever in heaven. Amen. C. S.

Me, Special?

James had an awful day. In fact, the whole week stunk. Nothing was going right.

Last night during the ball game, he dropped the ball every time it came to him. Today, he had trouble understanding math. He failed a history quiz. He just knew that his teacher hated him! James wondered why God even made him. He must have been a mistake.

Have you ever felt like James? It might be hard to see any good in your life. It may seem like everything you do is a failure. Maybe you don't look the way you want to look. Maybe it's hard for you to see any talents you have. You may question whether God really meant for you to be here.

But God tells us that He made each one of us, even if we have unique needs. Before we were born, He knew what we would be like. Even though we may not see it, God has a plan for us. He made us exactly the way we are for a reason. We are so important to Him that He even sent a Savior to die for our sins.

So how can we feel good about ourselves when everything seems to be going wrong? Remember that our worth doesn't come from what others say or what we do or don't do. Our worth comes from God and what He has done for us through Jesus. We are special because God says we are!

Journal: Write down three things that are special or unique about you.

Pray: Dear Lord, thank You for making me just the way I am. Help me to see the special gifts You have given me as ways I can serve others. Thank You for the most special gift, Jesus. In His name I pray. Amen. C. K.

Helpful Hands

"Mom, let me give you a hand with those grocery bags," Lucas said.

"Take my hand so you don't slip," said Kara to her friend Sophie as they hiked across the shallow creek.

"Let's give the fifth-grade class a hand for their hard work at our playground clean-up," said Principal Baker as she led the other students in applause.

Our hands can provide help and encouragement for others.

In the Bible, the right hand symbolizes strength. The "righteous right hand" (v. 10) of God powerfully fights for us in the troubles and battles we face. As God has done for all His people, His "righteous right hand" upholds us and gives us victory over our enemies.

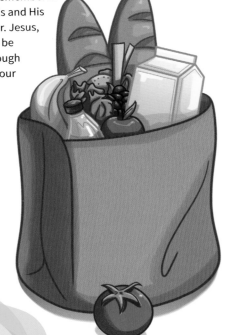

On Good Friday, Christians especially remember in worship the time when Jesus gave His hands and His whole life to give us the greatest victory ever. Jesus, our Suffering Servant, allowed His hands to be nailed to the cross as He was crucified. Through His death and resurrection, Jesus defeated our worst enemies of all: sin, death, and Satan.

God's "righteous right hand" is the victory God has won for us through Jesus, the Messiah. God's "righteous right hand" will always fight for us, uphold us, and carry us safely to our heavenly home.

Journal: Make a small, palm-side-up drawing of a hand. On the palm, write down a way you can use your hand this coming week to share with someone the strength we have in Jesus, our Savior.

Pray: Lord Jesus, thank You for using Your hands to serve, save, and uphold me. Help me use my hands to share with others the victory You give over sin, death, and Satan. Amen. D. G.

Preparing for Easter

Four words can help us compare the children of Israel and the blessings of Easter. Like the word *resurrection*, all four words begin with *r*.

The first word is *rescue*. In Exodus, we read how Moses led the people of Israel out of Egypt. It was God's rescue plan. Life in Egypt was hard for the Israelites. They had hardships like making bricks in the hot sun. We have the hardships of sin and suffering too. But Moses led the people out of Egypt as God rescued them. In the death and resurrection of Jesus, God rescues us too.

The second word is *relationship*. At Mount Sinai, God established a new covenant with the children of Israel by giving them the Ten Commandments. The Commandments were not just rules to follow. They focused on the relationship of the people with God and with one another. God sent Jesus to suffer and die for us because God wanted us to have an eternal relationship with Him through faith in Jesus.

The next word is *repent*. Sadly, the Israelite people did not always obey God's Law. We don't always obey God either. When we sin, God calls us to repent. To repent is to turn back toward God, where He rescues us again through His forgiveness and love.

In response to God's rescue, we can *rejoice* over His love and mercy in our lives. The Israelites did that. They rejoiced after crossing the Red Sea and seeing their enemies destroyed. We can rejoice over the victory of Jesus, who returned to life from death.

As you celebrate the resurrection of Jesus, use those four words to help you remember what Easter is all about—**rescue, relationship, repent,** and **rejoice.**

Journal: Make a list of other words that help you remember the real meaning of Easter.

Pray: Dear God, thank You for loving me enough to rescue me from my enemies through Jesus, my suffering Savior. Amen. D. G.

APRIL 9

Romans 6:13

Grandpa's Tackle Box

Billy loved to go fishing with his grandpa. They would spend hours in a boat out in the middle of the lake, trying to catch fish. Billy especially loved looking inside his grandpa's tackle box. It was full of brightly colored lures. Some were made with feathers. Others were made of plastic and looked like real worms. The lures were used to "tempt" or trick the fish into being caught. Billy spent hours talking to his grandpa about lures. He even knew which lures were used to catch which fish.

Fishing can remind us of how Satan tempts us to sin, to fall away from Jesus. Just as different lures are used to catch different fish, Satan uses many different temptations to get us to sin.

For some people, a certain brand of shoes in an open locker can be a temptation to steal. Others are tempted to gossip in order to make fun of someone. Some are tempted to take drugs or visit bad websites. Others are tempted to cheat during a test.

Whatever temptations we face, we can be comforted by the fact that God is always ready to help us. The Bible reading reminds us that God will provide a way out for us. Jesus suffered all the consequences of sin, including all the times we yield to temptation. He stands ready to help us turn away from temptations. He will not allow us to be tempted beyond what we can bear. His love is that great.

Journal: What lures does the devil use to tempt you?
Draw some lures in your journal. Draw a cross
beside each one to remind you of God's strength
in temptation and His forgiveness when we sin.

Pray: Dear heavenly Father, when I am tempted, help me turn
away and not give in. Thank You for sending Jesus to take
away all my sin. In His name I come to You. Amen. J. D.

A Lasting Crown

"Hosanna! Hosanna!" Taylor was waving two palm branches from yesterday's church service.

"Will you cut that out?!" Kole yelled. Kole was not in the mood for his little sister's parade. "Besides, those branches are falling apart and making a mess." Kole looked up and saw Mom staring at him. Her look was a mixture of disappointment and worry.

Kole sighed, "Look, Mom, I'm sorry. But I just can't get this project to look right, and Taylor's distracting me. I'll never win that geography trophy. Nothing's going the way I planned."

"I have a question for you," Mom said. Kole set down his glue and turned toward her. "How long do you think that geography trophy will last?"

Kole smiled a little. "Probably longer than the soccer one from last year—the pieces are still in my room somewhere. But definitely longer than Taylor's palm branches!"

Mom chuckled. "You know, it's great to do your best. It can also be fun to win. But the best prize of all has already been won for you."

Kole had heard this before. "Heaven, right?"

"Some Bible verses describe a crown of life or a treasure that never fades away," Mom added.

"Yeah, I remember that," said Kole.

His mom continued, "On Palm Sunday, people called Jesus the King of Israel. It's hard to believe that a few days later He wore a crown of thorns. It surprised the disciples, but that week went exactly as God planned, and Jesus won the crown of life for us all."

Journal: Are you proud of a certain award? How does it feel to know God will give you the crown of life?

Pray: Dear God, thank You for Jesus, the King of kings, and my lasting crown. Amen. L. C.

He Understands

Mrs. Alexander slept after her emergency surgery. Mr. Alexander yawned as he sat next to his wife's hospital bed. David rubbed his tummy; he was hungry for comfort food. Theresa paced the floor or patted her mom's hand.

The Alexander family was going through a difficult time. Mom had pain and then surgery, Dad was exhausted, David was hungry, and Theresa was concerned. Their day was filled with stress. Each person, in his or her own way, needed comfort.

Mark 11:12 reads, "On the following day, when they came from Bethany, [Jesus] was hungry." What comfort could the Alexanders find in that simple verse? Here are some ideas. Jesus had just ridden into Jerusalem while the people shouted "Hosanna" and waved palms. During that Holy Week, Jesus experienced tiredness, stress, concern, pain, and even death—and oh, yes, also hunger. Here is the comfort: whatever emotions or struggles we go through, Jesus can relate to it!

It is a wonderful gift to have a friend who can relate to our experiences. But Jesus is more than a friend. He is our God. He can do all things and help in all situations. He died on the cross to pay for our sin, rose again to guarantee us eternal life with Him, and lives in our hearts through every joy and pain of ours. What a comfort to trust in Jesus through it all!

Journal: What did you experience today that Jesus also experienced?

Pray: Jesus, help me when I am going through difficult times. Give me Your comfort. Amen. T. W.

Jesus' Love

How are you feeling today? Are you excited because of Easter? Are you worried about grades? Are you anxious about making the team? Maybe your feelings are so strong right now that you're not sure how to describe them.

During Jesus' last week before the cross, He experienced many things. On Palm Sunday, He must have been thrilled. Later, He was furious at people who cared more about money than about respecting God's temple.

In the Garden of Gethsemane, Jesus struggled with what He was about to go through—the pain of the cross and the sin of every person for all time. Then He was betrayed by someone close to Him. (Do you remember his name?) He was denied by one of His best friends. (How about his name?) He was bullied and mocked by people. How terrible this all must have felt! On the cross, He was completely alone.

You know what? No matter how *you* feel, there is one thing Jesus *always* feels for you: love. He loves you, and He knows what it feels like to live in this world. In fact, He went through that emotional week before Easter out of love for you. Jesus knows what we're going through. But Jesus didn't just experience suffering, did He? He also experienced joy and victory because He won over the sinful jeers, hurtful thoughts, death, and the devil. We can experience that joy with Jesus—here on earth and when we live with Him forever.

Journal: How do you feel today? How does Jesus feel about you?

Pray: Jesus, thank You for going through so much for me. Thank You for Your love. Amen. L. C.

What No One Knows

Macy gazed out the window. "I cleaned my room, put away my toys, and combed my hair. I am ready. When are my cousins coming?"

"I don't know exactly, but they said sometime today," Dad said. "Why don't you find something to do while you wait?"

"I want to be ready when they come, so I'm going to stay right here and watch for them." Macy turned back to the window.

Christians are waiting too. We are waiting for Christ to return and take us to heaven to live with Him. It could be today or tomorrow, or it might not be for years and years. But Christ will return. There will be no more sickness, no more crying, and no more pain. We will spend eternity celebrating with Him in heaven.

What do we do while we wait? Jesus tells us in the Bible to be on guard and to keep awake. That doesn't mean no sleeping. It means to be on guard when Satan tries to tempt us. It means asking Jesus to forgive us when we sin. It means trusting that Jesus is the Son of God and the Savior of the world.

While we wait, Jesus has given us work to do. He wants us to serve others. When we are able, we can tell our friends and family how Jesus died to take the punishment for our sins. He wants us to help others and show God's love to them.

Macy was thrilled when her cousins arrived. Our greatest joy will be when we see Jesus and begin our new life in heaven with Him.

Journal: What are you doing while you wait for Jesus to return?

Pray: Dear Jesus, come quickly and help me to be ready for Your victorious return. Amen. G. G.

Never Alone

APRIL 14

John 16:32–33

Karly clung to her friend's hand as she was pulled toward the Sunday School classroom. Karly was a visitor and wasn't sure she wanted to go to Sunday School. But Faith was excited for her to meet the other kids.

"Welcome to our class!" the teacher greeted them at the door. "We're so glad you came." Faith introduced Karly, and soon the lesson began.

Sometimes it's hard to face things alone. You'd rather not go at all. It's so much easier when you have a friend at your side.

Jesus knew that soon His friends would all leave Him. But He knew He was not alone. His heavenly Father was with Him.

Your heavenly Father is with you too. He loves you so much that He sent His Son to this earth. Jesus gave His life for you to save you from eternal death. And He comforts us in our troubles because He has overcome all of them.

After Sunday School was over, the teacher thanked Faith for bringing Karly. She told Karly she hoped she would see her again. Smiling, the girls left the classroom.

Looking at her friend, Karly said, "Thanks for asking me to come today, Faith. I was scared, but I really had fun. Everyone was so nice."

Laughing, Faith replied, "I knew you'd like it! And it was fun bringing a friend with me. I hope you can come again soon."

Journal: What are some things you do not like doing alone? How will knowing Jesus is always with you help you when you're feeling all alone?

Pray: Heavenly Father, when I am afraid, help me to run to You and not away from You. Thank You for sending Your Son to die for me and for being with me in all my troubles. In Jesus' name I pray. Amen. B. S.

Rest

"I just want to get home and go to bed," Jimmy yawned. "It's been a long, long week."

"Whatever happened to the kid who was going to stay up all night and watch videos?" his dad teased.

He got no answer. Jimmy's eyes were shut and he was slumped to one side. Jimmy's dad smiled. He parked the car as quietly as he could and got out. Reaching into the back seat, he scooped up his son to carry him into the house and to bed.

Holy Saturday is a day of waiting. It involves rest. On that day, the terrible events of Good Friday are over. The suffering is past; the dying is over. Jesus' body rests in the tomb, and His disciples wait in their hiding place in Jerusalem. Though they don't yet know it, tomorrow will be the start of an explosively exciting day—the day Jesus rises from the dead and begins to send them out into the whole world to tell the Good News of forgiveness. But until then, there is just waiting for the good to come. And resting.

God sends you times of rest too—days when everything is quiet and nothing exciting is happening. You may even complain, "I'm bored!" But God has great plans for you, and you will need the rest He is giving to you now. Never forget that you are God's own child, the one Jesus suffered, died, and rose again for. And He has plans for your life, just wait and see. Enjoy your rest!

Journal: When are you usually the busiest? When do you rest? Write a sentence prayer thanking God for both of these times.

Pray: Dear Father, thank You for the rest You give me. Please let it make me strong to serve You. Amen.
K. V.

Unique Voices

Alligators swim easily. They can jump as high as six feet and run on land between twenty-five and thirty miles per hour. They are fierce predators. The adults have no natural enemies except larger alligators. The babies, however, have many enemies.

The female alligator uses leaves, twigs, and mud to build a nest on the ground. She digs a hole in the center of the mound and lays a lot of eggs. Then she covers the hole with dirt and stays near the nest to guard it from any predators.

After about seventy days, the baby alligators begin to yelp and grunt inside their eggs. When the mother alligator hears them, she recognizes their voices and scratches the dirt off the top of the nest. Many of the babies hatch out of the eggs by themselves, but some need help. The mother rolls these eggs around in her mouth until they crack and the babies are freed.

Our Bible verse tells us that God knew us even before we were born. God is all-knowing.

Before Jeremiah was born, God had a plan for him. God has a plan for you—a special plan. In Baptism, He marked you as His. He freed you from sin, death, and the devil and gave you power to live under Him in His kingdom.

God planned for Jeremiah to be a prophet. What are His plans for you? You might not know yet, but God does. And He is leading you.

Journal: What are some things God has for you to do today?

Pray: Dear Lord, You know each person You have made. Thank You for making me in a special way and remaking me to be Your child in Baptism. Bless all I do today. In Jesus' name I pray. Amen. C. H.

APRIL 17

John 20:19–20

Jesus Is My Savior!

The year is AD 30, a long time ago. The place is Jerusalem. It is Monday evening, and the sun has already gone down. It had been a long Monday for Hannah and Rebekah. And now Father was late getting home from work. Hannah and Rebekah were excited. They wanted to hear the latest news about Jesus.

"Happy day!" Father said when he came in the door. "I've got some good news about yesterday. It's true! Jesus is alive! Two disciples saw Him yesterday afternoon. He was walking with them on the road. And then last night, the disciples were together with all the doors locked. They were still afraid that the temple leaders might be after them. Suddenly, Jesus appeared, even though the doors were still locked."

"How did He do that?" Rebekah asked.

"Jesus can do anything. Remember?" Hannah said.

"Were the disciples sure it was Jesus?" Mother asked.

"Yes!" Father said. "This is the best part. At first, they thought He might be a ghost. But Jesus talked to them and held out His hands. He showed them His feet too. They could see the places on Jesus' hands and feet where He was nailed to the cross."

"It's true," Mother said. "Jesus is alive. But what does it mean?"

"It means that Jesus is our Savior. He died for us and then came alive again," Father explained. "It means Jesus paid for all our sin."

"God has kept His promise!" Mother added.

Journal: Make a list of all the things you remember that happened on Easter Day.

Pray: Thank You, dear Jesus, for dying and rising from death for me. Remind me that I can always trust in You. Amen. L. E.

Easter Certainty

It has been said that Jesus was one of three things: a liar, a lunatic (crazy), or the Lord. Why? Jesus claimed to have risen from the dead. This means He was lying, was crazy, or told the truth, which would mean that He's the Lord of all, since no one can rise from the dead except by God's power.

On Good Friday, we felt with the disciples their pain and confusion on seeing Jesus die in such a terrible way. But then the women came with some amazing news after visiting Jesus' tomb on Easter. Angels appeared to them, telling them that Jesus was not there, but risen.

The disciples' first response to the women was that either they were lying, talking crazy, or . . . just maybe . . . it was true! Peter rushed to the tomb; he had to see for himself. He peered inside and found no bloodied, beaten body. In fact, he found no body at all—only linen cloths.

On seeing this, Peter knew that Jesus was not a liar or a lunatic. He was convinced that Jesus was the Lord. Since that was true, Peter went on to become a bold spokesman for Jesus, baptizing and communicating this amazing message.

This kind of certainty is ours too. We can trust that Jesus is who He claimed to be, and knowing that, we can trust Him for everything—including forgiveness, salvation, and eternal life. And that's good Easter news!

E _____

A _____

S _____

T _____

E _____

R _____

Journal: Using the letters of "EASTER," create an acrostic, with each letter signifying a name for Jesus, like "Emmanuel, God with us" and "Alpha and omega, the first and the last."

Pray: Dear Jesus, thank You for Your death on the cross and Your glorious resurrection. Give us faith to share Your message with others. Amen. J. S.

Seeing Open Doors

Volleyball tryouts had just finished. There were twelve spots on the team; fifteen girls had tried out. Some girls wouldn't make the team. Coach Wallace was talking to each girl individually. Megan sat silently, praying. When coach called her name, Megan's skin felt prickly.

"Megan, I'm really sorry," Coach began. "I know you wanted to be a part of the team, but it won't happen this year." Then Coach paused. "I know it might not make you feel better now, but I've found that when the Lord closes one door, He opens another one. Maybe He has something else in mind for you."

Megan nodded, muttered a tearful thank-you, and left. The next day, she noticed signs at school announcing auditions for the musical. "We should try out," Megan's friend said.

Three weeks later, the girls were busy with rehearsals, getting costumes, and practicing lines. When Megan saw Coach Wallace one day after school, she said, "Coach, you know what you said about the Lord closing one door and opening another? Well, He did!"

"I'm so happy for you, Megan," she said, "I hope you can always remember that the Lord loves you."

"Thanks, Coach. I'll try." Megan smiled at Coach Wallace. "Well, got to go. I have a rehearsal now."

Because we are God's children through Jesus, we can be sure that He can use even our disappointments to redirect our lives for good purposes. Even in sadness and weakness, God is at work.

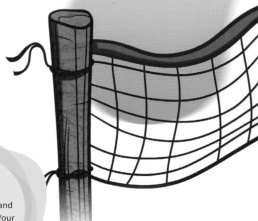

Journal: Write about a disappointment in your life that became God's blessing.

Pray: Dear Lord, thank You for knowing what's best for me. Give me power to trust You and place my disappointments and hurts in Your hands. In Jesus' name I pray. Amen. M. W.

Power to Stay on Top

"I need two volunteers," Mr. Hernandez told his Sunday School class. Eager hands went up as the teacher pushed a small sturdy box into the room.

"Nick, will you stand on top of this box? And Jason, please stand next to the box." The boys took their places.

"Good," said Mr. Hernandez. "Now, Nick, you pull Jason up. Jason, you pull Nick down."

Looking a little nervous, the boys joined hands. After a few moments of pushing and pulling, Nick gave up and landed on his feet on the floor next to Jason.

"Thank you, gentlemen. What happened here?" the teacher asked.

"It wasn't fair. Jason had gravity helping him pull Nick down," said Amy. "Nick never had a chance of winning."

Mr. Hernandez nodded. Then he said, "Sometimes, Christians find themselves in situations like Nick's. They believe they can hang out with friends who are headed for trouble and still resist temptations to sin themselves. They might even believe they can change things for the better. But when you're with someone who is involved in sinful things, it's like being on top of the box. It's easier to be pulled down into sin than to pull up someone."

Today's verse from God's Word tells us to "be wise as serpents and innocent as doves." We can't always avoid people who are trapped in sinful living. God wants us to share the Good News about Jesus with those who don't know Him. We also need to be wise, asking God for His power to resist temptation. His Word makes us strong. His Word makes us wise.

Journal: How can you be innocent as a dove around others who may not know Jesus? Why is it important to also be as wise as a snake in those situations?

Pray: Heavenly Father, plant Your Word in me, that I may find my wisdom and strength in You. In Jesus' name I pray. Amen. D. N.

Buried to Grow

Anastasia sat with her spade. She dug a row of holes in the ground. She buried some seeds in the dark dirt and gave each mound a pat and a splash of water from her can.

She remembered Pastor's sermon on Sunday. He said that for a seed to grow, it has to be buried. A seed won't grow if it's just thrown above the ground. But once it's buried and in the darkness of the earth, it can shoot up into the light. He talked about Baptism and life with Jesus.

Jesus was buried in the dark tomb, Anastasia remembered from the sermon. And then He rose to the light of Easter morning. In Baptism, we're buried with Jesus so that we can rise with Him.

Anastasia cried as she read her grandma's name on the gravestone in front of her. The seeds she just planted would be in the darkness of the dirt for a while, but they would grow and have life in the light.

Anastasia thought, Grandma won't stay buried either. When Jesus returns, Grandma will rise up and live with Him in His light forever. And so will I.

She looked up at the bright sky and prayed.

Journal: Write about your loved one or someone else's loved one who is now with Jesus for eternity.

Pray: Come quickly, Lord Jesus. Amen. R. A.

Jesus, the Bread of Life

The country of France has many bakeries to delight the tourists and nourish the countrymen. Every neighborhood has its own fresh pastries. You might like to sample a basket of baguettes or a cream cheese delight.

Fresh bread is an important part of every meal in France, so people buy it every day. With such a daily demand, there are many bakeries. Boys and girls often help their parents get their supply. They run to the bakery to buy bread for breakfast.

Getting daily bread can be a big problem because of another French tradition— long summer vacations. Businesses close for weeks. Even bakeries shut down for a whole month while the owners go on vacation. Imagine being hungry for some bread, only to find out that your favorite bakery is closed for a month.

Praise God that our bread of life, Jesus Christ, doesn't go on vacation. He is always available to us by the power of the Holy Spirit. Through His Word, our hungry souls are fed.

Unfortunately, we sometimes go on vacation from Jesus. We do that when we neglect His Word or stop going to church. Then we miss out on God's blessings, our daily bread. But God never gives up on us! He is always ready to feed us with His Word, to forgive all our sins, and to guide us daily until we reach heaven.

Journal: Why is bread important to you? Why is Jesus important to you? Why do we say Jesus is the bread of life?

Pray: Lord Jesus, when I go "on vacation" from listening to Your Word, please forgive me. Send Your Holy Spirit to guide me back to You, the true bread of life. In Your name I pray. Amen. J. D.

APRIL 23

Luke 24:46–47

Stale Jelly Beans

"May I please have a piece of candy from my Easter basket, Mom?" asked Ashley. "Sure, if you have any left." Ashley found a few jelly beans and popped them into her mouth. After a few chews, she made a face. "Not as good as they were last week!" Then her brother Sam started digging through the plastic grass in his basket. Near the bottom, he found a foil-wrapped egg. "Look at this chocolate egg. It's turning white!" Mom laughed, "I think that might be left over from last year!"

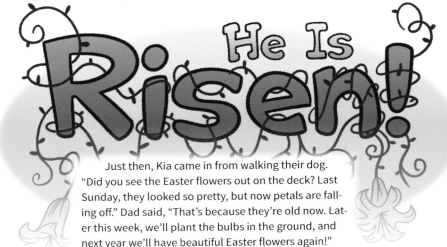

Just then, Kia came in from walking their dog. "Did you see the Easter flowers out on the deck? Last Sunday, they looked so pretty, but now petals are falling off." Dad said, "That's because they're old now. Later this week, we'll plant the bulbs in the ground, and next year we'll have beautiful Easter flowers again!"

On Easter Sunday, everything is so beautiful and special—the flowers on the altar, the music from the choir. Maybe you get new Easter clothes. Perhaps you have a special meal with family. But after Easter, everything seems back to normal. However, in church the pastor still declares, "Christ is risen!" That's because every Sunday is a celebration of Jesus' death and resurrection. Every week we confess, "The third day He rose again from the dead." And, when we're old enough, we share His body and blood. That's why today, and every day, we can shout with joy, "He is risen indeed! Alleluia!"

Journal: How can you continue the Easter celebration today?

Pray: "Your name we bless, O risen Lord, And sing today with one accord The life laid down, the life restored: Alleluia!" (*LSB* 475) N. D

Beautiful Feet

I smoothed out my dress and wound my hair into a tight bun. I looked down at my skates. They were polished and beautiful, with perfectly white laces.

Ever since I was a little girl, I had dreamed of performing in front of hundreds of people. And my dream would come true.

Many people thought I'd be a missionary or a church worker. They weren't sure that being a figure skater would serve others in God's kingdom very well. Sometimes, I wondered too. But then, God showed me something wonderful!

I learned that all types of people, with all types of jobs, can serve in God's kingdom. This meant that I put on Christ everywhere I went, especially at the rink. I was able to tell figure skaters and hockey players about the Savior! And I skated in front of many people to songs about God's love.

Our Bible reading speaks about those who proclaim God's Word. It says, "How beautiful are the feet of those who preach the good news!" (v. 15). Even though you aren't a pastor, you have beautiful feet. You are God's child with Good News to share. My feet have skates on them. What's on your feet? Skateboard shoes? Cowboy boots? Baseball cleats? Flip-flops?

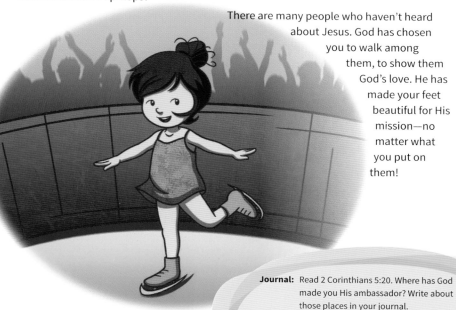

There are many people who haven't heard about Jesus. God has chosen you to walk among them, to show them God's love. He has made your feet beautiful for His mission—no matter what you put on them!

Journal: Read 2 Corinthians 5:20. Where has God made you His ambassador? Write about those places in your journal.

Pray: Lord, help me to spread Your Word, right where You've placed my feet. In Jesus' name I pray. Amen. L. M.

Beloved

At dinnertime, a favorite family activity is to go around the table and either ask questions or share thoughts for the day. We try to come up with a way for everyone to participate in the conversation.

Of all the topics we have come up with, I think our kids' favorite is when we go around the table and say something we appreciate or love about the person next to us. The joy and anticipation of what their parent or sibling will say shows on each of their faces and on my husband's and my faces as well! We all soak in the heartfelt compliments and tender words that are shared across the table. This topic is a safe go-to and a reminder of how much we love one another.

While it is wonderful to be the recipient of kind, loving words from family members and friends, how much more amazing is it that God shows and tells us that He loves us? Soak in the words from Colossians 3:12 and marvel at the fact that God says we are "beloved."

Take a moment to picture yourself sitting across the table from God. You wait in anticipation to know how He feels about you, and He whispers, "I love you dearly. I love you so much that I sent My Son to die for you so that you can eat at My table for all eternity."

Journal: The Bible clearly communicates God's love. What are other examples of how much God loves you?

Pray: Dear God, thank You for loving me dearly. Please help me tell others about Your love, especially how You loved us enough to send Your Son to be our Savior. Amen. L. D.

Rescued!

"Dog Saves Woman's Life"—that was the newspaper headline about a dog that dialed 911 and saved a life.

Here is what happened. The dog's owner had a breathing problem so she slept with an oxygen mask over her face. While she was sleeping, the breathing machine's plug fell out, and oxygen was cut off. Without oxygen, she would have died.

The dog, which had been specially trained as a service dog, heard the oxygen alarm and first tried to awaken her owner. When the woman did not respond, the dog knocked off the telephone receiver and bumped a button programmed to dial 911. Help arrived in time; her owner's life was saved.

God rescued us. His story is even more amazing. Why should a holy God rescue people who had turned away from Him? Romans 3:10–12 says, "None is righteous, no, not one; . . . no one seeks for God. All have turned aside." God could have walked away from us, but He didn't.

Because of His great mercy, God provided a way for us to be free from sin's curse. He sent His life-giving Son, Jesus. He paid the debt we owed for sin. Through Him, we are restored to God and made part of His family.

And there's even more to this rescue. Though we sin daily, God freely forgives us. He cares for us (1 Peter 5:7) and promises never to leave us (Hebrews 13:5). That's truly amazing love!

Journal: What price did Jesus pay to rescue us from sin? What are some good things about being part of God's family?

Pray: Thank You, Jesus, for rescuing me from sin. Be with me always. In Your name I pray. Amen. M. J. G.

APRIL 27

Romans 6:4

Creating Anew

"Look, Mom! The first spring flower!" Megan pointed to a yellow daffodil.

"Yes," Megan's mom said. "Spring brings lots of new things."

Megan thought for a moment. "Like baby calves on Uncle Roy's farm."

Megan and her mom walked along, naming new things. "Blossoms on trees," said Megan, looking at the budding trees along the sidewalk.

"Cousin Dawn and her new husband," Megan's mom said.

"Our neighbor's new baby," Megan said.

"Your new friendship with Alyssa," Megan's mom said.

"My new teeth!" Megan said. "The baby ones came out, and new ones came in. Just like that."

"Just like that," Megan's mom said. "How do you suppose all these new things came to be?"

Megan stopped. "God did it. He made all these new things because He loves us."

Megan's mom smiled. "I think you're right. God created all life." She took Megan's hand. They started walking again, swinging hands as they walked. "God even makes us new."

"What do you mean?" Megan asked.

"Yes. When you were baptized, the Holy Spirit came to you in the water combined with God's Word. You became God's child." They walked past the pond and watched the ducks. "God sent His Son, Jesus, to be our Savior. He took our sins to the grave with Him when He died on the cross. He forgives our sins, so we are made new."

"New and improved . . . every day!" Megan said.

Journal: List or draw some things that are new this spring.

Pray: Creator God, thank You for making the universe and everything in it. Thank You for my new life in Jesus. Thank You for new-life opportunities to grow in faith and serve others. Amen. J. H.

Eagerly Waiting

Have you started counting how many days until the last day of school?

What do you like to do in the summer? Do you go swimming? Do you go to the library? Do you visit your grandparents? What about Vacation Bible School? Summer is a special time.

The people in Jesus' time were also counting the days. For thousands of years, the Jewish people had been waiting for the Messiah to come and deliver them. Many thought He would be a warrior who would make the children of Israel into a powerful nation. But Jesus was not coming to save them from their political enemies. He was coming to save them from their spiritual enemies of sin, death, and the devil.

Jesus came to earth to suffer and die for the sins of all people. Many wouldn't accept this, and they turned away from Him. Sadly, millions of people today are still waiting for a savior to make their nation great. They don't want to believe that Jesus is their Savior.

Christians all around the world are also waiting, but we know that Jesus is our Savior. On the Last Day, Jesus will take to heaven everyone who believes in Him, both the living and the dead. We will live there with Jesus forever!

What will heaven be like? No one knows exactly, but we know there will be no sadness, pain, or tears. Heaven will be better than the best summer vacation.

Journal: Read Titus 2:11–14. What does Paul say about waiting?

Pray: Dear Jesus, please forgive me when I forget that Your salvation is the most exciting thing of all. I am waiting for You to come again and take me home to live with You. Thank You, Lord! Amen. N. D.

Just the Facts, Please!

Did you know that a hard-boiled egg will spin? An uncooked or soft-boiled egg will not. Were you aware that the kiwi bird of New Zealand has a nostril at the end of its beak and finds food by smell? Did you know buttermilk does not contain butter?

You might be surprised to learn that the famous physicist Albert Einstein never wore socks. And his favorite pastime was sailing. Although he won the Nobel Prize in physics, he didn't accept it in person because he was on a voyage to Japan.

Facts can be surprising, interesting, and even funny. But one thing we know about all of them—if they are facts, they have to be true.

Paul gives us some interesting facts in today's Bible reading: "Christ died for our sins. . . . He was raised on the third day" (vv. 3–4). Those things really happened.

The fact that Jesus died and rose again is a wonderful truth. It is a fact that He gave His life for us. It is a fact that He rose again. And it is a fact that those who believe in Jesus have their sins forgiven. It is a fact that they will spend eternity in heaven with their Savior.

This world is full of interesting facts. But only the truths of Jesus' death and resurrection can save us. And in Baptism and through God's Word, we have faith to believe the most wonderful facts of all!

Journal: Why is it so important to know Jesus' death and resurrection are facts and not fiction?

Pray: Lord, I am happy that You really lived, died, and rose again. Thank You for the faith to believe the facts in the Bible. Help me share the facts of Your Word with others. Amen. C. A.

Family Gatherings

Have you ever been to a family gathering? Parents, grandparents, aunts, uncles, and cousins come together just to see one another. There is usually food, games, and storytelling. You may have relatives that you see only at these gatherings. You may even meet a family member for the first time.

People who believe in Jesus have one more family—the family of God! God gives many gifts to those who are baptized in Jesus' name. Forgiveness of sins and the Holy Spirit are two gifts. Becoming God's child is another gift. After a Baptism, the pastor welcomes the baptized person as a brother or sister in Christ and invites him or her to hear God's Word, receive His gifts, and proclaim His praises. Then the members of the church say, "We welcome you in the name of the Lord" (*LSB*, p. 271).

As the members of God's family gather every Sunday, they hear God's Word read from the Bible, receive God's grace, and remember how they became part of God's family through Baptism. You might say that every worship service is a special family gathering!

In heaven, all God's children will gather to praise God together. There will be people from every country who have heard and believed the message that Jesus is God's Son and their Savior. There will be many people whom you have never met, yet they are your brothers and sisters in the Lord. What a great family gathering that will be!

Journal: Choose a country other than the one you live in. Find out and write down three facts about that country, and then pray that God would bring many people from that country into His family through Jesus Christ.

Pray: Father, thank You for making me Your child. Keep me firm in my faith in Jesus so that one day I will be part of a family gathering with all of Your children. Amen. C. R.

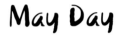

May Day

People used to observe a custom to give secret presents on May 1. A person would fill a May basket with flowers and other treats, leave it on a friend's doorstep, knock on the door, and then run away. When the person answered the door, he or she would find the flowers and treats but wouldn't know who gave them.

God surprises us too. He gives us wonderful things while we're not looking! In spring, we see new flowers, leaves, and birds just outside our doorstep. He also gives us other blessings we don't expect, like kindness from family and friends, help with problems, and happy times at school.

Of course, not every basket is perfect. Sometimes, bugs crawl into May baskets or the fresh flowers in them wilt. Sometimes, problems crawl into our lives or beautiful situations wilt.

We all have the problem of sin, sin against God and against other people. Others also sin against us. To deal with sin, God gives us the best unexpected gift of all—His love and forgiveness.

Jesus won God's forgiveness for us on the cross, and because of that, we can be sure of God's love. God's love is a blessing on a day of beautiful surprises or on a day of sadness and trouble.

Journal: What beautiful surprises have you had today? Write about them. Can you give one to someone else?

Pray: Dear heavenly Father, thank You for giving me beautiful surprises every day and for Your love and forgiveness, which are with me always. In Jesus' name I pray. Amen. E. G.

The Work Surprise

"I'm sick of working!" Missy complained to her dad. "I worked at school. I've done my homework. And then I set the table!"

"Ouch," replied her dad. "But work is a good thing. We can rejoice in our work."

"Are you kidding?" said Missy. "Rejoice?"

"I am not kidding," explained Dad. "God gives us work for a reason. We work in His kingdom. Our service benefits those around us."

"Oh, Dad," Missy said. "How does doing thirty math problems benefit anyone?"

"God has a purpose for the work you do, even if you cannot see it right now. He knows what the future holds. The work you do today may have a great effect on something or someone at a later time."

Missy thought about her dad's encouragement. Then she went to the kitchen. "Mom," she said, "I'm here to help."

"Oh, thank you, Missy," Mom said. "I wasn't sure how I was going to get everything done before my class tonight."

Missy was embarrassed. "You're welcome," she said softly.

Dad peeked around the corner and said, "God does have a purpose for your work!"

We can praise the work of others, especially God's work. He sent Jesus to do the work of saving us on the cross. That wasn't fun, but it was essential for our salvation. And God's works of love, forgiveness, faith, and salvation in us enable us to carry out our work every day in surprisingly important ways.

Journal: What work has God given you to do today?

Pray: Dear Lord, thank You for the work Jesus did for my salvation on the cross. Thank You for the work You do in my life every day! Amen. C. K.

MAY 3
Joshua 1:7–9

Strong and Courageous

Riley often felt afraid. If her mom was late to pick her up from school, her stomach tightened. The tight feeling crept up into her throat, and she felt like crying. Riley didn't like this at all, but she didn't know how to stop.

One night, Riley's parents were late getting home. Even while Riley played a card game with her babysitter, she felt a "pit" in her stomach. She listened for her parents' car in the driveway. Her sitter must have sensed Riley's anxiety.

Sarah shared, "I used to feel afraid."

"You did?" Riley was surprised.

"I sure did. A friend told me to memorize Joshua 1:9. A few months later, my fiancé broke up with me. I waited to feel afraid and anxious, but I felt calm. I remembered that verse, 'Be strong and courageous. Do not be frightened, and do not be dismayed, for the LORD your God is with you wherever you go.' Jesus, my Lord and Savior, was with me right then! I already believed, but at that moment I really knew He was at work, comforting me. I knew that His Word was powerful and that faith in Jesus made a lifelong difference!"

Riley's eyes welled up with tears of comfort and joy. She was thankful Sarah had shared this special experience. Riley believed God's promise was for her too. Just as Riley realized she wasn't afraid anymore, she heard a car door. Guess who was home?

Journal: Draw a picture of a fearful situation. Draw Jesus beside you.

Pray: Dear Jesus, thank You for being with me in all situations. When troubles come, give me a calm heart and trusting faith. Amen. C. R.

Take It to the Lord

The National Day of Prayer is held in May. Many Christians will pray in public, in churches, in schools, and in homes. You can use today's devotion as a time of prayer. Here are some starters. Add to them your own petitions.

I praise You, Lord, for Your loving presence and for the gifts of forgiveness and eternal life won for me through Jesus. Thank You for hearing and answering my prayers!

Make me thankful, God, for Your gifts that support my body and life, such as food, clothes, a home, and much more. Make me satisfied with what You give me.

Dear Jesus, thank You for the people who provide for me and help me— family and friends, teachers, coaches, and others.

Heavenly Father, thank You for my country, where I am free to pray in the name of Your Son, Jesus. Protect and watch over our nation. Guide all leaders to govern wisely and honestly.

O Lord, show me those who need to hear about Your Son, Jesus. Let Your Holy Spirit guide my words and actions as I witness to others about Your grace and mercy.

Thank You for churches where Your Gospel is proclaimed and taught. Bless all pastors and other church workers as they teach and care for Your people.

Healing Savior, be with those who are sick or have troubles. Help and heal each of them according to Your will.

I pray all these things in the precious and powerful name of Jesus. Amen.

Journal: Use each letter of the word *prayer* to make your own prayer list.

Pray: "O God, hear my prayer; give ear to the words of my mouth" (Psalm 54:2). Amen. D. N.

MAY 5

Matthew 28:16–20

One at a Time

Paris called to her brother, "Scott, it's time to go swimming. Put your Spanish book away."

Scott surprised her when he said, "I'm not going. I want to study my Spanish so I can speak with our new neighbor Juan. Now, all I say is *hola* or *adios*. If I can't talk to Juan, how can I tell him about Jesus?"

Paris thought a bit. "Maybe Juan can help you with your Spanish while we are swimming, and you can help him with his English, telling him about Jesus along the way."

"That's a great idea!" Scott agreed. "For now, I'll show Juan my swimming trunks and towel. Maybe he will understand, and his parents will let him come with us."

Shortly after His resurrection, Jesus told His disciples, "Go therefore and make disciples of all nations" (Matthew 28:19). The risen Christ, who overcame death and the grave, sent His disciples out to tell others that their sins had been removed through the suffering, death, and resurrection of Jesus. He sent them to tell the Good News of the Gospel.

Scott had the right idea about sharing God's love—start nearby in everyday activities. The Holy Spirit gives pastors to teach and preach about God's love and to administer the Sacraments. The Holy Spirit works through His Word and His Sacraments to reach around the world with the Good News of salvation. The Holy Spirit works through Scott and you, as you go about your day.

Journal: List the names of five people who have shared with you the Good News that Jesus is your Savior.

Pray: Thank You, Lord Jesus, for the opportunity to tell others about Your love. Send Your Spirit to bless my parents, my pastor, and me. In Your name I pray. Amen. R. S.

Spring Cleaning Day

Adam's family did spring cleaning the first Saturday in May. In the morning, they washed windows, cleaned the garage, cleaned carpets, and arranged things in the basement. In the afternoon, each person cleaned his or her own room.

Adam worked hard all morning. He helped his brother in the garage and washed windows upstairs with his mom. He and his sister tackled the playroom in the basement.

Right after lunch, Adam started on his room. He put his shoes away and arranged his baseball cards.

Then Adam was distracted by his comic books. When his dad poked his head in the room, he made Adam put them away. Adam arranged the video games. Then he found the Sunday School Bible that he'd misplaced three weeks ago. He also found a permission slip for the spring movie night at church tomorrow night. The slip was stuck in the Bible at 2 Kings 22, where the message told about cleaning the temple.

Adam read that Josiah became king at eight years old—his same age. Adam wondered what it might be like to be king. He imagined a life without cleaning and smiled.

He read about how the book of God's Word had been lost. He couldn't imagine going for years without reading the Bible! Suddenly, he was glad for spring cleaning. He was thankful for a chance to go to church and Sunday School, where he could hear God's Word of love and forgiveness through Jesus Christ.

Journal: What have you misplaced? How important is it?

Prayer: Dear God, thanks for Your Word, the Bible, which tells me how You clean up my life with Your forgiveness. In Jesus' name I pray. Amen. J. G.

Marshmallows

How do you eat marshmallows? Right out of the bag? Toasted on a stick over a campfire? Smashed in a s'more between chocolate and graham crackers? Delicious!

My favorite way to have marshmallows is melted in hot chocolate. Before I pour hot water into my mug, I drop a handful of mini marshmallows on top of the cocoa mix. When I add the hot water, the soft marshmallows melt and make the cocoa creamy.

But the last time I made hot chocolate, something strange happened. The marshmallows didn't melt! Even though I stirred and stirred, they just floated on the top. Why? The marshmallows were as hard as a rock! The bag had been open too long, and the marshmallows were stale.

Sometimes, Christians get stale too. We forget to say grace before we eat or say our prayers at bedtime. We don't listen to the Bible story our teacher is reading. We skip church or Sunday School because it's cold or it's raining or we're tired or we want to do something else.

When we forget about Jesus, our hearts grow like stale marshmallows. To stay fresh, we need the Holy Spirit to renew us. How do we receive the Holy Spirit? Every time we hear God's Word, the Holy Spirit works in our hearts, keeping us fresh. He helps us to pray and to worship. The Holy Spirit pours Jesus' love into our lives and gives us opportunities to serve others! Thank God for the refreshing Holy Spirit!

Journal: What are some ways God flavors your life with His love?

Pray: Holy Spirit, forgive me when I avoid Your Word and become stale. Keep my heart fresh with God's Word. In Jesus' name I pray. Amen. N. D.

V-E Day!

Everyone in Miss Jensen's class was excited. This morning, during chapel, their classmate Tyson had been baptized. The class was going to have a party to celebrate, but first they had to finish social studies.

"Today is an important day in history," announced Miss Jensen.

"I know," Tyson said. "It's my Baptism day!"

"That's not a holiday," argued Olivia.

"Actually, it is," Miss Jensen replied. "In fact, Tyson's Baptism *is* a part of our lesson. Almost eighty years ago, our country was fighting a terrible war. The war had been going on for years. Both sides suffered terrible destruction and loss of life. Finally, the war in Europe was over."

"I'm glad the war ended," Brooke said. "War is scary."

"Me too," agreed Cole. "But why is today a holiday?"

"May 8, 1945, was V-E Day. On that day, Germany officially surrendered, and the whole world celebrated the Allies' victory in Europe." (V-E comes from *Victory in Europe*.)

"But what does Victory Day have to do with Baptism?" asked Tyson.

"Baptism is a victory," said Miss Jensen. "The catechism says that '[Baptism] works forgiveness of sins, rescues from death and the devil, and gives eternal salvation to all who believe this, as the words and promises of God declare.' "

"I get it! When Jesus died and rose again, He defeated Satan. Because Jesus won, I'm a winner too! Today *is* my victory day!"

Journal: Ask your parents about your Baptism day, and ask your older relatives about V-E Day. In your journal, write something that you learned about each.

Pray: Thank You, Jesus, for the blessings of Baptism. You have brought peace to my soul. Please bring Your peace to this world too. Amen. N. D.

Spreading Seeds

Renee had a neighborhood friend named Jenny. The girls both loved baseball, reading, and word puzzles. But Jenny didn't love Jesus.

So Renee invited Jenny to come to church and Sunday School with her. Renee had tried to tell her about the love of Jesus. Jenny had always listened politely, but she hadn't seemed really interested. Occasionally, she came to special events at Renee's church, but that was all. Renee wondered if her best friend would ever believe in Jesus.

Renee also had a garden. She planted seeds of her favorite vegetables: green beans, sugar peas, and carrots. The spring weather was unusually cool, so it was taking a long time for her seeds to sprout. She became discouraged and asked her dad, "What can I do to make my seeds sprout?"

He replied, "You planted the seeds and watered them, but you can't make them grow. God does that." So Renee waited. Eventually, the seeds sprouted.

One warm afternoon, she was weeding her garden when Jenny came over to visit. Jenny said she was interested in coming to church and Sunday School! She said, "I've been thinking about what you told me about Jesus, Renee, and I'd like to learn more." Renee was so happy. She thought, It's just like my garden—only God can make the seeds grow.

Journal: Who plants seeds in your church? Who plants seeds in your family? Where can you plant seeds of opportunity to hear God's Word?

Pray: Dear Jesus, thank You for opportunities to hear and learn about You. Thank You for saving faith through Your Spirit. Thank You for friends whom I can invite to know more about You and Your love. Amen. E. G.

Grateful Words!

G rave, open and empty

R eal body and blood for us

A ngels who protect us

T he Savior, Jesus Christ

I n time and into eternity

T he forgiveness of sins

U nder the Spirit's guidance

D efended against all danger

E ternal thanks and praise

The acrostic above builds on the word *gratitude*. The words that come after the first letter in each line explain things for which I am grateful.

When you think about all of God's goodness to you, what would you name? You could list God's earthly blessings such as your family or life in a free country. You could also name healthy foods and exercise and sports. How about your school, books, and technology? They are for learning and fun. God also gives you friends and a place to live. When you think about it, God gives you *everything*!

In Baptism and through His Word, the Holy Spirit gives us faith in Jesus. And because of Jesus' life, death, and resurrection, we have a victory over our enemies and a home with Him in heaven.

Yes, we can express our gratitude to God for so many things. With the apostle Paul, we can say, "Thanks be to God."

Journal: Make a list of your physical and spiritual gifts.

Pray: Thank You, heavenly Father, for Jesus, my Savior, who gives me the victory He won on the cross. Amen. J. L.

MAY 11

Psalm 51:7

Filtered

The mechanic finished working on Timmy's mom's car and came over to where they were waiting. Holding out what looked like a round accordion, he said, "Here's the part I took out."

"What is it?" asked Timmy as he studied the dirty black object.

"It's an air filter," the mechanic explained. "It keeps your car's engine clean by removing the dirt from the air."

"We have a water filter on our faucet in the kitchen, but it doesn't look like that," said Timmy.

"Well," the mechanic laughed, "if you took it apart, there would be something similar inside. Your house's air conditioner and furnace also has a filter. They don't all look the same, but all filters do the same thing. They are designed to remove dirt."

In our Bible passage for today, David asks God to cleanse him with hyssop so he will be clean and whiter than snow. Hyssop was a plant used in a cleansing ceremony. When lepers who were free of their disease came to the high priest, he would dip the hyssop in blood and sprinkle the blood over them. Hyssop carried the blood that showed the leper was free from his deadly sickness.

Jesus has cleansed us from our deadly sickness of sin. When He died on the cross, He became our sacrifice. His blood was sprinkled out when He died. He removed our dirty sins from us. He took our sins upon Himself. Through Him, we are clean.

Journal: What are some things that need to be cleaned? Don't forget to put your name on the list.

Pray: Dear Lord, thank You for sending Jesus to give Himself as my sacrifice and make me cleaner than even the purest snow. Amen. C. H.

Mother's Day Cards

Most of the students at school made Mother's Day cards in art class, but not Alex.

"I don't know what to put on this card," Alex complained. "Why can't I just buy a card, like my dad does?"

"Making a card is special," his teacher answered, "because of the effort you put into it. Mother's Day is about the love shared between you and your mom. Think of all the things your mom does for you, and you'll find your own special 'card' for her."

That gave Alex an idea. Instead of a card, he asked his dad to buy a sponge. On Sunday, Alex's mom was delighted when she received a sponge with this note attached:

For taking me to soccer, basketball, and track,

This Mother's Day, I have to say how much I love you back!

This card is good for two free car washes!

Alex discovered that love is the best gift to his mom.

God gave us His best gift when Jesus was born to be the Savior of our sinful world. God did all that because He loves us; we are His children. Any love we experience on earth is also a gift from God—a gift that comes through other people.

Your mother loves you and cares about you. Her love is a gift from God for you. The love and respect you show her honors God. You are God's gift to her, and she is your gift from God.

Journal: Plan an extra helpful thank-you for your mother.

Pray: Dear Jesus, thank You for Your love and those who show Your love to me. Teach me to be faithful. Amen. S. R.

Standing Apart

In many places around the world, Christians have freedom to pray, sing, and gather in worship; however, this is not true everywhere. A woman in Sudan faces death because she will not deny her Christian faith and become a Muslim. In China, a man who opened a Christian bookstore has been imprisoned for two years because he wanted to sell Bibles.

Jesus told His followers that they might suffer because they believe in Him, but do we suffer because of what we believe? Most of the time, we don't. In our desire to fit in with others, we become so much like nonbelievers that no one would know if we believe in Jesus or not. This doesn't mean we have to go around in a monk's robe or wear a giant cross necklace. But our lives should look different.

Our Sunday mornings should not be filled with soccer games or sleeping in, but instead should find us in the pew at church, at the foot of the cross, learning about our Savior. Our comments to others should not make them feel belittled or hurt, but should encourage. Our daily reading should not only include the latest best seller, but also the Bible to remind us of God's gifts.

None of our efforts will be perfect; in fact, we'll fail a lot. But in Christ, because our lives are washed in the baptismal grace of God, we are forgiven and redeemed. So don't be afraid to stand apart from the crowd!

Journal: What are some ways people know you are a Christian?

Pray: Dear Lord, we pray for all those around the world who suffer greatly because of their faith in You. Please help me to live a life worthy of Your name. In Jesus' name I pray. Amen. J. S.

Memories

The sixth graders were working on Mother's Day cards, but Carlee just watched sadly while her classmates made their cards.

You see, Carlee's mom had died in a car accident. Carlee missed her mom a lot. She wished that she had a reason to make a pretty card this year.

"This is a hard week, isn't it?" said Carlee's teacher. "My mother died of cancer when I was in high school. I always miss my mother. But Mother's Day helps me to remember the good things about my mom too." Suddenly Carlee had an idea. She took paper from the art table and worked on something special.

After church the next Sunday, on Mother's Day, Dad took Carlee and her brother to the cemetery. Dad put purple hyacinths on the grave. Her brother laid down a little wooden cross. Carlee had two cards, one for her Dad and one for her brother. Dad's card had a picture showing how he helped Mom in the kitchen. Her brother's card showed Mom reading him a story in their "special chair." No cards for Mom this year, thought Carlee, but special memories about her.

Mother's Day can be a chance to thank God for the many ways He cares for us through the people in our family and through His only Son. Jesus' death and resurrection brought forgiveness of sins to those who believe in Him. The promise of eternal life with Jesus in heaven comforts us when we are sad.

Journal: Ask your mother about a special Mother's Day she celebrated with her mother when she was younger.

Pray: Dear heavenly Father, thank You for Your goodness and love shown through mothers. Bless and protect my family. Amen. S. R.

MAY 15

Joshua 1:9

Sad Endings

Good-bye, Mrs. Buckman. Trevor would miss her, but he was moving on to seventh grade.

Good-bye, Olivia. Montenae would miss her friend. But Montenae was moving to Houston, and Olivia lived in Little Rock.

Good-bye, Langston School. Ossario would miss going to school with his mom, the principal. He would miss knowing everyone—well, almost everyone. But high school was only three months away.

Changes can be hard, even good changes. When you move from one grade to the next, you will probably look back and miss the way things used to be. Sad changes are even harder, especially being separated from friends.

Whether changes are good or bad, they are almost always a little bit scary. That's where today's Bible reading comes in. Joshua was about to have a big change as a leader of his people. He was going to move them from their forty years of wilderness wandering into the Promised Land. He had said good-bye to Moses and had taken Moses' place. Now God was giving him the reassurance that he wasn't alone at this important and difficult time. Wherever Joshua went, God would be with him.

Wherever you go, be strong and courageous. Do not be frightened. The Lord your God is with you in His Word and in His Sacraments of Holy Baptism and the Lord's Supper. God's Son has redeemed you from any sin that could threaten you.

Good-bye to the old. Hello to the new with the Lord your God.

Journal: What is changing in your life right now? How is God changing you?

Pray: Thank You, Lord God, for Your strength and courage to meet the changes in my life, now and forever. In Jesus' name I pray. Amen. E. G.

A Perilous Bridge

Dan was a missionary in the Philippines. Some people there are terrified to die. They believe that when they die, they must cross over a razor-thin bridge to get to heaven. If they fall off the bridge, they will go all the way down to hell. They say it is such a long way down that if a coconut fell off the bridge, it would be a coconut tree when it reached the bottom!

One day, Dan asked a man, "What if you didn't have to cross that bridge to get to heaven?"

"Oh!" gasped the man. "That would be wonderful!" Then Dan told him about Jesus.

We don't have to accomplish impossible tasks to get to heaven. Jesus did that in our place. First, He lived perfectly in our place. Then He paid for the sins of the whole world on the cross. When He came out of the grave, He proved He was stronger than death and hell.

Those who have faith in Jesus don't have to be afraid to die. There won't be a perilous bridge to cross, a tough exam to pass, or even a secret password to remember. There will just be our Savior.

People like Dan are so excited by this good news that they want to share it with others. Some Christians leave their homes and live in different cultures so they can do this. There's nothing like the joy of seeing Jesus' love come alive for people all around the world!

Journal: Do you know anyone who is afraid to die? How could you share the Good News of Jesus with them?

Pray: Dear Jesus, thank You for saving me from sin, death, and the devil. Bless all those who share Your Good News at home and around the world. Amen. E. G.

A List of Wrongs

Shantel's parents went out for the night and left her big sister, Natalia, in charge. Shantel wasn't listening to her sister, but Natalia's parents didn't allow her to punish Shantel. So, Natalia started to make a list of everything Shantel did wrong. She planned to give the list to her parents so they would punish Shantel when they got home.

Natalia's list was long! "Shantel jumped on the couches after I told her not to. Shantel hit me when I told her to stop jumping on the couches. Shantel wore her shoes on the carpet. Shantel left three candy wrappers on the end table by the lamp." The list went on and on!

When Shantel's parents got home, Natalia gave them the huge list of wrongs that Shantel had done. Before her parents could say a word, Shantel yelled, "I know, I'm in trouble!" Then she ran to her room and slammed the door.

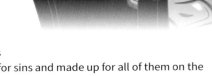

Can you imagine what it would be like if someone followed you around, just waiting for you to mess up. Then, when you do, they add it to a list of everything you've done wrong. That would be embarrassing!

God does see everything we do. He knows when we are on our best behavior and when we fail. Thankfully, He doesn't keep a record of our iniquities—that means our sins. Instead, He took the punishment for sins and made up for all of them on the cross. Instead of punishment, He gives us forgiveness because of Jesus.

Journal: How would you feel if someone wrote a list of all the things that you did wrong.

Pray: Thank You, Lord, for not keeping track of everything I do wrong. Thank You for forgiving my sins and loving me anyway. Help me to live in a way that would make You proud. Amen. F. S.

Everyday Greatness

Many schools give awards to celebrate things that students have achieved.

One school principal gives an award for something he calls Everyday Greatness. For this award, he chooses students who are not outstanding in any one way.

Does this seem strange? Most awards go to students who have the best grades or who excel in the arts or sports or who have perfect attendance. However, this principal believes students who go to class, do their homework, and are respectful of others set an example of greatness.

God also measures greatness differently than the world. The Son of God was not born in comfort to a rich family. His parents were not rich. Jesus did not live among wise or powerful people. He chose fishermen and an unpopular tax collector to be His disciples. Jesus taught that little children, a poor widow, and a sinful woman were examples of greatness in God's kingdom.

Jesus wants us to know that all people are equal in God's eyes, equally lost in sin and equally loved by our heavenly Father!

No matter how smart or strong we are, we cannot save ourselves or earn God's favor. We are great because our God is great. God's glory was shown when Jesus died for our sins and rose again so that all might have eternal life. Followers of Christ shine with greatness every day, not because of what we accomplish but because of what Jesus accomplished for us.

Journal: What talents or gifts has God given you? How can you use these things to serve Him every day?

Pray: Great God, help me serve others in Your name and show them Your greatness every day. In Jesus' name I pray. Amen. D. N.

Wonderful Truths

Allow me to introduce you to some of my young friends. These boys and girls have suffered more than many children.

Carol was eleven when a police officer came to her home one evening. The officer arrested her brother and held him at the police station overnight. Then they let him go. Carol was scared. The kids next door teased her because they had heard about the arrest.

Then there was Sean. He was in fourth grade when his mother got sick with cancer. She had many treatments, and her health was fragile. Sean became quiet and sad because he was concerned about losing his mother.

Andy was eight years old when his dad lost his job. With no income, his parents could not make the payments on their home. Finally, the bank took back their house, and they had to move out. Andy and his family moved in with relatives.

Each of my young friends felt alone and scared. But through their experiences, they discovered the wonderful truths in today's Bible reading. Their family and friends reminded them that God knew about their troubles. He cared and had power to help.

God raised Jesus from suffering and death. He promises to keep us in His love no matter what happens in life. Jesus is proof of how much God loves us. God won't let anything get between Him and His love for us. Nothing can separate us from Him.

Journal: What might you say to a friend who is going through a scary time?

Pray: Dear Father, there are times when I feel sad and see those I love suffering. Thank You for Your love that surrounds me. Bring me through my troubles either now or in heaven with You. In Jesus' name I pray. Amen. D. S.

Rock Solid

For the fifth day in a row, Sam's family sat around his aunt's dinner table. Last week, Sam's home was destroyed in a flood. Sam, his parents, and his younger brother had moved in with his aunt.

After dinner, Aunt Sally handed a devotion book to Sam's dad. As he skimmed the devotion, his eyes filled with tears. Then he said, "This devotion was written just for us!" Dad read Matthew 7:24–29 aloud and then started singing this hymn:

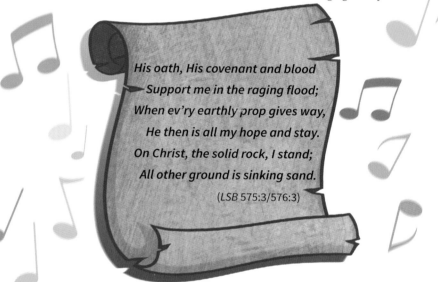

*His oath, His covenant and blood
Support me in the raging flood;
When ev'ry earthly prop gives way,
He then is all my hope and stay.
On Christ, the solid rock, I stand;
All other ground is sinking sand.*

(*LSB* 575:3/576:3)

The family joined in. Then Mom took a small rock from her pocket and set it on the table for all to see. "One day last week, I walked away from our ruined furniture on the trash heap," said Mom. "As I looked out over the field of mud, I sang this same hymn. It comforted me to know Christ sustains us through difficult times now and forever. This rock was on the ground where I was singing and praying. Since then, I've carried it in my pocket. I thank Jesus for being our Rock. And I ask Him to send us to other hurting people so we can share the story of His love with them."

In all life's troubles, we can lean on Jesus, our Rock and our Redeemer. Through faith, He gives us the hope of heaven, a brand-new home.

Journal: Draw a large rock in your journal and write the name "Christ" on it.

Pray: Father, thank You for Jesus. When problems flood my life, sustain me through Him. Give me comfort and hope. In His name I pray. Amen. C. R.

Relay the Message

The dictionary says that an ambassador is "an official envoy; an authorized representative or messenger." Ambassadors represent their home government to foreign countries.

An ambassador carefully relays the message from someone who is not there to someone who is. If your teacher has ever sent you to the office or to another teacher to deliver a message, you were an ambassador. You brought information. You didn't make up the information.

Pastors are God's ambassadors. They preach God's Word. They bring His message to others. They don't make up new Bible stories. They proclaim what the Bible teaches. That news tells us we are sinners. How sad. It also tells us that God sent Jesus to save us from our sins. How wonderful!

In our Bible reading, Paul says that he is God's ambassador. He wants people to know that Jesus died for their sins. God does not want us to quarrel but to treat one another as God's loved children. God sends us His messengers to remind us of that message too.

The devil wants us to ignore that ambassador's message or even get angry. The devil doesn't love us. He wants us to be miserable and separated from God. But God is more powerful than the devil.

Thank God for His ambassadors. And when you have a chance, you can be one too. You can tell someone about God's great love. It is so great that He sent His Son to die for the sins of all people.

Journal: Write down the names of people who have told you about Jesus.

Pray: Lord Jesus, You love for me to hear Your Word. Thank You for those who correct me and tell me about Your love and forgiveness. Help me to show Your love to others. In Your name I pray. Amen. J. D.

There's No "I" in Team

Have you ever heard the saying "There's no 'I' in team"? Michael Jordan, one of the greatest basketball players ever, could not have won six championships without his team. As the team captain, Jordan always included everyone on the court. An effective team involves a group of people who come together to achieve a common goal. There is no room for selfish attitudes when you are part of a team.

Did you know that you are part of God's team? God wants all His children to be saved, but some people do not even know about God. As part of God's team, you can share the Good News that God loves them and sent Jesus to die for them. You even have teammates to help you share the Good News!

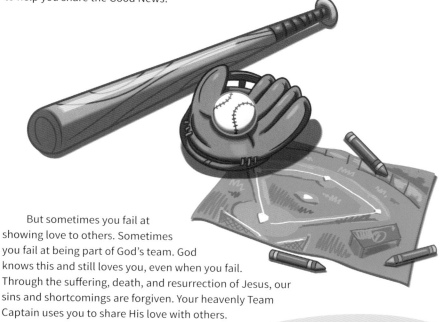

But sometimes you fail at showing love to others. Sometimes you fail at being part of God's team. God knows this and still loves you, even when you fail. Through the suffering, death, and resurrection of Jesus, our sins and shortcomings are forgiven. Your heavenly Team Captain uses you to share His love with others.

Journal: What does the word *team* mean to you? How have you been part of God's team?

Pray: Dear God, help me be a better team player for You. Thank You for being the best Team Captain ever! Amen. A. G.

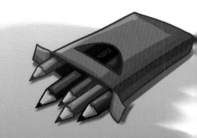

MAY 23

Psalm 103:11–13

Given and Gotten

Jerry was in trouble. He told his parents a lie and was caught. The next day as his dad drove him to school, Jerry seemed better. "How are you doing?" his father asked.

"I'm okay now," Jerry replied confidently, "because everything is given and gotten."

"I think that you mean 'forgiven and forgotten.'"

"No!" Jerry said. "I mean given and gotten!"

His father asked him to explain what he meant.

Well," he explained, "when I've *given* Jesus my sin, I've *gotten* forgiveness."

Psalm 103:12 reminds us of Jesus' gift of sacrifice on the cross. It shows us the endless power and strength of God's grace. When you confess your sins and give them to God in prayer, He remembers your sins no more.

Through His Word, God reminds us that we can give away what we have gotten from God. We can forgive the sins of others.

Journal: Write about a time when you forgave someone. Was it hard to forget what they had done?

Pray: Dear heavenly Father, I have often sinned and tried to hide my sins from You and others. Help me to confess them so that I may hear the sweet words of Your forgiveness. Thank You for sending Your only Son to die for my salvation. In His name I pray. Amen. J. H.

Fulfilled Promises

Dillon didn't know if he was sad or angry or relieved. It wasn't a huge surprise when his mom and dad told him they were getting a divorce. He knew they weren't getting along, but he had prayed to God to please fix the problem.

Right now it felt like God was not listening. Why didn't God keep his parents together? Dillon felt all alone. Everyone had disappointed him.

When things seem to go all wrong, it is easy to feel neglected. Does God forget our situation? Is He really helping? How can we trust Him? Throughout the Bible, we see examples of God fulfilling His promises. Remember these? God saved Noah and his family from the flood. Abraham and Sarah finally received a son after so many years of being childless. David became king after fleeing for his life. The most important promise God fulfilled was when He sent His one and only Son to die for our sins.

We can have faith that the Lord will be with us during hard times because He says He will. We can trust His promises. He tells us,

"When you pass through the waters, I will be with you" (v. 2).

Dillon can find comfort in knowing that, while his parents go through the waters of divorce, God will be with him every step of the way. We, too, don't have to be afraid of difficult situations in our lives. God, who has saved us, also guides and protects us throughout our daily lives.

Journal: What are some scary things you are facing right now?

Pray: Dear God, help me trust You during the tough times. Amen. C. K.

ımer:

Cloud Watchers

Have you ever watched the clouds float slowly across the sky? Sometimes, you can see shapes in the clouds like rabbits, dogs, or houses. The clouds form and then reform into something else.

In our Bible reading, the disciples were watching the clouds. Jesus had promised them that soon the Holy Spirit would empower them to speak the Word of God. He had commanded them to go into all the ends of the earth witnessing for Him. Then He had ascended into the sky. What did the disciples do? They stood watching Him until a cloud covered Him.

They just kept staring until two men in white stood next to them. The men in white spoke to them and wanted to know what they were looking at.

The disciples were confused and wondered when Jesus would be back and afraid of what the future would bring.

The two men in white said Jesus would come back the same way He left. That was all the reassurance the disciples needed. After that, they returned to Jerusalem and waited to start their ministry to the world.

We, too, have that same reassurance. We do not have to be confused and wonder about it. He will be back. Until that time, we have the assurance that He is with us every day in our Baptism and in His Word. These things make it possible for us to be His witnesses to the ends of the earth and in our own neighborhoods.

Journal: List all the places God has sent you to live or visit.

Pray: Dear God, thank You for sending Jesus to die and to rise so that my sins could be forgiven. With my new life in Christ, give me Your power. Send me to love others as I am able. Amen. C. H.

A Special Family

To Molly the Rottweiler, two newborn lambs would normally be nuisances to be chased. But when Lucky and Charm were born, their mother could not care for them. Molly adopted these helpless creatures as her own. She slept with them, kept them warm, and protected them. Without her care, they would have died.

God brings children into families through the process of birth, and another way He joins people in families is through adoption. Just as Molly cared for the lambs, adoptive families care for their children.

By nature, Rottweilers and lambs don't get along. By nature, we are sinful and unclean. We are God's enemies. But in Baptism, God adopted us. The blood of Jesus became the seal of our Baptism, the guarantee of our adoption. The power of the Holy Spirit brought the new life of faith.

Some people wish they would be adopted by a movie star or a king so that they could become rich and famous. But you don't need that. You have been adopted by the King of all, and you will inherit God's riches. While we wait for heaven, God gives us a life full of everything He knows is good for us.

As a part of God's family, we have many brothers and sisters in the Church. We are related to everyone who believes in Jesus! God has plenty of love to go around. In fact, He wants His family to grow even bigger—until His heavenly home is full of His children.

Journal: Have you been adopted, or do you know someone who has been adopted? What makes being adopted special? Your Baptism birthday is actually your adoption day into God's family. How could you celebrate it?

Pray: Thank You, God, for loving me and making me Your own child. Forgive my sins for the sake of my Savior, Jesus Christ. Amen. C. S.

Real Beauty

"I can't wait for Saturday, Bridgett, when you come over," exclaimed Darnae. "Marcy is coming too. She's beautiful. You'll like her."

On Saturday, Bridgett was a little nervous. If Marcy was so pretty, she thought, she might be stuck up. Bridgett looked for Marcy when she walked in. She saw a girl in a wheelchair. Her legs seemed too small for her body, and one arm hung limply. She wore thick glasses and had a brace on her neck.

"Hi, Bridgett. I'm Marcy," said the girl. "I'm glad to meet you."

The girls played together all afternoon. Marcy was one of the nicest people Bridgett had ever met. When Bridgett left, she whispered to Darnae, "Marcy really is beautiful!"

Bridgett learned something important that day—beauty is on the inside. The prophet Samuel learned that too. God wouldn't let Samuel pick a king because he was handsome. God told him, "the LORD looks on the heart" (v. 7).

God sent Jesus to die so that our ugly, sinful hearts could become beautiful. He gives us the Holy Spirit, who beautifies our hearts through faith.

God led Samuel to choose David as king. He became one of the greatest kings of Israel. David loved the Lord. Through faith in the coming Savior, God made David's heart beautiful. He does the same for us so that we, too, can shine from the inside out.

Journal: Explain in your own words what makes someone beautiful. Are you beautiful in God's eyes? Why?

Pray: Thank You, Jesus, for dying for me. Thank You for forgiving my sins and making me beautiful. Amen. C. A.

Life in the Shadows

Jeff didn't turn on the light in the bathroom. He opened the door of the medicine cabinet so he wouldn't see himself in the mirror. He'd seen more than enough of the red spots and pits in his skin. Jeff remembered the young boy who came up to him at camp last summer. "What's wrong with your face?" the boy asked.

The doctor called it acne. Jeff called it ugly. He lathered up with a special cleanser from the drugstore. He'd tried several kinds of ointments and soaps, but they didn't clear things up. Jeff's mom had made an appointment for him with a specialist, a dermatologist. Maybe there would be a prescription that would help.

All of us are spotted with sins, and they're more than skin-deep. We can't cure ourselves, no matter how hard we try.

Thank God there is a prescription to heal us. It is given by Jesus, the Great Physician. He understands our condition. He took our infirmities and sorrows upon Himself. His wounded, bleeding body hung on a cross. Even though people looked away from Him and made fun of Him, He stayed there. He died to clear up our lives now and forever.

Now we can come out of the shadow of sin because through Christ's sacrifice we live in the shadow of the cross. And in that shadow, we claim spiritual health and life in Jesus, our Savior. Our sins are forgiven. Our wounds are healed. Our lives are made whole and holy, now and forever.

Journal: Choose one verse from the Bible reading that is especially meaningful to you, and write it in your journal.

Pray: Lord Jesus, I see that sin covers me and my life. Please forgive me for Jesus' sake and make me clean. Amen. M. A. K.

MAY 31

John 15:12–14

A Day to Remember

Memorial Day is observed on the last Monday of May every year in the United States. We remember the brave men and women who lost their lives in war. Actually, they did not really *lose* their lives; they *gave* them. They knew they would be in danger and might die.

Why would a person be willing to do that? Their leaders command them to go into battle, but it's easy to get out of obeying a command. They took an oath to serve their country, but promises can be broken. They have the skills they need to fight the enemy, but they could use those skills in other ways. Only one thing makes a person willing to give up his or her own life, and that is love.

A soldier who has served three times in Iraq said, "I want to make this world safe for my children so they don't ever have to go to war." His love for his children is greater than his fear of dying. "If I die, I will be in heaven," he said, "I will be all right. I am not afraid."

Jesus was a brave soldier. He was willing to die on the cross because He loved His children. His death won freedom for us from the power of sin, death, and the devil. On the cross, Jesus ended the war with sin, death, and the devil. Now the cross reminds us of His sacrifice. Sacrifice, love, and thanks.

Journal: Do you know people who died in service to our country? Thank God for them. Thank their families too.

Pray: Dear heavenly Father, thank You for sending Jesus to give His life for me. Thank You for those whose love for You and others led them to give their lives so I can live in freedom. In Jesus' name. Amen. C. S.

Hello, my name is
Christina

Isaiah 59:20
_____

Matthew 16:16
_____

What's in a Name?

Matthew 25:31
_____

Imagine for a minute that you have no name. That would be a big problem! What would Mom say when she wanted you right now? What would Dad yell to encourage you in a ball game? When someone wanted your attention, he or she might call out, "Hey, Nameless Kid!"

Luke 2:11
_____

Of course, we all have a name. In fact, our names were probably chosen by our parents even before we were born. Names are very important because they identify us.

John 20:28
_____

Jesus has many names. They tell us who He is. They tell us what He did for sinners like you and me in need of a Savior. Look up these Bible verses to find some of those names. Then write them down.

Acts 5:42
_____

Fit the names that you found into these sentences to learn more about Jesus.

Jesus is the **L** _O N d_ of the whole world. He is the **S** _ae i na_ of **M**_____ and the **S** _o n d_ of **G** _o d_. Jesus is called **C**_____ because He is the promised Messiah. Jesus is our **R**_____ and the **S**_____ of the world.

The Bible says, "At the name of Jesus every knee should bow, in heaven and on earth and under the earth" (Philippians 2:10). In Jesus' name, God forgives us all our sin.

Journal: Write a sentence using one of Jesus' names.

Pray: Dear Jesus, thank You for being my Lord, Savior, and Redeemer. Help me to honor Your name in all I do. Amen. J. D.

Answers: Isaiah 59:20: Redeemer; Matthew 16:16: Son of God; Matthew 25:31: Son of Man; Luke 2:11: Savior; John 20:28: Lord; Acts 5:42: Christ.

A Special Message

Ellie picked her friend Tito's birthday card very carefully. The one she chose said just the right words: Happy Birthday to someone who is special in every way

"Why did you choose this card?" asked Mother.

"Tito doesn't hear that he's special very often," she replied. "I want him to know that he is."

Ellie was speaking Jesus' words to her friend. She was letting him know he was loved and accepted by his friends and by God.

Each of us is a special creation of God. Jesus loved us enough to die for us to save us from the penalty of our sins. He gives us talents and skills to use for His glory and to help others. We are special because of Him.

Do you know someone who needs to know that he or she is important? Some kids are bullied at school or not treated well at home. Some may be different from others or have trouble making friends. You can share God's love and care. That's why God put you in their lives to help and encourage them.

You can share the love Jesus gives you through your words and deeds: God loves you; you are special. I am your friend in Jesus.

Journal: Write a note of encouragement to a friend in need.

Pray: Dear Jesus, please help me encourage others by being their friend and reminding them that they are special to You. Amen. C. S.

Gospel Art

Colin twisted the crushed soda cans. Then he glued them together. He added some rusty bottle caps and crumpled paper. His assignment was to transform litter into an art project.

Colin wasn't sure if he liked the finished piece, but his grandfather did. "Look," said his grandfather, "you've turned trash into art!"

We're like those twisted soda cans and rusty bottle caps. We're not perfect or always pretty. We're sinners. We say sarcastic words instead of kind ones. We are stubborn and decide not to do our chores. We're silent even though we know we should tell the truth.

God's Law demands that we be perfect to live with Him forever; in that case, we sinners deserve to be trashed. There's no way any person can be perfect through his or her own thoughts or acts. But God loved the world and sent Jesus. Through the righteousness of His death and resurrection, we are no longer trashy sinners. And through the work of the Holy Spirit, God gives us faith and uses us.

The Holy Spirit's power is at work within us. His power changes our acts and thoughts into treasures. And His power leads us to share the love of Jesus to others. He uses us, imperfect as we are, to bring His Gospel message to others. God turns our spiritual trash into Gospel art!

Journal: Make a cross using something from your trash. In your journal, describe what you made.

Pray: Lord, thank You for loving me instead of throwing me away. Help me to share Your love with others. In Jesus' name. Amen. K. M.

JUNE 4

John 10:28

Hold On

Sophie and her parents went to visit her grandparents on their farm. She looked forward to running in the wide-open spaces and flying her kite.

As soon as Sophie and her parents arrived, Rex, the family dog, greeted them with barks. After a while, her dad said, "Sophie, are you ready to fly your kite?"

"Yes, sir!" she said.

Her dad helped her find just the right spot, and she started running. Rex ran too, barking with each step. They ran together until Sophie tripped. She went down; the kite went up. The string slipped from Sophie's hand. The wind snatched away her kite. In an instant, Sophie's joy turned to tears.

That night, Sophie and her dad talked about the kite. She was still sad that she dropped the string and the wind blew the kite away. Her dad hugged her. He reminded her that Jesus has a perfect grip. He is the Good Shepherd who cares for us, His sheep. He says, "No one will snatch them out of My hand" (John 10:28).

Do you know why Jesus' grip is so strong? Because He knows the devil will try to snatch us away from Him. He knows we may be tempted to go away from Him. Our Good Shepherd laid down His life for His sheep. He defeated our enemies. We need never fear that the devil can take us away. Jesus holds on to us.

Journal: What is God's promise for you in today's Bible verse?

Pray: Dear God, thank You for holding me tightly when temptations come or doubts make me question Your love. Keep me as Your sheep, always hearing Your voice and following You. In Jesus' name I pray. Amen. D. G.

But I'm Tired of It!

Ariel sighed. She put her assignment folder in her backpack. She sighed again after she got in the car. "I can't wait for school to be over," she told her mother.

Ariel's school had been closed too many days during the year because of bad weather, so she and her classmates were still doing makeup days in June.

Her mother said, "It's only a few more days, honey."

Ariel replied, "But I'm so tired of it!"

Ariel's mother was often patient. She looked at God's plans as opportunities, even when things changed. She prayed for the right words to tell her daughter. She said, "I love you very much, Ariel, even when you complain! I want you to know that complaining isn't good for us. When we complain, we focus on what we don't have instead of on God's blessings."

Ariel's mother wanted to encourage her. Even when we're tired of what we're doing, God is at work in our lives. He surrounds us with many blessings. God gives us reasons to offer Him praise and to share His mercy as we do good to others, as our reading today tells us.

Jesus loves sinners and is very patient with us. He loves us even when we complain, forgives us as we repent, and sends us out in His name to encourage and help others. He even fills us with words of thanks and praise!

Journal: Think of someone who seems unhappy. How can you bless and encourage him or her? Think of someone who has cheered you up. How can you thank that person?

Pray: Dear Lord, forgive me when I'm not patient. Use me to help others. In Jesus' name I pray. Amen. C. O.

Nobody Knows

Maria dropped her schoolbooks on the table and ran into the kitchen, where Dad was cooking supper. "Dad, Consuela says we shouldn't bother doing homework because the world is about to end."

Dad stirred the beans and checked the rice. "Where did Consuela get this interesting information?" he asked.

"She says it's in the Bible. Does the Bible really say that?"

"Well, let's check to see." Dad put down the spoon and picked up a Bible. "Jesus did say He was coming soon, but He didn't say what 'soon' means. It's already been hundreds of years since Jesus said that." Dad found the verse he wanted. "Jesus says nobody knows the day or the hour. It might be today or tomorrow. It might not be for many, many years."

Maria read the verse and other verses near it. "A lot of frightening things are going to happen," she said.

"Yes, but frightening things have been happening for hundreds of years. We've had wars and all the rest going on for a long time," Dad added. "But Jesus is still in control. On the cross, He paid for the sin that causes these things. When He comes again, the world will be perfect."

Maria sighed. "Does that mean I still have to do homework?"

"That's right, kiddo. You still have to do your homework," Dad said with a smile.

Journal: How can you practice your faith today as you wait for Jesus to come again?

Pray: Jesus, help me live as Your child in Your kingdom as I wait for the life eternal to come. Amen. S. T.

God with You

When Ishmael was a child, he was taken from his family and friends. The same happened to Joseph as a teenager. They must have both been scared. They probably felt lonely.

But God was with them!

God was with them while bad things were happening to them. God didn't stop the bad from happening, but He took care of their needs. And God did more—He made good come from the bad. Ishmael grew up to become a beloved father, grandfather, great-grand-father, and so on; in fact, his family became a nation! Joseph grew up to become what today we might call a vice-president of the ancient world's greatest country.

And God is with you!

When you are afraid or lonely, it may not feel like God cares. But He does. He cares so much that He gave His only Son to live and die so that sin would no longer be a barrier between you and Him.

When you wonder if God cares, pick up your Bible and read about Ishmael, Joseph, Moses, Samuel, David, Esther, Daniel, Mary, Timothy, and Jesus. Then it will become evident to you that God will take good care of you too.

Journal: Why can you know that God is with you?

Pray: God, I want to believe that You care for me. Help me when I don't believe. Amen. C. L.

Blowing in the Wind

Anna whispered, "Here she comes again." She and Luisa watched the bird return to the tree outside the window. The girls were watching the mother going in and out of the nest in the wind chime that hung in the tree.

The wren looked around for several seconds. An insect wiggled in her beak. The bird ducked into the wind chime. After a bit, she emerged and off she flew.

A wind chime seems an odd place for a bird nest. Wind chimes are meant to be tossed about in the wind. That seems dangerous for fragile eggs and baby birds. But inside, the mother bird had layered twigs, leaves, and grass into a tightly woven nest. Although the wind chimes blew around, the baby birds were safe in the nest.

Our homes can be like that wren's home. There are many spiritual winds that try to blow us around. There are bad messages on television. Whoosh! There are temptations on the Internet. Whoosh! Even our sinful nature wants to lie, cheat, and steal. Double whoosh!

In all this turmoil, God's children have a safe home. We are built on the rock of Jesus Christ and fed by His Word. We are baptized children of God, safe from the evil one. We are His, and He is ours.

Journal: Write about a time God protected you from the dangers of this world.

Pray: Dear Jesus, my Lord and Savior, thank You for being a solid rock in my life. Amen. C. H.

Still One in Christ

Brittany grew up in Ohio near her cousins, Teresa and Shea. The three girls attended the same church and school and enjoyed being together.

But that all changed when Teresa and Shea's father got a job in Pennsylvania. Their family moved when the girls were in sixth grade. Three years later, it changed again when Brittany's uncle died.

Brittany's family traveled from Ohio to Pennsylvania for the funeral. After being apart for three years, she wondered if she would have things in common with Teresa and Shea. When she saw her cousins, her fears disappeared. She was surprised at how easily they became friends again. All three had remained close to God in prayer, and they were active in church and youth events. During the funeral, they sang the hymns of faith and heard hope-filled messages from God's Word.

Today's Bible reading is from the Book of Acts. It tells us that the disciples had been scattered to different countries. Wherever they went, they shared the same message and the blessing of God's grace. And when they crossed paths again, they prayed, sang, and told one another about God's goodness.

Like Brittany, Teresa, Shea, and the disciples, we are part of the family of God. In Baptism, we became bonded. We are one in the name of the triune God—Father, Son, and Holy Spirit. Now, nothing can separate us from the love of God in Christ Jesus—not even death!

Journal: Satan tries to divide God's family. What are some ways he does that?

Pray: Christ, my Savior, through Your Holy Spirit, keep me strong in faith, so that I may be faithful to You and a friend to others. Amen. C. O.

Invitations

Madison's friend Olivia invited some girls to a sleepover. The girls would eat pizza, watch a movie, and talk late into the evening. For an early morning treat, Olivia's mother planned to make strawberry pancakes.

Madison was excited, but she told her mom, "I don't want to miss church and Sunday School. Will you pick me up early?"

"Sure, darlin'," said her mother. "Be ready by 8:30."

Madison's parents took her to church each week, reminding her, "Once you're baptized, you're still like a young plant that needs to be watered. You grow as you hear God's Word." Madison loved to go to church and Sunday School, sing, listen to God's Word, and spend time with her friends. She joined in the liturgy and added her offerings to the plate.

At the sleepover, Madison explained to her friends why she would leave early. Then she told them about Jesus. Not long after her explanation, she called her father and asked, "Dad, can you bring the van tomorrow? Everyone here wants to come to church with us!"

God uses us to invite others to church and to tell them about Jesus. When people hear God's Word, the Holy Spirit is busy.

It is His job, not ours, to call, gather, and enlighten people as they hear the Good News about Jesus!

Journal: Name one reason you look forward to going to church.

Pray: Holy Spirit, enlighten me through Your Word. Thank You for those who tell me of You and Your love. Remind me to invite others to go with me to church and Sunday School. In Jesus' name I pray. Amen. C. O.

I Need the Lord

Grandma and Grandpa stopped by to visit Sunday afternoon. "Church was good, and there was Communion," beamed Grandpa. "All in all, it was a great way to start the day!"

Their grandchildren Amy and Caitlyn loved Grandpa's smiles. He often laughed while he talked and made everyone feel comfortable.

Grandpa turned his attention to the twins. "You girls are almost ready for confirmation, aren't you? Pretty soon, you'll be receiving the Lord's Supper. You girls make me so proud!"

Amy and Caitlyn were already learning about the Christian faith in classes with their pastor. He was instructing them with the Bible and Luther's Small Catechism. They had read about Jesus offering a special meal to His disciples.

Caitlyn said, "Confirmation will be in the spring next year, Grandpa. I'm looking forward to Communion. Our pastor says that's where Christ gives us His body and blood. It is in, with, and under the bread and wine."

This time it was Grandma who spoke up. "I need the Lord every day," she said. "The Sacrament gives me the strength I need to live out my faith. I hope you'll remember it gives forgiveness."

Holy Communion is a gift Christ has given believers. Jesus gave bread and wine to His disciples, saying, "This is My body," and "This is My blood." He gives the same to us so we know we're His forgiven children—forever and always!

Journal: Write out Jesus' words about the Lord's Supper from the Gospel of Mark.

Pray: Father in heaven, prepare my heart to receive Holy Communion. Thank You for my salvation. In Jesus' name I pray. Amen. C. O.

JUNE 12

Proverbs 23:4

Growing Up

"What do you want to be when you grow up?" It seems like adults always want to know how you plan to spend your life, even though you may have no idea.

You may wonder about your future, but you don't have to worry about it. You don't have to fret because God has many special things for you to do, starting now. He has given you the saving knowledge of Jesus, your Savior. With faith, you can trust, rejoice, and find comfort in Him.

What will you be when you grow up? You will be just what you are now—God's child. Each day, the Holy Spirit will renew your life so you can overcome sin and do work, good works.

That's good news. It means God's children can study, play, clean, practice, relax, and chat as they speak and act in faith according to the Ten Commandments. They do these things to the glory of God and to benefit others.

What does God have for you to do today? Are you a son or daughter? Are you a brother or sister, a friend or team member? Think of the possibilities.

And if you sin and don't feel like being nice to others, remember that the Holy Spirit brings comfort to you. Each day, you can confess your sins and find comfort in God's forgiveness.

So what do you want to be when you grow up? You want to be God's own child, declaring His praises.

Journal: What are some things you have to do today?

Pray: Dear God, create in me a clean heart, and renew me each day to do the good works You have for me to do. Amen. S. H.

A Treasured Heirloom

Jasmine pulled the quilt tightly around her shoulders. "Grandma," she said, "I like sitting out here at night to watch the stars with you, but I get cold, so I'm thankful for this old quilt."

"Jasmine, that quilt is very special."

"What's so special about this old thing?" Jasmine asked as she examined its faded patterns of red, blue, and green.

"It's special because my grandmother made it. It is an heirloom that has been passed down from one person to another in our family. Someday, I will give it to you because you are my heir."

Jasmine thought about Grandma's words and said, "Wow, this is special! Not only does it keep me warm, but it also tells the story of how our family has loved and taken care of each other. When it is mine, Grandma, I am going to take good care of this quilt."

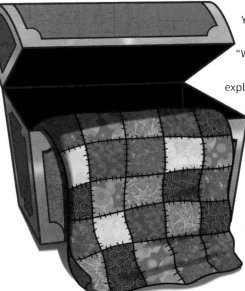

"Here's another thought, Jasmine. You are an heir to another gift, an even more valuable one."

"What gift is that?" asked Jasmine.

"When you were baptized," Grandma explained, "you became part of God's family of believers. Because Jesus paid for your sins, you are an heir to all that He won for you. Those gifts include forgiveness, life, and salvation." Then Grandma wrapped her arms around Jasmine and said, "You see, my dear, Jesus wraps you in His love. You are an heir and a child of heaven."

Journal: Grandma will someday pass on the quilt to Jasmine. What has someone passed on to you? What will Jesus give to you?

Pray: Dear God, thank You for making me Your child and an heir of heaven through Jesus Christ. In His name I pray. Amen. C. H.

JUNE 14

Galatians 6:14;
Psalm 60:4–5

Flag Day

Today is Flag Day in the United States. A flag is a banner that represents a nation and stands for victory.

During the War of 1812, Francis Scott Key watched from a ship in the Chesapeake Bay while a battle raged all night at Fort McHenry. When dawn broke, he saw that the American flag was still flying, which inspired him to write our national anthem.

As Christians, we are citizens of God's holy nation of believers, and we have a powerful symbol of what we believe in. It is the cross on which Jesus died for the sins of the whole world—including us.

The empty tomb also reminds us of our victory over death and the devil. The sight of the empty grave on Easter morning inspired much more than a poem. Because of it, we can be certain that our bodies will rise too, and that we will live forever in heaven. The battle has been won. The victory is ours.

Journal: Draw a banner that Christians could fly to declare their faith.

Pray: Dear Jesus, thank You for the blessing of our country. Let us show respect and love for it and for our flag. Thank You especially for Your empty cross and vacant tomb. They remind us of Your victory over sin and death. That is the greatest blessing of all. Amen. C. S.

Baseball

Do you like to play baseball? Baseball reminds us of our lives as Christians.

Baseball is a team sport. Teammates work together, and all the positions are necessary. We, too, work together with other Christians. God gives us different talents, but every person is needed.

Being a good baseball player requires listening to the coach and practicing faithfully. Christians, too, listen to God's Word and practice doing what He says.

In baseball, players run the bases focused on getting home. We, too, focus on going home to be with Jesus in heaven. The devil and his team would like to keep us out so we must beware of his tricks.

There is one important difference, however. Baseball players are chosen by how good they are. They must earn their place on the team. God chose us to be His own not because we are such great players, but because of the greatness of His love. We receive His blessings in spite of our errors, by His grace alone. And at the end of the game, we know the victory is ours.

Journal: Can you think of other spiritual lessons we can learn from baseball?

Pray: Dear God, thank You for choosing me. Please continue to teach me Your ways until, by Your grace, You bring me home. Amen. C. S.

JUNE 16

Ecclesiastes 4:12

For the Birds and Us

Trey's golf ball soared and just missed a bird. "That was close!" said Dad. Trey and his dad were golfing in Florida while visiting Trey's uncle Stuart.

"Did you see how one bird got the other bird to move out of the way?" Dad asked. "The bird got nudged out of the way just in time, almost like one bird was looking out for the other."

"Those are sandhill cranes," Uncle Stuart said. "We see them in pairs—a male and a female. They look out for each other."

"I guess we all need someone to look out for us, especially when danger is near," said Dad. "There's plenty of evil in the world. That's why your mom and I picked Uncle Stuart to be your Baptism sponsor, Trey. He prays for you and has promised to help us raise you as God's child."

"That's right, Trey," said Uncle Stuart as they walked down the fairway. "We know the devil, the world, and our own sinful nature try to turn us away from God. When you were just a little guy, I saw you being baptized. There, God gave you the Holy Spirit and the gift of faith. Now you can study His powerful Word. And soon you will take the Lord's Supper. And when you do, I'll be there with your parents." Just then the sand cranes scurried by again.

"Yes," said Dad, "God designed these birds to watch over each other. And He blesses us with faith-filled friends to help us keep Christ as the center of our lives."

Journal: Write down the names of your Baptism sponsors. Then contact them to thank them for praying for you.

Pray: Dear God, thank You for putting people in my life who not only care about me as a person, but who also care about me as a disciple of Jesus Christ. Amen. D. G.

Homeward Bound

Immigrants are citizens from one country who have moved to another country. Many countries welcome immigrants. The foreigners can have homes in your neighborhood. They can have all kinds of jobs. They can go to schools and get an education. They can play sports and have friends. Maybe you or your church have helped immigrants to learn the language and customs of your country. Or maybe you are an immigrant who has had this experience.

We could say that Christians are immigrants because we live away from our home in heaven. In Philippians 3:20, we read, "But our citizenship is in heaven." We often forget that we belong to our heavenly Father. Our sinful nature wants to crown us as ruler of our own "little kingdom" on earth. We ignore the truth that God is the creating Ruler of all and Lord of our lives.

We don't deserve to be citizens of His wonderful heavenly home. But because Jesus died on the cross for our sins, God forgives our sins and promises to be with us in heaven. Jesus made it possible for us to be members of God's household. Now we have access to heaven. Now we can tell others about Jesus, who made heaven our home.

Journal: How are Christians like immigrants? This week, say a prayer for someone from another country.

Pray: Dear Lord, thank You for the promise of a true home in heaven. Help me to tell others of Your great love and forgiveness. In Jesus' name. Amen. K. M.

Added Blessings

"Hey, Dad. Billy asked if we could go fishing with him and his dad for Father's Day. What do you say?"

"Sounds great, Ethan! When are they leaving?"

"Sunday morning, around six o'clock."

Dad paused. "Well, then, I don't know. It would be fun to go, but I would love to begin Father's Day in church with our heavenly Father and our family together.

"Jesus said, 'Seek first the kingdom of God and His righteousness, and all these things will be added to you' (Matthew 6:33). Jesus knew it would be tempting for us to think it's no big deal to miss the blessings of the church service. But it is. By choosing fishing, we would miss out on our heavenly Father's gifts—the ones Jesus gives us."

"I didn't think of that," Ethan confessed. "I'll tell Billy we can't go."

"Not on Sunday morning anyway," Dad said. "But I have another idea. I have tickets to the baseball game Sunday afternoon. Let's ask Billy and his dad to join us at church. Then they can go to the game with us that afternoon."

Ethan and his dad had a Father's Day of added blessings—the morning at church and an afternoon at the ballpark with special friends and family. And Ethan thought it was the best day of all!

Journal: Write down four blessings God has added to your life.

Pray: Dear Father in heaven, thank You for the time I am able to spend with my family and friends. Thank You for being my heavenly Father and for giving me wonderful gifts, including Jesus. Amen. D. G.

Summer Days

"This is the good life," sighed Colton as he stretched out on the porch swing. "I love summer!"

"Me too," agreed his brother Dakota. "No homework."

"We can fish and ride our bikes," Colton said.

"Yeah, but remember last summer," said Dakota, "when someone stole your bike?"

"I remember," said Colton. "And you got poison ivy, really bad."

The screen door banged as Dad joined the boys on the porch. "Hi, guys. What's so interesting?"

"We were talking about how summer can be good and not so good," said Dakota.

"That's true," Dad said. "Here on the farm, summer is a lot of hard work. So maybe not so good. But you boys are great help. So that is good. We can be sure we'll have troubles. And sometimes, we don't get along. But no matter what happens, we can count on God to give us the truly good things."

"Like His forgiveness and the help of others," said Dakota.

"We sure needed lots of helpers last summer," added Colton. "Dr. Berry helped Dakota get over poison ivy. Mom found me a better bike at a garage sale."

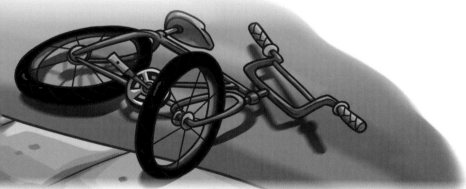

"And God used us to help one another," Dad reminded them. "We served the Lord while we worked."

"Thinking about work as service in God's kingdom," said Colton, "will make our chores easier to do."

Dad grinned and said, "Well, I need some help. Anyone feel like being a servant?"

Journal: How has God made you a blessing to others?

Pray: Heavenly Father, give me eyes to see all the good things You have given me and a heart that wants to serve others. In Jesus' name I pray. Amen. J. D.

For Ever and Ever

Have you ever watched leaders of different countries on TV? They talk about how to share products, how to support troops, how to divide land, and how to provide care for people. Sometimes leaders get along. Sometimes they don't.

This happened in Bible times too. Instead of presidents and prime ministers, there were kings and pharaohs. Those leaders didn't always agree with one another. When disagreements couldn't be resolved, they often went to war. People who had been neighbors might be separated by conflicts and battles. People who had gathered in worship might be scattered.

Then, as now, the spread of God's Word was affected by how leaders destroyed or controlled lands. Elijah worried about the survival of worshipers in his day. "I, even I only, am left," said Elijah (1 Kings 19:14).

Civilizations and governments may disappear or change, but God's Word never changes or gets lost. The Holy Spirit remains in the hearts of those who believe and are baptized, even if they can't always go to church. Faith grows in people, even if they must study God's Word in secret. God's love and forgiveness don't change, even during times of hunger and war. Just as Elijah learned to trust the Lord, we also can trust in the eternal power of God's Word. In a constantly changing world, God is always present.

Journal: Write down some attributes of God that never change.

Pray: O Lord, I thank You for the everlasting power and truth of Your loving Word, even in times of trouble and war. Thank You for Your presence. Amen. K. M.

The Sin Within

Have you ever heard of the Great Wall of China? The Great Wall is a series of many sections of wall, built of stone or mud, all across the vast lands of China. The walls were built over several generations to protect Chinese people from invaders. People wanted to keep fighters out of their land. They wanted the walls to protect them from danger.

We could build walls to protect us from bad things. But walls cannot protect us from the worst problem of all—sin.

We cannot get rid of our own sin since it comes from inside of us. The root of our sin is a broken relationship with the Lord. That relationship was broken in the Garden of Eden when Adam and Eve sinned. And it continues. Whenever we think or say something unkind, whenever we disobey, or whenever we hate, we show our sinful nature.

Only God can heal this kind of broken relationship. Only God can protect us from the results of our sin. This God loves us. Our sin cannot keep God's love away from us! God's great love, shown through Jesus, who died for our sins, is the perfect and only protection there is against sin. God sends the Holy Spirit into our hearts to heal the wounds of sin and to bring us to faith and obedience in Him.

God's love is a stronger defense than any great wall.

Journal: What should be the result of sin (Romans 6:23)? How did God save us from this sin? Why does God want to save us?

Pray: Lord, I praise Your holy name. Thank You for the power of Your love. In Jesus' name. Amen. K. M.

Guardian Donkeys

"There's another one. That's the fourth one I've seen."

Danny's mother looked at him in the rearview mirror. "The fourth what?" she asked.

"The fourth time I saw a donkey in a pasture full of sheep. I wonder why people put sheep and donkeys together."

Danny and his mother were on their way to visit his great-grandma Schmidt. They had been driving through farmland and green pasture.

Mother replied, "Oh yes. I noticed that too, the last time I drove this way. When I asked Grandma about it, she said the donkeys were there to protect the sheep. Donkeys have a natural dislike of animals like coyotes and foxes that might harm the sheep. When a coyote or fox comes too close, the donkey starts braying and scares it away."

Danny thought about that and then said, "That's pretty cool. The sheep have a guardian to protect them. And we do too."

"In what way, Danny?"

"Well, the devil is our enemy. He wants to separate us from God. But God loves us and protects us from the evil one. Even Jesus prayed to God for protection for us. It is good to know that He is our guardian, protecting us from the evil in this world. I think I understand exactly how those sheep feel."

Mother smiled at Danny's words and said, "I think I understand how they feel too, Danny! And it's a good feeling."

Journal: Write about a time you needed protection from something bad.

Pray: Dear God, thank You for sending Jesus, who loved me so much that He took time to include me and all believers in His prayers. Amen. C. H.

Thriller, Filler, Spiller

"Today is La Flor Day!" sang Rosa as she twirled around. "This is La Flor Day when Abuela Muñez plants flowers, and I get to help!"

Rosa was on her grandmother's patio, surrounded by bags of soil, trays of plants, and lots of containers. Rosa watched as Mrs. Muñez filled a large container with soil and plants. "Abuela, that's beautiful!" said Rosa. "How do you know which plants to put in the pots?"

Mrs. Muñez said, "I have a formula that I use. When planting a container, you need a thriller, a filler, and a spiller. This tall plant is the thriller, and these small colorful flowers are the filler. And this vine that hangs over the side is the spiller."

"That's so cool!" exclaimed Rosa.

"Our Christian life is kind of like the three parts of this planting," Mrs. Muñez continued. "The thriller part is the Good News that Jesus died for our sins and rose from the dead. Now we are forgiven and will go to live with Jesus someday. The filler is the Holy Spirit, who fills our lives and helps us to live as God's children. And we are the spillers as we live each day as God's children and tell and show others what we believe about Jesus."

"Abuela," said Rosa, "I learned how to plant a container of beautiful flowers. And when I look at it, I will think about my life as God's child—the thriller, filler, and spiller."

Journal: What are the "spilling" things you get to do today? Ask the Holy Spirit to fill you with opportunities to share God's love in words and actions.

Pray: Dear God, thank You for sending Jesus to be my Savior. May Your Holy Spirit guide me so I can spill out the Good News about Jesus. Amen. J. D.

Sticking Together

"Oh, Mom," Rachel whined, "Dad is upset with me. I'm upset with Bingo and myself. Do we even love each other anymore?"

Hugging her daughter, Mom asked, "Rachel, what is love?"

The twelve-year-old said, "I'm not sure. I suppose it means to feel good about someone."

"Do you feel good about your puppy?"

Rachel answered, "Not right now. I didn't think Bingo would do his business on the carpet. What a mess! Dad was yelling at both of us. He made me clean up everything. Gross!"

Mom smiled. "You still love your puppy. And I know Dad loves you. Love is more than a feeling. It's a pledge to stick together."

"Stick together?" Rachel echoed. "Even when we're angry?"

Her mom answered with a question. "Do you suppose God gets angry?"

Rachel responded, "I think Pastor read a passage last Sunday about God's anger."

"That's right," Mom explained. "On Calvary, God gave Jesus the anger we deserve. Without Jesus, God would still be angry with us because of our sins, but we know He forgives us each day."

Rachel said, "I guess love is like glue—sticking us together even though we don't always feel good about one another."

Mom nodded. "Love is cleaning the mess on the carpet even though it is gross. By the way, I see a puppy outside needing love."

"I'll take care of that," said Rachel as she headed out the door.

Journal: Suppose a friend asks, "How can you be my friend and still be mad at me?" What would you say?

Pray: Father, through the cross of Your Son, my sins are forgiven. You have restored me to Yourself. Let my love for You never come undone. In Jesus' name I pray. Amen. M. P.

The Food of Life

Alex poured the seeds into the new bird feeder and asked, "What happens if the birds don't come?"

"Just wait," Dad said. "They will."

Sure enough, by the end of the week, the birds had discovered the feeder. Soon, Alex and her dad had to fill the feeder almost every day. "What would happen to the birds if we didn't put any more seeds into the feeder?" asked Alex.

"That would be a problem for a while because they are depending on us," Dad replied. "But we aren't the only source of food."

God provides us with vegetables, meat, and other foods. But God also gives us spiritual food—the Word and Sacraments. Jesus said, "I am the bread of life; whoever comes to Me shall not hunger, and whoever believes in Me shall never thirst" (John 6:35).

Jesus was talking about heavenly life. He wants us to live with Him forever, and He provides the only way to get there.

Later in the Bible reading, Jesus said,

> **"For this is the will of My Father, that everyone who looks on the Son and believes in Him should have eternal life, and I will raise him up on the last day"** (John 6:40).

When the end of the world comes, the people who have believed that Jesus died for their sins and rose again will go to live in heaven with Him. What a wonderful, exciting day that will be!

Journal: Why do we need the food of life that God gives us?

Pray: Dear Jesus, You are the bread of life. You suffered and died for me so that I can live forever with You. Nourish me so that I can tell this Good News to others. In Your name I pray. Amen. P. L.

What Friends Do

Jake had a great time his first day at VBS. One thing his teacher said stuck in Jake's mind. She said that Jesus came to save the world from sin. Without being mean or judgmental, she said that people who don't know Jesus are not going to be saved. She said that part of a Christian's purpose for living is to serve in God's kingdom. Christians serve others and use those opportunities to tell them the Good News of salvation.

Jake thought about it after VBS that day. He made up his mind to call and invite Kyle. But then he had another thought. Kyle already knew Jesus. It would be fine to have Kyle come to VBS, but James, one of the boys on the baseball team, had said, "What's VBS?" Jake decided to ask James to come to VBS.

When Jake got home, he called Kyle to invite him. He also called James, who seemed happy to hear from him and said he was bored and would come to VBS. Jake offered to ride his bike to meet James so they could go together.

On Tuesday, James had a great time. With Kyle there, the two boys were able to explain to James the story of Jesus' birth—the story James had missed on Monday. They also explained what Jesus' Baptism meant.

In baseball, Jake's team lost, but he didn't care. He was excited that James had heard about Jesus and said he believed in the promise of forgiveness in Jesus.

Join the Fun!
June 26 / 6:00 - 8:00 PM

Journal: Make a list of people you might invite to church or VBS.

Pray: Dear Jesus, through Your Word, work faith in the hearts and lives of my friends, that they may be saved from sin and death and live in eternity with You. Amen. J. O.

Natural Disasters

Mariah heard about a flood in Asia. Many houses, people, and animals were swept away by the water.

She wondered why God didn't stop the flood. Wouldn't it have been better if the flood had never happened? Mariah asked her pastor where God was during the flood.

He replied, "God is everywhere. He was there during this flood, just like He was with Noah and his family during the great flood."

"Why didn't He stop it?" Mariah asked.

"You and I know how powerful God is," said her pastor. "We believe He made the world, parted the Red Sea, made the sun stand still for a day, and raised Jesus from the dead. I don't know why He didn't stop the flood in Asia. But His Word says death is not His will. He cares for all people and wants them to trust in Jesus as their Savior."

Mariah had been worried that God wasn't in control. But she realized that earthquakes, tornadoes, floods, and fires happen in a sinful world. She said, "People everywhere need to hear God's Word and believe that Jesus died for their sins and rose from the dead. Then they can be His children now and go to heaven when they die."

"Yes, Mariah," her pastor answered. "That's why missionaries all over the world tell people about Jesus. God is still doing great deeds today. He's bringing salvation to the world through the Good News of His Son."

Journal: Learn about people in another country. What country did you choose and why? Pray for God to provide pastors, teachers, and missionaries who will tell them about Jesus.

Pray: Dear God, please help children throughout the world to hear and believe that You have sent Your Son, Jesus, to be their Savior. In Jesus' name I pray. Amen. C. O.

What's in the Bag?

Niki noticed the musty smell in her room. It must smell this way because of the rain, she thought.

But later that day, her mother noticed the smell too. "Do we have a dead mouse? Is there a wet towel in here? What is it?"

A quick search of the room turned up a gym bag under Niki's bed. "Yuck," said Niki. "It's my clothes from the game Thursday night. Sorry, Mom."

Sweaty clothes in a zipped-up bag make an unpleasant smell, but there is something worse. What if all our sins were zipped up in a bag? And what if God found the bag and opened it?

Our sins would smell rotten. We would be ashamed of all the sins our Lord would see. We would also be afraid of getting into trouble. The Bible says that "the wrath of God is coming" because of our sins (Colossians 3:6).

Thankfully, the Lord won't have to open a bag of our sins. Jesus bore God's wrath against sin on the cross. He traded His sinless life for our sinful ones. He took away the smelly clothing of guilt and, in our Baptism, clothed us in His righteousness.

Our Bible reading is a prayer of thanks that "my transgression would be sealed up in a bag, and You would cover over my iniquity" (Job 14:17). Jesus Christ has covered our guilt and sin.

Journal: Compare the bad behavior in Colossians 3:5–8 with the faithful living in Colossians 3:12–14.

Pray: Father, You love an unworthy sinner like me, and I am thankful. Forgive me, and lead me to clean living. In Jesus' name I pray. Amen. C. O.

June Blessings

Summer gives us the opportunity to spend time outdoors enjoying God's creation.

From the tiniest bug to the most magnificent constellation, our world is full of God's wonders.

His most awesome work and proof of His amazing love for us, of course, was sending Jesus to be our Savior. But He shows His love in other ways as well. When I was a baby, my father made toys for me. He made a tricycle out of a wheelbarrow and pieces of old machinery. He made a little red chair and bench and even a doll buggy. Those toys are special to me because my father made them, and he made them because he loved me.

That's why the beauties of nature are so special to those of us in God's family. Our Father made them, and He made them because He loves us.

He also gave us our senses so we can enjoy the gifts of nature in a variety of ways. Try doing this:

* Sit someplace outside and list all the colors you see.

* Close your eyes and name all the sounds you hear.

* What smell is the strongest?

* Touch a piece of tree bark and then a smooth rock.

* Go inside and drink a glass of cool, fresh water.

Now try writing a poem or a description of what you experienced in nature and as a member of God's family.

Praise the Lord!

Journal: List three things found in nature that you really love. Do some research about them to learn more about God's wisdom in creating them.

Pray: Dear heavenly Father, Your love for us is beyond description. Thank You for this world and all its wonders. Thank You most of all for sending Jesus to love this world and all of us in it and to be our Savior. Amen. C. S.

Many Ways or One Way?

"I'm studying about different religions," Kelly told Heather as they waited at the library checkout desk. "That way I'll be able to decide what I want to believe."

"But Kelly," asked Heather, "aren't you worried that you might not get to heaven?"

"Heaven? All religions lead to some kind of heaven," answered Kelly. "It doesn't really matter what you believe—only that you have faith and try to live a good life."

Later, Heather told her father about her conversation with Kelly. "Is it true, Dad?" asked Heather. "Can a person get to heaven by being a Hindu or Buddhist or Muslim?"

Dad said, "People follow many different religions, Heather. Some of them encourage their followers to do good to their neighbors. Others teach the great thoughts and words of someone who lived long ago. Some religions tell people they must follow certain rules to live in a God-pleasing way."

"But Dad," interrupted Heather, "those are things we do. Are all religions just the same?"

"No, Heather. Christianity is very different. In all other religions, going to heaven depends on what a person does. Christians know that no one can keep God's Law perfectly. That's why God sent His Son, Jesus, to keep it for us and then to die for our sins. Jesus is the only way to heaven. Jesus makes all the difference!"

Journal: Write three ways that Christianity is like some other religions. What makes it different?

Pray: Lord Jesus, You are the way, the truth, and the life. No one comes to the Father or goes to heaven except through You. Keep me in the faith that trusts You alone for salvation. Amen. E. R.

Living with Jesus

California was a long way from Virginia, where Michaela lived, but she wasn't afraid. Michaela was spending a month with her grandma in California.

She would have to take an airplane all the way across the United States. She would have to be away from her mom and dad. She would have to leave her friends behind. But she was not sad. Why?

Michaela would be with her grandma, who loved her. She thought about all the fun and exciting things she and Grandma would do. They would go to the beach. They would bake cookies. They would go to museums and an amusement park. But the best thing wasn't what they would do or where they would go. The best thing was that they would be together.

Someday, we will go on a trip to heaven. The Bible doesn't tell us all the things we will do in heaven, but we know it will be wonderful. There will be happiness and no more tears. We will live there forever with Jesus, who died and rose so we can come in. He loves us even more than our parents and grandparents. He takes better care of us than anyone else ever could. What an adventure heaven will be!

It will probably be many years before we go to heaven, but whenever you are having a great time with someone you love, think about the eternity you will spend with Jesus.

Journal: Draw a picture of what you think heaven will look like. Be sure to include yourself and Jesus in the picture.

Pray: Dear Jesus, thank You for the promise that I will live in heaven with You. You made that possible because You died on the cross to take away my sins. I love You because of Your great love for me. Amen. C. C. S.

All the Water You Need

During a drought, one family had trouble milking their goats. The goats gave a gallon a day, then a half-gallon, and then nothing at all. Living through a hot time meant the goats could no longer produce milk.

The goats suffered because the grass was scorched and their natural sources of water dried up. Can you imagine what it would be like to be hungry and thirsty all the time?

God's Word reminds us, "The grass withers, the flower fades, but the word of our God will stand forever" (Isaiah 40:8). Everything in this world—our body, house, clothes, and toys—will turn to dust with age. But the Word of God remains forever.

When you were baptized, the pastor called you by name and said, "I baptize you in the name of the Father and of the Son and of the Holy Spirit." He poured water on your head, just as Jesus commanded His disciples to do.

That's when you were changed by the Word of God! Your sins were washed away, and you "put on Christ." Jesus offers the water that leads to eternal life. It is a river that always flows and never goes dry.

As you remember how you received saving faith in Baptism, give thanks to God. Feed your faith by reading His Word, listening to your pastor's sermons, and singing hymns of praise with the church. Fed and nourished, your faith will never "dry up"!

Journal: What does Jesus promise He will give you in John 4:13–14?

Pray: Heavenly Father, increase my faith each day. Lead me to be nourished by things that are good and godly and to avoid the temptations of the world. In Jesus' name I pray. Amen C. O.

A Better Plan

Isaac was bummed. If only he hadn't tripped over that tree root and broken his ankle. Now he had to wear a cast for six whole weeks! That meant no baseball, no soccer, and no swimming.

At least he had his iPod. He could sit in the sunshine and listen to music. His uncle had even bought him an app with Bible stories on it, which was pretty cool.

He was so intent in listening to one of the stories that he didn't notice the boy who sat near him on the bleachers.

"What are you listening to?" the boy asked.

"Oh, just a story," answered Isaac. "It's from the Bible."

"I don't know any stories from the Bible," the boy, named Moshi, responded. "Are they any good?"

"You mean you've never heard about Noah or David or Jonah or Jesus?" Isaac asked.

"No. What's the big deal?"

Then Isaac began to understand why he was sitting on those bleachers that day. Having a broken ankle was a pain, but being able to tell someone about Jesus was worth it all. So that's what he did. Many days that summer, Isaac and Moshi listened to the stories together. Soon, Moshi knew all about Jesus too.

God kept His promise to work all things together for good for those who love Him. When Isaac asked Moshi to sign his cast, this is what he wrote:

"Thank you for telling me about Jesus!"

Journal: Write about something that seemed bad at the time, but later God turned into something good.

Pray: Dear Jesus, when I feel sad because of sin or disappointed by injuries, help me trust You to work everything together for good according to Your will. At those times, work in my life for Your purpose. Amen. C. S.

JULY 4

Psalm 20:7

Fireworks and Freedom

A warm day was dawning. Coolers were packed with cold drinks and refreshing snacks. Blankets and lawn chairs were loaded into the car. Sunscreen was rubbed onto arms, necks, and noses. American flags were waving.

"I can't wait for the fireworks," Morgan squealed. "That's the best part!"

"No, the parade is best—bands, horses, and candy!" James grinned.

"Don't forget about singing the national anthem while the giant flag is raised," their dad chimed in.

"I know. That's the whole point of Independence Day, I guess," James said.

"No, silly," Morgan chided. "It's called the Fourth of July!"

"Either name is correct," Dad said. "What is more important is realizing that the day is about more than fireworks and parades. Today we celebrate a country that allows us to worship our God and share our faith. But even though God gave us a country where we can be independent, He still wants us to be dependent on Him."

James and Morgan thought for a minute. "Like how we depend on Him to provide everything we need?" Morgan asked.

"Exactly," Dad said. "We enjoy our independence in America, knowing we are always dependent on God."

"So the reason we can celebrate Independence Day is because we are dependent on God, right?" James asked.

Dad smiled. "We can be independent only because of our dependence!"

Journal: What is your favorite part of the Fourth of July?

Pray: Dear Jesus, thank You for the gift of being able to freely worship You. This Independence Day, let me be dependent on You. Amen. J. D.

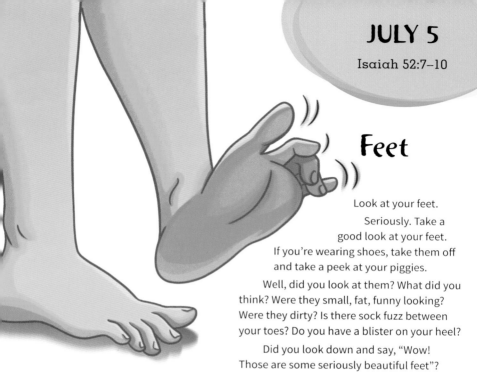

Feet

Look at your feet.

Seriously. Take a good look at your feet. If you're wearing shoes, take them off and take a peek at your piggies.

Well, did you look at them? What did you think? Were they small, fat, funny looking? Were they dirty? Is there sock fuzz between your toes? Do you have a blister on your heel?

Did you look down and say, "Wow! Those are some seriously beautiful feet"?

Feet are not beautiful, if you ask me. They can get pretty dirty, especially in summer. And they can even be a little bit stinky.

There's a verse in Isaiah that says, "How beautiful upon the mountains are the feet of him who brings good news" (52:7). Now, if you were going to run around in the mountains, taking a message from one place to another, how do you think your feet would look? Not very clean, that's for sure.

So, what's so beautiful about these feet Isaiah's talking about? They are bringing good news. And what's the good news that they carry? It's that Jesus is our Savior. It's the news that God's in charge and mighty. They bring the news that God loves us enough to take care of us all the time and that we are never, ever alone.

Feet may be funny looking, but they can do amazing things. They can carry God's good news to us. And they can carry us to others, so that they can hear the good news too.

Journal: Where will your feet carry you today? How can you share some good news there?

Pray: Jesus, help me to be Your beautiful feet today! Amen. J. R.

A New Language

If you read today's Bible reading out loud, you might have had trouble pronouncing the names of all the countries mentioned. Just imagine—people from all those places heard the Word of God preached in their own native language. The Holy Spirit gave the disciples the ability to speak in languages they had never heard before so that they could tell people about Jesus.

Can you speak more than one language? It usually takes years to learn and speak a language well, but there is a new language that you probably know even better than your parents and teachers. That language is called texting.

Sometimes when people text, they shorten their words. For example, instead of writing, "I see you," you might text, "I C U." See if you can translate the following messages about God from "texting" into English.

1	**SRV 1 ANTHR N LV**
2	**THX B 2 GD**
3	**GD S LV**
4	**GD CRE8D TH HVNS N TH RTH**
5	**GD S GR8**
6	**JC S UR BFF**

The translations are printed below. No matter what language you use, remember to tell people about Jesus and His love.

Journal: Write three more text messages about God. With your parents' permission, send them to a friend.

Pray: Dear heavenly Father, thank You for translating Your Word, the Bible, into many languages so all people can learn about You. Please help me read and understand it so I can tell others about You too. Amen. C. S.

(1) SERVE ONE ANOTHER IN LOVE. (2) THANKS BE TO GOD. (3) GOD IS LOVE. (4) GOD CREATED THE HEAVENS AND THE EARTH. (5) GOD IS GREAT. (6) JESUS CHRIST IS YOUR BEST FRIEND FOREVER.

Prepared

Flashlight. Bug spray. Sleeping bag, hiking boots, marshmallows. Griffin and his dad were going camping. They had been preparing all week for their trip, and Griffin was excited. "Dad, we've got enough stuff. Can't we just go?"

Dad made another check mark on his list. "I need to make sure we've got everything we need. Did you pack your hat?"

"It's on my head, Dad. Let's go!"

"Here's the map and the first-aid kit and the magnifying glass. Okay, we're ready."

"With all this stuff, Dad, we're ready for anything!"

Camping trips, piano recitals, and social study tests all take preparation. So do spiritual things.

God uses the Bible to get us ready to do the things He has planned for us to do. The more time we spend with it, the more prepared we are to face challenges. God's Word comforts us, strengthens us, and gives us peace. He gets us ready to help others and to share the story of Jesus' love with them. His Word completes and equips us for every good work.

Jesus was prepared to do what He was born to do—die on the cross for our sins. Through the Word, God has given us faith in Him. Now, we have the joy of spending time in His Word, being strengthened in faith and prepared for a life serving others in His name.

Journal: Do you have a favorite Bible verse? How might it prepare you for something you will face tomorrow?

Pray: Dear Jesus, thank You for being ready to give Your life for me. Help me to be ready to share Your Word with my friends. Amen. J. R.

The Day Made by God

"Time to go home! It's time to meet your mom," called Tasha's dad. Tasha and her friend Olivia looked up from sorting shells.

"One more swim, Dad?" Tasha begged. Tasha held up one of her shells. "Look, Dad. This looks like the one in church."

"It does. It's a symbol of Baptism, a reminder of when God's Spirit brought you to faith and you became God's child," he said.

"May I keep it?" Tasha asked.

"Sure. Did Olivia find one too?"

Olivia held up her favorite shell. Then they picked up the rest of their things.

They took Olivia home and drove toward Tasha's. Tasha sighed. "Did you have a good time?" her dad asked.

"Yes!" Tasha shouted. She sang, "This is the day, this is the day that the Lord has made." Her dad joined in. By the time they got to Tasha's house, they were singing with gusto. "We will rejoice and be glad in it. This is the day, this is the day that the Lord has made!"

Tasha got her things out of the car. "I wish we could sing that every day, Dad."

"You can, Tasha. Just call me." Tasha's dad hugged her. "The Lord gave us a beautiful day, and He promises to be with us every day." Tasha nodded.

"Jesus loves us so much! He died for our sins so that we can live with Him forever. We can rejoice every day." He kissed Tasha and said, "Call me tomorrow, and we'll sing together."

Journal: Write new stanzas to "This Is the Day," or write your own song of rejoicing to God.

Pray: Lord, You made this and every day. I am alive in You and rejoice in Your everlasting love, which forgives me and helps me live. Amen. J. H.

The Test of Time

"Think about something you really want to have or something you want to do," said Ms. Cain to her Sunday School class.

"I want these shoes I saw online," said Phong.

"I've always wanted to go to Disney World," added Hannah.

Everyone smiled when Martin complained, "I want a cell phone, but Mom says I have to wait."

"I would like my grandfather to get well," Javier said quietly.

Ms. Cain continued, "Now put your ideas to the Hundred Years Test. Think about how the world and people will be affected one hundred years from now by the shoes you wore, where you went on vacation, or when you got a cell phone."

"We need to think more long term," said Jenn, grinning.

The teacher said, "Something like the Hundred Years Test helps us see more clearly what's truly important. It helps us make good choices about how to spend our time and money.

"God always thinks long term. Our heavenly Father looks far beyond today. He looks at things from an everlasting perspective. He loves us so much that He sent His Son to die for our sins so that we can spend eternity with Him."

God wants us to live life fully and enjoy the things and experiences He gives us. However, what will matter in the future is if our words and actions help take the Good News of forgiveness in Jesus to others.

Journal: Make a list of things in your life that pass the Hundred Years Test. What things could you add?

Pray: Everlasting Lord, forgive my selfishness. Help me to live in ways that matter in Your eternal kingdom. In Jesus' name I pray. Amen. D. N.

JULY 10

Ecclesiastes 3:1–7

Summer Plans

Are you ready for school to start? That's probably not the question you want to hear in the middle of summer. But vacation days pass quickly. Here are some ways to make the best use of the remainder of your free time.

1. Have fun.
God designed our minds and bodies to need rest and relaxation. Take time to think, imagine, and dream.

2. Learn.
Choose two books to read before school starts. Ask your parents to take you someplace new.

3. Give.
Take flowers to an assisted-living facility. Help your mom make dinner. Gather canned goods for a homeless shelter. Look around for the opportunities God is giving you to show and tell of His love to others.

4. Thank God.
He has given us His world and time to enjoy it. Jesus, too, spent lots of time outdoors. He loved learning and helping people. On the cross, He died for our sins so that we can enjoy the gifts He gives us here. We can look forward to being raised from the dead and living forever with Him.

Along with all the gifts God gives us, we have the gift of time. We can make plans to have fun, learn, and give, but we cannot control what time will bring. We don't even know exactly what will happen tomorrow. Only our eternal God does. And He can bless our time no matter what—that's another reason to give Him thanks.

Journal: Make a list of the things you plan to do before school starts. Ask God to help you accomplish your goals, and thank Him for all the opportunities He gives you.

Pray: Dear God, thank You for loving me so much that You gave me a world to enjoy and time to explore it. Through faith in Jesus, I know You will also give me the eternal joys of everlasting life. Amen. C. S.

Facing a Bear

When I was young, my family camped during summer vacations. Sleeping on the hard ground isn't as comfortable as sleeping at home. However, it's a wonderful treat to roast marshmallows over a fire, to hike through the woods, to see spectacular scenery, and to spend time with your family.

One night, Dad and I walked from our campsite to an outdoor theater to watch a nature movie. Halfway through the movie, I decided I wanted to go back to our tent. I took the flashlight and set out on the trail. I came to a stream that had to be crossed on a narrow bridge. As I started to cross the bridge, I looked up. There in the distance, standing nine feet tall, was a huge black bear.

I backed away slowly and went back to my father. I would wait and walk home safely, holding my father's hand.

This experience I had with my father reminds me of my heavenly Father. Whenever I face a big problem or temptation, I realize that I need to return to my heavenly Father. In His Word and in Baptism, He gladly promises to be with me.

The Lord will keep you safe from all threats to body and soul. He also keeps His promise to be with you through all your problems. May you always turn to your heavenly Father for help and comfort. May you also share with your friends the news of His love and protection.

Journal: What's the worst danger you've ever faced? How did God keep evil from happening to you?

Pray: Dear Lord, thank You that I don't need to face the "big bears" of the devil and sin in my life alone. I believe that You've defeated sin and that You're always watching over me. Amen. P. L.

Braces

Sam stared into the mirror. In the front of his mouth, where his freshly brushed and flossed teeth should be, were braces!

What would the kids say when they saw him tomorrow? He had heard them tease others, calling them names. But his mom said he had to wear them so his teeth would grow straight instead of staying kind of crooked and spaced funny. If only he could take the braces out when he wanted to and then put them back in when nobody was looking.

"No," Mom explained. "Only the doctor can remove them, and if he takes them out too early, your teeth will go right back to being crooked."

We are like those crooked teeth. God's Law shows us how crooked our hearts are by nature. On our own, we would never be straight with God. But Jesus died to take away that crookedness, called sin. Through Baptism and the preaching of God's Word, the Holy Spirit works in us to create faith in Jesus. He sends parents and teachers into our lives to train us in His Word. The Bible says if we are taught that Word when we are young, we will, by the power of the Holy Spirit, remember and trust it as we grow older. When you see braces on your teeth or on the teeth of others, let the braces remind you that you are in training to live as God's redeemed child.

Journal: Draw pictures of three teeth. On each tooth, write or draw a picture of something you want to remember about living as God's child. Then draw a cross over the teeth as a reminder of the forgiveness, life, and salvation God has given you in Christ Jesus.

Pray: Dear Jesus, teach me Your ways while I am young, so that when I am old, I will continue to believe that You love me and died to take away my sins. Amen. C. S.

Serving

"I'm bored," Travis sighed. "There's nothing to do."

"Hmm," his dad said thoughtfully, "let's see if we can solve your problem." He opened up the church bulletin from Sunday's worship service that was on the kitchen table.

He ran his finger down the list of bulletin announcements. "Pastor Jim has a request in here for someone to make Scripture cards he can take when he makes hospital and home visits."

"What's that got to do with me?" Travis asked.

"Remember that birthday card you made for Grandma?" his dad asked.

"Yes," said Travis. "Grandma really liked that card."

Dad smiled. "Perhaps you could add some Bible verses with your drawings and make cards for Pastor Jim."

"Oh, Dad, I don't know," Travis replied. "What drawings should I make, and what Bible verses should I use?"

"I'll help you select some verses," his dad said. "Go get your markers and I'll be right there with my Bible."

Sometimes when presented with an opportunity to serve God, we don't know what we can do. We may be unsure of how to use the talents and abilities God has given us.

Today's Bible reading reminds us that God wants us to serve others. Whenever we share Jesus with others, we bring God glory. Serving God and others is exciting! How might God use you and your abilities to serve someone today?

Journal: Write down a way you'd like to use your talents and abilities to serve others. Talk with your pastor about how to do it.

Pray: Heavenly Father, thank You for the gifts You've given me to serve others in Your kingdom. Bless me with willingness to share these gifts and bring glory to You. In Jesus' name I pray. Amen. D. G.

Waiting

Today was the day. Lina bounced with excitement. "Mom, when will we go?"

Mom smiled. "For the twelfth time, Lina, we leave at nine o'clock."

Lina squeezed the rubber bone on the table. "I just can't wait to go pick up Buster. We finally get a dog!"

For ten years, she had looked at pictures of dogs, drawn dog pictures, and dreamed about dogs. And now, finally, she was going to get the dog she'd wanted for so long.

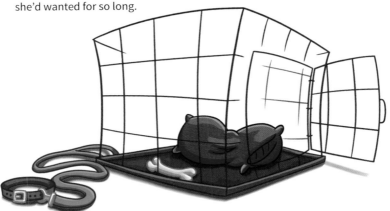

"Mom, thanks for letting us get a dog," Lina said as she gave her mom a squeeze.

Her mom squeezed her back. "Good things are worth waiting for. And speaking of good things . . . it's nine o'clock. Let's go!"

Have you ever had to wait for something you really, really wanted? How did you feel when you finally got that special thing? Pretty excited, right?

Did you know that angels get excited too? The Bible tells us that when even one person becomes a new child of God, the angels rejoice. And if the angels are happy, then God must be thrilled! What a joy it is to Him when He adds one more son or daughter to His family.

Because of Jesus, you are a part of God's family. And that means He is excited about you! On the day of your Baptism, on the day you became His child, He was truly happy. You were something worth waiting for.

Journal: When have you waited for something special?

Pray: Heavenly Father, thank You for making me a part of Your family through water and the Word. You are waiting for other people to join Your family. Help me to share Jesus' love with them. Amen. J. R.

Break for Church

"I'm glad we'll be out of town for the softball tournament next weekend. I'm ready for a break from church," Lisa confessed.

"A break from church? Why?" Allison asked.

"Boring, boring, boring," Lisa said. "Don't you feel that way?"

Allison paused and then went on, "Well, actually, no, I don't. When we travel, my family visits other churches. We meet lots of interesting and friendly people."

"My family skips church all the time. It doesn't make any difference to us," Lisa said.

"That's sad. It would to me. The blessings we receive by going to church often seem hidden, but they are there," Allison said. "And it's a sin to ignore God's Word. In the Third Commandment, God commands us to 'Remember the Sabbath day by keeping it holy.' We do that when we gladly hear and learn His Word."

"It's not like God is going to punish us," Lisa said.

"We don't go to church because we're afraid of God's punishment. We know He loves us and forgives us. We go because we can. When we go to church, we hear about God's love. We confess our sins and God forgives us because of Jesus. I don't know about you, but I need to hear that every week," Allison confessed.

"Well, I never thought about church as something I *get* to do," Lisa said. "Maybe we should all take a break for church next week. You can help me understand what it's all about."

Journal: What about the church service is important to you?

Pray: Heavenly Father, help me to be faithful in attending church. Give me opportunities to encourage others in their worship also. In Jesus' name I pray. Amen. G. G.

A Care Package

"One toothbrush, one toothpaste, and one comb," counted Arianna. She and her Sunday School class stood in an assembly line. Each person added one thing to the care packages they were making for residents of a nearby senior citizens' home. Arianna and her mom volunteered to deliver the gifts.

When it was time to go, Arianna told her mom, "My stomach feels funny." Then tears streamed down her face. "I'm a little afraid, Mom."

"Oh dear, what's wrong?" said her mom.

"Remember when Great-Grandma was in a nursing home? She used to smile when we came. But when it was time to go, she cried. I'm afraid some people will be sad today."

"Oh, honey." Her mother hugged her close. "It's okay to be happy with happy people and sad with sad people. It's one way God uses us to show His love to others. God uses us as His care packages. It's a great honor God gives us. He tells us, 'Rejoice with those who rejoice' and 'weep with those who weep.'"

Arianna and her mom knew the best care package had come from God. He gave us His Son, Jesus Christ. Jesus came to suffer and die for our sins. That was a day to weep. Then He rose again, proving that someday we, too, will live again with Jesus. That was a day to rejoice.

Each day we can be Jesus' care packages as we rejoice or cry with others.

Journal: Who has been God's care package to you? How can you care for someone today?

Pray: Dear Father, You have given me Jesus, the best caregiver of all. Thank You so much. Help me to be a caring gift to others in His name. Amen. S. H.

Always There

At the dinner table, Dad said, "I've been offered a good job in Chicago. On Friday, I'm flying there to check it out."

"Chicago—home of the Cubs, the White Sox, the Bears, and the Bulls!" cheered Ted. "A pro team for every season."

Rachel frowned. She didn't share her brother's enthusiasm. After dinner, she went to her room and threw herself across her bed. She absolutely did not want to move.

When Mom came in, Rachel started crying. "I want to stay right here, Mom," she sobbed. "I have lots of friends. I won't know anybody in Chicago."

"I know you're upset, Rachel," Mom said. "It's hard when things change. But whether we move or stay, one thing never changes. God is always with us, no matter where we are."

In Joshua 1:5, God encouraged Joshua, who was leading the Israelites on the move, by saying, "I will be with you. I will not leave you or forsake you."

The Israelites were about to enter the land of Canaan. But they couldn't just move in. The Canaanites didn't want them there. So the Israelites had to fight many battles.

God reminded Joshua of His love and care. How does God speak to us? He speaks in His Word and Sacraments, where He is always to be found. God reminds us there that He will never leave us. No matter where He moves us, He is there.

Journal: How did God help you with a big change in your life?

Pray: Dear God, thank You for always being with me. Help me to trust You in every situation. In Jesus' name I pray. Amen. J. D.

Not Ashamed

Brody joined Trent and Tyler at the bus stop. "We're going to the movies tomorrow. Wanna come?" Trent asked.

"I'd like to, but I'm serving lunch at the homeless shelter tomorrow."

"Why?" Tyler said.

"I want to. Jesus said we should help others. This is one way I can do that, and I like it," Brody answered.

"'Jesus said'? Jesus talks to you?" Tyler asked.

"The Bible tells me what Jesus said and did, it tells me who Jesus is," Brody said.

Trent and Tyler looked at each other. "Oh yeah? Who is He?" Trent asked.

"Jesus is God's Son, my Lord and Savior," Brody answered. "He loves me so much that He died for me. He loves you that much too."

Tyler raised his eyebrows. "Why would God's Son die for me?"

"Everyone does things they aren't supposed to do. And they don't do the things they should." Brody paused. Trent and Tyler nodded. "We call it sin. Sin separates us from our perfect God."

"So?" Tyler asked.

"God created us and wants us to be united with Him. The only way for that to happen was for Him to send His Son, Jesus, to earth. Jesus lived perfectly, without sin. And when He died on the cross, He took the sins of the world with Him." Brody took a deep breath. "He promises us forgiveness and life after death forever."

"Wow!" Trent said. "How can I get that?"

Journal: If you were Brody, what would you say?

Pray: Dear Savior, thank You for Your Word and Your very life. Keep me faithful, and strengthen me to be Your witness. Amen. J. H.

Sing His Praise

Have you ever been someplace where people were talking in a language you couldn't understand? Wasn't it confusing? How could you know what was said? Can you imagine going to church and hearing the liturgy or sermon in another language week after week after week?

By the 1500s, most people could not understand the church services they were attending. Worship was in Latin, and only the rich could go to school to learn Latin. People couldn't read either. Even some priests couldn't read, so they taught what they had been taught or what they thought people should believe. God's truth began to get lost. Martin Luther and others wanted to teach God's truth so people could understand it. They began to worship in German, because the people understood German, and hymns were added in the service.

Many hymns are based on Bible words and describe Bible teachings. Hymns teach the truth about Jesus. They remind us that we are sinners, and they invite us to repent of our sins. They remind us that Jesus is our Savior. Hymns lead us to recall God's promises as we rejoice on Christmas, and to see Jesus revealed as God during Epiphany. Hymns guide us as we look to the cross during Lent and allow us to sing alleluias, rejoicing in Jesus' Easter resurrection. Hymns help us to stand in awe on Ascension Day and to experience the power of the Holy Spirit on Pentecost.

Journal: What is your favorite hymn? What does it teach you about faith?

Pray: Dear heavenly Father, thank You for the truths of Your Word taught in hymns. May You always be the way, the truth, and the life for me. In Jesus' name I pray. Amen. C. S.

Anger and Comfort

Cheyenne sat in her room with the door closed, bored out of her mind. She was supposed to be at her swim meet, but she got in trouble. Her parents decided the consequence would be for her to miss something she liked.

When her mother came in from mowing the lawn, she invited Cheyenne to have lunch. Cheyenne was surprised that her mom was so nice. They ate macaroni and cheese, one of Cheyenne's favorite foods. Her mother asked how the morning had gone, and then she laughed as she told about her shoe falling off while she mowed the lawn.

Cheyenne asked, "I guess you're not upset with me anymore?"

Her mother looked at her with compassionate eyes and a loving smile. "Honey, of course I'm not upset. You did something wrong, but I still love you!"

Isn't it surprising when someone forgives us? It was that way for people living in Jerusalem. After sinning and worshiping other gods, they were punished by the Lord.

Suddenly, He turned off His anger and said, "Comfort, comfort My people" (Isaiah 40:1). He assured them that their sins were forgiven.

God has already provided forgiveness for our sins through Jesus' death on the cross. Even when we think God is upset with us, He surprisingly releases us from guilt. He looks at us with compassionate eyes and a loving smile and says, "I still love you!"

Journal: Draw a picture of a Bible with a heart on the cover. Your drawing can remind you that God gives His love through His Word.

Pray: Dear Lord, sometimes when I think You are upset with me, remind me of Your love. In Jesus' name I pray. Amen. C. O.

Choices

What will you do today?
Will you go swimming? Will you read a book?
Which game will you play? Which chore will you do first?

Life is full of choices. Some choices lead to happy results. Other times, our choices are mistakes with consequences that hurt us and others. When that happens, we wish we would not have made that choice.

After Adam and Eve sinned, they were sorry they had disobeyed God. Their choice brought sin and death into our world.

Then God chose to love and save all people. God sent His Son, Jesus, to earth to suffer and die the death we deserved so that we could be redeemed. Through God's Word and Sacraments, the Holy Spirit comes to give us faith and to let us know that God has chosen us to be His children. In John 5, Jesus says that when we believe in Him as our Savior, we will have eternal life.

Will everyone have eternal life? Sadly, no. Not everyone who hears about Jesus will believe that He is their Savior from sin. Some people will reject Him, make fun of Him, and ignore Him. They will choose not to believe. But what they might do doesn't keep us from living as God's children.

Every day, God chooses us to be His agents in the world. We can love and serve others so that they might know more about Jesus and how much He loves them.

Journal: What are some ways you can choose to serve others today?

Pray: Dear God, thank You for giving me faith and for choosing me to be Your child. Help me choose to love, forgive, and serve others in Your name. In Jesus' name I pray. P. L.

Who Knows?

"Huh—1.84 billion years old?" Bryce was confused by the brochure. He and Uncle Ramon sat at the rim of the Grand Canyon.

Uncle Ramon laughed. "That's what some scientists say."

Bryce went on, "This brochure says the Colorado River wore away all this rock to form the canyon."

Uncle Ramon patted Bryce's arm. "It's true. Erosion from wind and rain helped shaped the canyon too. But that's not the whole story, is it?"

Bryce shook his head. "The Bible says God created the heavens and the earth. Everything in it, God made. Even this canyon."

"That's right. People try to explain creation in ways they understand. Sometimes, they are wrong, especially when they leave God out of the story. Just look out there. God has done amazing things."

Bryce said, "You can't know things about God unless you know His Word."

Uncle Ramon smiled. "That's just what I was thinking, Bryce. God's Word tells us about creation. And it tells us about sin and salvation. As we hear and read it, we learn about Jesus' death and resurrection. And we learn that in Baptism, God creates faith in us so that we have the power to believe in Jesus as our Savior from sin."

It was quiet again as the two looked over the canyon's layers. Finally, Bryce said, "Someone should write a brochure about God."

"Someone did," said Uncle Ramon with a wink and a smile.

Journal: Write about some wonderful things you have seen this summer.

Pray: Dear God, Your works are amazing. Thank You for sending Jesus and for His saving work on the cross. Thank You for creating faith in me. Amen. C. S.

Songs of Praise

Have you ever tried to make up a poem in praise of God? Try it now. Start by making a list of words that rhyme with *sing*. It might be fun to have someone else do it too. Then you can compare lists. Also make lists of rhyming words for the following: *joy*, *grace*, *shine*, and *love*.

When you are ready with your lists, put them together into a poem.

The Book of Psalms is full of poems—150 to be exact. These poems depend on the rhythm and beauty of the words to remind us of God's greatness and His ever-present love. Maybe you have worked with similar kinds of poetry in school.

Look through the Book of Psalms. Some are long and some are short. Some have phrases that repeat over and over. You'll find many prayers and songs of praise to God. Some of the psalms are prayers written in times of trouble. Others are prayers of thanks to God. God inspired all of them so that we may benefit from reading them.

Psalm 67 is written as a song. You can see the chorus in verses 3 and 5: "Let the peoples praise You, O God; let all the peoples praise You!" The psalmist wrote this song of praise long before Jesus was born. Yet the poem reflects a strong faith. With the psalmist, we write and sing about our faith. We join in praising God for His salvation through the Messiah, Jesus.

Journal: Write your own psalm of praise to God, or set your favorite psalm to music.

Pray: Dear Lord Jesus, "I will be glad and exult in You; I will sing praise to Your name, O Most High" (Psalm 9:2). Amen. S. V.

JULY 24

God's Help in Dark Places

You might not know what happened fifteen years ago. But many people in Pennsylvania and across the United States do remember what happened on July 24, 2002.

Coal miners at Quecreek Mine in southwestern Pennsylvania made breaking news on radio and TV. Nine men were trapped and were close to drowning in the coal mine where they worked. Rescuers worked for seventy-seven hours, pumping out water and drilling through the rock to save the miners.

To this day, people still talk about the brave people and the amazing technology. But many locals say God's hand was in this event. They strongly believe it was a miracle that all nine survived.

We will all struggle with something scary, maybe even something life-threatening. You may already have been saved from death or know someone who has. You or someone you know may feel awful about some sin.

If so, be brave. Use technology if it is helpful. But the most important thing is to ask God for forgiveness and help. You can draw near to His throne of grace, trusting Him for forgiveness, life, and salvation through His Son, Jesus. He provides mercy and grace in our time of need.

Even in the scariest, darkest mines or times, God can hear and answer prayers. He is there. He offered mercy and grace to the coal miners in 2002. He offers mercy and grace to you too, no matter what today or tomorrow brings.

Journal: Describe a time when someone was sad or miserable. (Maybe it was you.) Tell how God answered prayers for help.

Pray: Dear God, sometimes life is really hard, and I am afraid. But I believe You have promised to hear my prayers no matter how happy or sad I feel, how great or bad life gets. Grant me mercy and help in my time of need. Thank You for Jesus, who overcame sin and death for me. In His name I pray. Amen. S. H.

Giving to Jesus

Georgina and her mom were cleaning out her closet. There were lots of clothes that Georgina couldn't wear anymore because they were too small.

"Why are you putting these in the box?" asked Georgina. "Why don't we just throw them away?"

"They are in good condition," Mom said. "We'll take them to the thrift shop at church. Lots of people can save money by buying them at low prices, and we'll have the good feeling that we're helping someone else. We all gain from it."

"What gave you the idea to take them to the thrift shop?" asked Georgina.

"Remember when Dad was out of work and we didn't have much money? That's where your clothes came from. People gave their used clothes to the thrift shop, and we bought some," said Mom.

"Wow, that's neat," Georgina said. "Is that what Pastor meant when he was telling about giving clothes and food to Jesus? When people give them to others, they're giving to God, right?"

"That's exactly right, Georgina. Jesus said that is a sign of our faith. It is our way of showing our love to Jesus because He first loved us. Now, let's keep working. When we take these to the thrift shop, maybe we can do some shopping there too."

Journal: Make a list of things that you might be able to give to help other people.

Pray: Thank You, God, for showing us true love. Amen. P. L.

A Message of Hope

Today is another day in your life—your new life. What does it mean to have "new life"?

Barry and his dad both have new lives. Barry's mother and father divorced six months ago. Barry's life changed. He went to church with his mom one week and with his dad the next.

Barry remembered when he and his dad played around the house, ate together, and practiced football. He asked his dad, "What's your new life like?"

Barry's father said, "Well, I'm learning a lot. I made some mistakes that I regret. I am sorry for the trouble I have caused you and your mom, but I asked God to forgive me. And He has."

"How do you know He really has?" asked Barry.

His father explained more about God's forgiveness. He said that when Jesus died on the cross, He paid the full price for our sins. That is how his dad knew that God had forgiven his sins. Then his dad said that in Baptism, God gives us a new spiritual life. Every day, God gives us power to overcome and bury sin. Every day we can live a new life as we grow in faith and in good works.

After his divorce, Barry's father had one kind of new life. He was a single man and a single parent. Because of his Baptism, Barry's dad had a new life in Christ, one in which he was completely forgiven. And Barry did too.

Journal: Believers sin daily, but daily God offers them a new life. How is this good news for you?

Pray: Dear Lord, when my sins make me feel terrible, remind me to confess them and to live the new life You give to me in Baptism. In Jesus' name I pray. Amen. C. O.

It Is Someone's Birthday!

Today is my birthday. It's a happy day because I had a second "birthday." That one came two weeks after I was born. Can you guess what happened that day?

My second birthday—the more important one— was the day I was baptized. That's the day when the Holy Spirit gave me faith. Oh, I didn't know about it. I was just a baby! But I didn't have to know. Faith is something that lives in the soul, even when a baby brain doesn't know about it. Later, I learned more about Jesus from my family, church, and Lutheran school.

Like me, you made history the day you were born. Your birthday was no surprise to God. He knew you were coming even back when He was creating the world. He knew you would be a sinner like everyone else. He sent Jesus to live, die, and come back to life—all to take away your sins. The Holy Spirit came to you on your second (and best) birthday to give you faith.

Talk about a great present!

Not all people have families, churches, or schools to tell them about Jesus. That is sad, but it also gives you a chance to tell them how Jesus took away their sins. Then, trust that the Holy Spirit will give them faith.

Journal: Write a birthday card to yourself as if it had come from Jesus.

Pray: Thank You, dear God, for bringing me to life. Thank You, dear Jesus, for taking away my sins. Thank You, dear Holy Spirit, for giving me faith to believe that Jesus is my Savior. Amen. E. G.

World War I Begins

On this date in 1914, World War I began. About sixteen million people died and another twenty-one million were injured. We still are fighting wars—including the war over you!

The devil does not want you to be a Christian. He would like to bury you in sin. He wants you to enjoy sin so much that you forget to ask God to forgive you. He just wants to take you away from Jesus.

Don't worry. You are safe.

Jesus won this war long ago. He didn't use stealth bombers or missiles. He used divine weapons built by God. His best and most powerful weapon was the cross. He died there to take away your sins. Unlike all other soldiers killed in war, Jesus came back to life. He took away the devil's power to take you to hell.

The fight against the devil still goes on. The devil has already lost the war, but he keeps fighting. He wants lots of company in hell. Don't worry. You're not going there. Angels are fighting to keep you safe. They cannot lose the battle over you unless you give up and choose to be on the devil's side.

The Holy Spirit gave you faith, along with truth and forgiveness. He gave you the Bible so you can learn more about how much God loves and protects you. The Bible is your weapon to fight against sin and the devil. Keep it open—and let the angels do the big stuff!

Journal: Write a newspaper headline about Jesus winning the war over you.

Pray: Dear Jesus, thank You for winning me from the devil. Amen. E. G.

Family Reunion

"I can't wait to play baseball with Ray and Julius," said Stanley, thumping his fist into his baseball glove.

"Well, I want to jump rope with Shawna and Ellie," Jasmine said. "I want to see baby Sam too."

Stanley and Jasmine and their family were on their way to the family reunion. All the aunts, uncles, and cousins would be there. Grandma and Grandpa were coming. Great-uncles and great-aunts and second cousins would show up too. It would be a day for lots of fun, food, and news.

Reunions of our extended families bring together different kinds of people. We are very old and very young. We are tall, short, and in between; farm kids, kids from the suburbs, and city kids.

Our reunions are full of laughter and love. We are family, and we like being with one another. But there is a more important thing that links us together: We are all part of God's family.

The family of God includes all people who have ever believed in Jesus as their Savior. This family includes people from the beginning of the world who looked forward to the coming of the promised Savior, and all believers till the end of time. Generations upon generations have the same heavenly Father—a Father who sent His one and only Son to be the Savior of the world, a Father who lovingly planned a heavenly reunion for all believers.

Journal: What is the best thing about being a part of your family? of God's family?

Pray: Father God, thank You for my family and for making me part of Your family. Help me to be a good member of both families. In Jesus' name. Amen. J. D.

Got Riches?

"I want to be rich so I never to worry," Susie said.

"People with lots of money have lots of things, but they still worry," said Aunt Jean. "And sometimes, they are so busy taking care of their things that they don't have time for what's important."

"Well, I wouldn't be like that," Susie promised.

"Maybe," Aunt Jean said. "But in 1 Timothy 6:9, God says that 'those who desire to be rich fall into temptation.' If we own lots of things and want even more, we might forget that everything comes from God. It's even possible to forget Jesus."

"I would never forget Jesus," Susie insisted. "I just want to be rich and have fun."

"I do too, but when you put being rich and having fun first in your life, it is easy to forget Jesus. That's why God tells us to 'pursue righteousness, godliness, faith, love, steadfastness, gentleness' (1 Timothy 6:11). These qualities are the real riches."

"How do I do that?" Susie asked.

"You're doing it now, by listening to His Word. Ask Jesus to give you a godly attitude toward money. Remember, Susie, He died on the cross to take away the punishment we deserve for our sins. It's not wrong to have money or use money, only to love it."

"That's good," Susie said with a grin, "because I was going to ask you to use some of your money to buy us ice cream."

Journal: What do you want to be when you grow up?

Pray: Dear Jesus, thank You for giving me so many treasures. Please forgive me when I love these things more than I love You. Amen. G. G.

Why Be Scared?

Are you afraid of snakes? thunder and lightning? darkness? speaking in front of your class? being alone?

Sometimes, fear is good because it teaches us to be cautious. We avoid places with poisonous snakes. We stay inside during a storm. We turn on a light instead of stumbling in the dark. We carefully prepare a report before presenting it to our class. But there are times when caution cannot protect us. We live in a sinful world where bad things happen.

The disciples were out in a boat. It was dark, and the wind caused the boat to rock on the waves. When they saw someone coming across the water, they were frightened. They did not know the figure was Jesus. He called out to them, telling them they didn't have to be afraid. He would not let them be harmed. With His almighty power, Jesus joined them and brought them safely to shore.

No matter what happens, we are never alone. Jesus is always with us. Through His Word and Sacraments, He strengthens us to face our troubles, and He can bring good from every wrong.

The same Jesus who walked on the water, who performed miracles to save others, who died on the cross for our sins, and who rose victoriously from death is with us. He tells us not to be afraid because He will save us from earthly troubles. Someday, we will live with Him in heaven forever.

Journal: List what frightens you. Then list where you can hear or read God's Word. Where can you hear that He forgives your sins?

Pray: Dear Jesus, thank You for Your promise never to leave me alone. Grant me trust in You when I am afraid. Bring me safely through the stormy troubles of this life to Your heavenly shore. Amen. G. G.

AUGUST 1

Psalm 46:10–11

Relax

Relax. That's what Gillian's teacher said, but Gillian held on to her with a iron grip. The teacher said she could trust the water to hold her up, but how could that be possible?

Still, Gillian really did want to learn to swim. All her friends loved the water, and she wanted to be a part of their summer fun. The Sunday School swim party was just a week away. Was it possible she could learn to relax and stay afloat?

Gillian decided to give it one more try. This time, instead of thrashing around and fighting the water, she took a deep breath. She let go of her teacher. She laid back her head. Can you guess what happened? Right. Gillian found herself being supported by the water—just as her teacher had promised.

In the Bible, God tells us to relax—to be still. That means instead of being afraid, we can trust God to help us. We can be still and know that our God is with us. We can count on Him. We can relax.

The most important thing God does for us is take away our sins. We could never do that by ourselves. But we can be still and know that God has forgiven us for Jesus' sake and made us His children.

Whenever you are afraid, remember that God is in control. Remember that He loves you. You can relax knowing you are in His care.

Journal: Make a list of things you are afraid of. Pray for God to help you face these fears, to relax, and to do what you need to do. Then write how God answered your prayers.

Pray: Dear God, thank You for loving me and taking care of me. Please help me relax because I know You are God and I can trust You for all things. For Jesus' sake I pray. Amen. C. C. S.

Big Book

For some people, summer is the perfect time to read a book. For others, summer is the time to take a break from reading.

Either way, you're probably able to read more than you used to. And your books are longer too! Instead of a book taking an hour or a day, it might take you a week or even a month to get to the end of a story.

Do you read the Bible on your own very much? Now, that's a long book. Some of the words are pretty hard. Sometimes, it might seem like it's too big of a job even to get started.

The great news about the Bible is that you're never alone while reading it. There are some great resources to help people read and understand the Bible. Some people even get into pairs or small groups to help talk about what they're reading. Parents, teachers, pastors, and friends can be helpers as well.

But the best Helper, the Holy Spirit, is always there with you as you read God's Word. God wants you to know more about Him. He wants you to know He loves you and sent His Son, Jesus, to be your Savior. He helps you along the way as you dig deep into His big book of blessing. Whether you're reading a Bible story for the first time or studying a familiar passage for greater understanding, God will help you as you learn.

Journal: Is there a Bible story you've always wanted to read? Is there a favorite part you want to learn better? Think about people or books that can help you in your learning, and jot down a plan to get started.

Pray: God, Your Word is so amazing! But it can be a little intimidating to read it on my own. I know You are always there to help. Please guide my thoughts as I learn more about You and Your love for me. Amen. L. M. C.

A Fantastic Reunion

Tam's family was busy getting ready to go to a family reunion. Tam had been only four years old when she came to the United States. Her relatives had settled in many different parts of the country, but this year, they planned to get together.

Tam was excited. She knew she would see her cousins, her aunts and uncles, and her grandparents. It had been so long since she had seen them that she couldn't remember what they looked like. But she knew there would be lots of hugs and fun.

Have you ever been to a family reunion? Did you find that you have relatives you didn't even know existed? As you get acquainted, you learn that you have many things in common. You realize that your family is much larger than you thought.

As children of God, we are part of His family. Our brothers and sisters in Christ live all over the world. Even though distance separates us, we have much in common. God loved us so much that He sent Jesus to live like one of us here on earth. Jesus' life, suffering, and death as our substitute make it possible for us to become part of God's family.

All of us who believe in Jesus as our Savior will be together in heaven someday. Best of all, we will see our Lord face to face. That's really a reunion to look forward to!

Journal: What will heaven be like? John, one of Jesus' disciples, gave a description of heaven. Read it in Revelation 21:1–4. Then write about it in your journal.

Pray: Thank You, Father, for making me part of Your family through faith in Jesus. Keep me as Your child in this life, and take me to heaven to live forever with You. I ask it in Jesus' name. Amen. J. W.

Our Daily Bread

As soon as Jason saw Mom and Dad sitting at the table, he knew something was wrong. "What happened?" he asked.

"I'm losing my job. We are planning how we can get by on Mom's salary until I find work. It's going to mean cutting corners," Dad told him.

"Will I still get a new bike for my birthday?" Jason demanded.

"I wish you could," Dad said. "But there won't be money for bikes, movies, and a lot of other things."

"Are we going to be poor?" Jason asked.

"No, Jason. We may not have as much as before, but we are still rich," Mom said. "God gives us many things that have nothing to do with money. This is a good time to remember our blessings so we can forget our worries."

"But shouldn't we worry if Dad doesn't have a job?"

"When we prayed the Lord's Prayer this morning, we asked our heavenly Father, 'Give us this day our daily bread.' Do you know what that means?" Mom asked.

"Of course, we ask God to feed us," Jason answered.

"It's more than that. God gives us everything we need to live. We may not understand why bad things happen, but we should never doubt God's ability to help us and to love us," Dad explained. "God loved us enough to send Jesus to die for our sins. He keeps the devil from depriving us of all that we have from God. We are safe in God's hands."

Journal: List all the things that you think are included when we pray for daily bread.

Pray: Dear Jesus, thank You for loving me so much that You died to take away my sins. Please continue to give me all the things I really need. I pray in Your name. Amen. G. G.

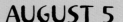

AUGUST 5
Psalm 118:24

Scheduling in the Savior

Did you sleep in today or watch television? Was it a day full of chores? fun with friends? Weekends are usually a nice change from the rest of the week. You can set your schedule and plan some things you'd like to do.

Did you plan some time with God?

If you go to church on Sundays, you might think of Saturday as a break from learning about Jesus. But imagine for a minute what your Saturday would be like if God took a break from you.

The truth is that God is always with you, whether you pay attention to Him or not. And He loves it when you take the time to talk to Him in prayer and to learn about Him in the Bible. Maybe think of it as a conversation: God talks to you through His Word, and you talk to Him through prayer.

This day is a blessing from God, and it's great to enjoy His gifts of friends, fun, family, food, and everything else. But don't cheat yourself out of one of God's greatest gifts—time with Him.

Did you know that Jesus took time to pray for you? Check out John 17:8–10. Shortly after praying this prayer, Jesus died for your sins and the sins of the whole world. It's such a comfort to know that no matter how your day goes, God cares about it. He loves you and loves spending time with you.

Journal: If this is morning, make a list of the most important things to fit in your day. If it is evening, write down some blessings God gave you today.

Pray: God, thank You for loving me and for giving me this day. Thank You for always wanting to spend time with me. Amen. L. M. C.

God's House

"Time to get up!" Dad said.

"I'm tired. Do I have to go?" asked Zoe.

"You don't have to go; you get to go," Dad answered. "Your clothes are laid out; hop to it."

"But Dad, I really am tired," Zoe moaned.

Dad sat on the edge of Zoe's bed. "I know you're tired, but going to church is important."

"Why? Why can't I just sleep in one Sunday?" asked Zoe.

"Because God never sleeps in on you," Dad said with a smile. "We're going to church because God is there waiting for us."

"God's everywhere, Dad," Zoe sighed.

"Yes, God is everywhere, but at church He is there for you in a special way. God comes to serve you when you are in His house. He forgives. He strengthens. And He blesses you. If you're not there, you'll miss out."

Zoe thought for a moment. "So God wants me to go?"

"He does. There's even a commandment about it," Dad smiled. "You can go because you have to, but my hope is that you'll go because you want to. At church, God's glory, Christ, is present. And that's a pretty awesome reality."

Zoe thought for a moment. "I'm coming," she said, "and not because I have to."

Dad smiled.

Journal: List some of the benefits of gathering with other believers in worship.

Pray: Dear Jesus, help me desire Your house, the place where Your glory dwells. Amen. M. B.

The Blessing of Work

Do you have chores to do each day? When your parent asks you to weed the garden, take out the garbage, or clean your room, are you happy to do the work? Do you ever ask for more work to do?

The Bible reading reminds us that we can find enjoyment in toil. These words mean we can be happy with work. Doing work helps us to grow because we learn how to complete the job. When you know how to stick with a job and get it done, without complaining, you become a better student and a good worker.

God also helps us to learn how to care for one another. When you weed the garden, you are giving your parents time to do other work, and you are helping to feed your family. These are things God wants you to learn.

Doing chores is not always fun, and most of the time we wish we could be playing instead. But God teaches us good things when we do the work He gives us. This is His plan for us to help us grow and serve Him in all we do.

Journal: How could your work help others in your community?

Pray: Dear God, sometimes I do not like work. But I thank You that I am able to do work. Remind me that work is a blessing. Amen. K. M.

Which Tent Do You Live In?

"Tommy," called Dad, "let's get a new tent for our camping trip."

At the store, Tommy picked out the biggest tent he could find. "How about this one, Dad?"

"We don't need such a large tent for just the two of us. Remember, we are hiking to our campsite. I don't want to carry a big tent on my back. How about this one instead?" Tommy's dad pointed to another tent.

On their way home, Tommy's dad remembered something people had talked about at Bible study that morning. "The apostle Paul says in Philippians, 'I have learned in whatever situation I am to be content' (4:11). Which tent did Paul live in, Tommy?"

"What do you mean, Dad?"

"Well, Paul said he learned the secret of how to be content in any situation. So, which tent did he live in? Content or discontent? Sometimes we are discontent because we don't have everything we want. But we can learn to be content with the blessings God gives us. After all, God gives us what we need the most—His forgiveness through Jesus Christ. God gives us His love, and He promises to be with us always. God gives us the promise of heaven. Knowing and believing this can lead us to be content, whatever the situation."

"Hey, Dad, can I make a sign for our tent that says 'Content'?"

"That's a great idea, Tommy."

Journal: What are some times in life when you feel content? What are some times when you feel discontent? How can your discontentment turn into contentment?

Pray: Dear God, help me be content in Jesus with the blessings You give me in life. Amen. D. G.

Not Just for Sundays

Have you ever thought about the first pencil? What about a paper clip or a car? We see these things every day, but there was a time when they didn't exist. Cell phones and microwaves make life so much easier, but they haven't always been around.

It's easy to take something for granted when you're used to having it around. However, try going a whole day without watching television or playing video games. It's not easy!

Sometimes we take God's Word for granted. This is especially true for those who grew up in a family that has always gone to church and read the Bible. Reading the Bible can become routine, something we always do. We might even start to think of God as only for Sunday. If that's the only time we read the Bible, we're missing out on a lot.

God's Word is timeless. Even though it was written years ago, it is living and active every day. God's Word is true; it is without error. God's Word is instructional. Through it, we learn of Jesus Christ, the Savior of the world. Jesus is the key to understanding the true meaning of the Bible. God's Word is a Means of Grace. When we read and hear God's Word, the Holy Spirit works faith that believes Jesus is our Savior. God's Word is profitable. It trains us in right living and equips us so we can do the good works God has for us to do.

Journal: Write about God's Word. What did you learn about it today?

Pray: Dear Father, forgive me when I've taken Your Word for granted. Remind me of the power of Your Word, so that I may delight in hearing, reading, and studying it. In Jesus' name I pray. Amen. J. A.

St. Lawrence Day

It's a special day today! There are no shamrocks like on St. Patrick's Day, no hearts and candy like on St. Valentine's Day, and no shoes filled with golden coins like on St. Nicholas's Day. So what makes this day worth remembering?

St. Lawrence was a Christian in the early days of the Church. He was known as a person who cared for the poor and needy. The governor demanded that Lawrence give all the riches of the Church to Rome. What riches did Lawrence bring? He brought the sick and needy people as examples of what God valued and treasured. The governor was angry and put Lawrence to death!

Many other Christians have died because of their faith in Jesus. While this may never be asked of us, sometimes acting as God's child and remembering His sacrifice comes with hurts and disappointments. A friend might reject us because we won't watch an R-rated movie with him or her. Our coach might bench us because we kept a commitment to sing in choir rather than play in a soccer game.

Thank God that we are His riches. He valued us so much that His Son, Jesus, died to pay the price for our sin. We are His children, and He is our priceless treasure!

So today, remember what St. Lawrence remembered: that Jesus is our priceless treasure, and we are His.

Journal: Look up another martyr or saint on the Internet, and write down what you can learn about God from him or her.

Pray: Dear Jesus, thank You for giving Your life for me so that I could be Your treasure forever. Be with me in troubles. Help me to tell others that You are my priceless treasure. In Your holy name I pray. Amen. B. T.

God's Creation

Have you tried snorkeling? I did. It felt strange to wear fins on my feet and walk like a duck. It was also strange to put my face into the water and float, while still being able to breathe. And it was no fun to swallow saltwater. But after a while, I caught on and so did the rest of my family.

Later, after our snorkeling adventure, we compared stories of what we had seen—beautiful blue and yellow fish, purple and pink coral, jellyfish, and a barracuda. We saw sights we had never seen before. We explored in areas we had never been before. It was a remarkable time for all of us. We viewed a part of God's created world in a way we had never done before.

When God created the world, He saw that it was good, very, very good. The perfect world God created had no sin or death. Sin entered the world when Adam and Eve disobeyed God. In order to save humans from sin, God promised Adam and Eve that He would send a Savior.

Many years later, God sent His Son, Jesus, to take our sins upon Himself. Jesus would live on earth perfectly. He would suffer, die, and rise again. Now, the risen and ascended Jesus is re-creating us through His Spirit while He is creating a remarkable new place—a heavenly home—where all who believe in Him will gather.

Journal: List something in creation that starts with each letter in the name Jesus.

Pray: Thank You, heavenly Father, for all You have created, including me. Thank You, Jesus, for saving me from my sin. Thank You, Holy Spirit, for keeping my faith strong. Amen. K. J.

A Bountiful Promise

Noah's dad sat in the chair, his leg covered in a bright orange cast.

"Can I get you anything?" Noah asked.

"I'm fine, but you could help me with this puzzle if you want to," Dad replied.

Noah sat near the card table and began sorting pieces.

"Dad, can I ask you something?"

"Sure, I'm listening."

"Why didn't God protect you when you fell?"

Noah's dad smiled at his son. "He did protect me, Noah; the accident could have been much worse. My leg is broken, but God will heal it."

"But He let you fall," said Noah.

"We don't always know why bad things happen, Noah, but we do know that in a sin-filled world, they will. And God is with us when they do. He has defeated our enemies, sin, death, and the devil; and He will never forsake us. Even now, God has blessed me with a bountiful promise."

"What promise?" Noah asked.

"God promises to heal me and to take me to be with Him in heaven one day. No matter what hardships I have to face on earth, even death, God will bless me always. And He makes that same promise to you too, Noah."

Journal: Write a note of encouragement to someone you know who is sick or is in need of healing.

Pray: Dear Jesus, help me to remember Your bountiful promise when I face hardship. Remind me that You are always with me. Amen. M. B.

No Longer Orphans

Joshua and Caleb are best friends. One week this summer they went with their parents on a mission trip to Honduras. They went to work with children at an orphanage located high in the mountains.

While in Honduras, Joshua and Caleb learned that children at the orphanage enjoy the same things they do. They like playing soccer, painting pictures, chasing lizards, climbing trees, and going to Sunday School.

Children at the orphanage welcomed Joshua and Caleb and were happy to share their games and activities with them.

One day during devotions, one of the children, Josué, shared his favorite Bible verse. Josué said, **"No os dejaré huérfanos; vendré a vosotros"** (Juan 14:18).

Do you know Spanish, or can you use the verse reference to figure out Josué's favorite verse? Joshua and Caleb used their English Bibles to discover the answer.

During their visit to the orphanage, Joshua and Caleb learned that we are all orphans. Sin has separated us from our heavenly Father. But Jesus promises that He will not leave us as orphans. Jesus came from heaven to earth and died on the cross to pay for our sin, so that we might become children of God. Although in Honduras Josué is an orphan, through Jesus' work on the cross, God has made him His child for eternity.

So, today we celebrate with Josué, Joshua, and Caleb that we are no longer orphans because of God's love for us in Jesus.

Journal: How is it that all believers in Jesus, no matter how old they are, are considered children of God?

Pray: Dear God, thank You for making me one of Your children. Help me to share Your love with others. Amen. S. S.

The Spanish Bible verse is from La Biblia de las Améric

North, South, East, West

Find these four places on the globe. Using latitude and longitude lines to measure, which is farthest north? farthest south? farthest east? farthest west?

1. Kaffeklubben Island   2. Attu Island, Alaska
3. Antarctica   4. Caroline Island, Kiribati

I had never heard of some of these places. Have you? The people living there probably have never heard of your town either!

The Bible tells us that in heaven, at God's table, there will be people from the East, the West, the North, and the South. Heaven will be filled with Christians from around the world.

God knows every person, his or her country, even his or her address! After all, He made us. He knows everything about everyone! He knows how we are alike and how we are different. He knows that we all sin. He knows my sins and your sins.

Each one of us was born with sin. We sin every day and need Jesus' forgiveness. Praise God that His forgiveness is for everyone! Whether you became His child in your hometown or in a place thousands of miles away, you belong to Him. There is nowhere on earth you could be that God could not rescue you from death and hell. Jesus paid for the sins of all people for all time. What a celebration it will be to sit together at God's table someday!

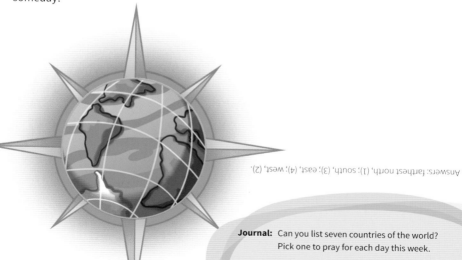

Answers: farthest north, (1); south, (3); east, (4); west, (2).

Journal: Can you list seven countries of the world? Pick one to pray for each day this week.

Pray: Dear God, please help the people in _____ to know about Jesus' love and forgiveness for them. In Jesus' name I pray. Amen. L. H.

Growing Up

"Too short," Mom frowned. Mom tilted her head to look at the slacks' length. Then she shook her head. "They're just too short, Jill. Put them in the box along with the other clothes you've outgrown. We'll take it to the shelter. It looks like we'll need to go shopping soon."

Jill shrugged out of the slacks and put them into the box. Trying on clothes wasn't her favorite thing to do on a summer day, but the thought of going shopping made it almost seem worth the hassle.

"Too small . . . too tight . . . too short . . ." Mom commented on each piece of clothing. "You must have had a growth spurt. Even your shoes are too small!"

Have you grown over the summer months too? Getting ready for school often means buying new and bigger clothing. Growing taller and bigger is usually a good sign—a sign that your body is healthy.

Did you know that your physical body isn't the only thing that God causes to grow? It's true! God also helps to grow your faith in Jesus Christ as your one and only Savior. God cares most about how your faith is growing.

Most people know that good food, proper rest, and exercise help healthy bodies grow. But what can help faith grow? The Bible says in 1 Thessalonians 2:13,

> "The word of God . . . is at work in you believers."

Journal: How can God "feed" your faith more? Here are two ideas to get you started: listen to the Word of God preached in church; attend Sunday School. Add your own ideas to the list—and get growing!

Pray: Thanks, Lord, for helping me grow physically and spiritually. In Jesus' name I pray. Amen. G. M.

A Summer of Riches

When the summer began, did you make a list of what you wanted to do?

1. Build a fort.

2. Beat a video game.

3. Read a mystery book.

4. Make a friend.

5. Start a pet-sitting business to earn money.

At the beginning of the summer, it felt like you had all the time in the world. Soon, however, summer will end and school will start. Where did the time go?

In the Bible reading, the rich man spent his life earning money and storing up grain to have food for a long time. What he did not know was that his life would soon end. His life went by, and he did not do what was most important. He did not remember God.

Add some new things to your list that help you to remember your faith in Jesus, your Savior.

6. Share Jesus with a friend.

7. Pray.

8. Think about God's mercy and grace.

Every day, God helps you to spend your time wisely. God knows that it is good to make plans and to work on those plans. It is even better to make plans that include God.

Journal: Make a list of the top five things you accomplished this summer.

Pray: Dear God, thank You for beautiful days. Thank You for Your mercy and grace. Be with me each day, and help me to share Your love with others. Amen. K. M.

The Earth Gives Praise

When we think about praising God, we usually think about singing hymns in church. Singing is a good way to praise God, but our praise for Him does not stop with hymns or daily devotions. We can praise God in all we do.

We praise God when we notice His wonderful creation. When you are playing outside, take a good look at God's beautiful world. It is interesting how all of creation works together to keep God's world going. The insects pollinate the plants and feed the birds. The birds make beautiful songs. The rain makes the plants grow and creates a rainbow in the sky. Humans care for animals and plants. Even the moisture in the air on a hot, humid day is a part of God's plan. God's creation is praising Him. We see this and thank God for taking care of us.

Every part of God's world is a reminder to us that we are His sheep and that He has given us the world as our pasture. When we care for the earth, we praise God and thank Him for caring enough to send Jesus as our Savior from sin.

Journal: What can you do for God's world today?

Pray: Dear God, You fill my heart with love for You. Show me the many ways I can praise You by taking care of Your world. Amen. K. M.

True or False?

There are many different teachings and beliefs about God. Some are true, but many are false. For example, are these statements **true or false?**

◯ 1. Jesus is both true man and true God.

◯ 2. Only good people go to heaven.

◯ 3. All religions are basically similar; any one will get you to heaven.

◯ 4. Faith is a gift from God.

◯ 5. The Bible is not true.

How do you keep false teachings from leading you astray? First, ask yourself if the teachings point to Jesus as our Savior. Then test the teachings against God's Word by reading, learning, and studying the Bible. Attend church and Sunday School. Ask your pastor, teacher, and parents to help answer your questions. And think about these responses to the statements above.

1. True.   **Jesus became true man to take our place; He is true God to save us from our sins** (Matthew 8:20; 1 John 5:20).

2. False. **All people are sinners. We get to heaven only through the saving blood of Jesus** (Romans 3:23–24).

3. False. **The only true religion is Christianity, where the name of Jesus is taught and confessed** (1 John 5:12; 1 Timothy 2:5).

4. True.   **We cannot by our own power believe in Jesus. Faith and salvation are gifts from God** (Ephesians 2:8–9).

5. False. **The Bible is the true Word of God, written by man, but inspired by the Holy Spirit. It teaches us to trust in Jesus for forgiveness** (2 Timothy 3:16).

Journal: What is a question you have about your faith? Write it in your journal.

Pray: Dear God, help me know Your truth. Guide me through Your Word to know You better. In Jesus' name I pray. Amen. C. K.

AUGUST 19

1 Peter 2:11–12

Sojourners

Reed spent the summer with his grandparents on a farm. He ate corn on the cob and fresh tomatoes. He fed chickens and mowed the lawn. He put up hay and made pickles. Reed had a wonderful time, but he missed his parents. He was glad when it was time to go home.

Reed experienced the feelings of a sojourner. He lived temporarily in one place.

Did you know that everyone on earth is a sojourner? Eventually, we are all going to live somewhere else, forever. In this world, we live with sin and face death. That can be so frustrating and sad. But all the while we are here, we know we are not citizens of this world. The children of God are citizens of heaven, baptized into the death and resurrection of Jesus Christ. We are members of His family, who now live earthly lives for a heavenly purpose.

The devil, the world, and our sinful nature will try to keep us from reaching heaven. They will try to keep us from showing and telling others about Jesus. God knows we are tempted, and He gives us His Holy Spirit as our Helper who instructs us through God's Word.

We can ask Jesus to make us aware of who we are: His own dear children. We can ask Him to bless us with a heart for those who don't know Him so that they may come to saving faith as they sojourn wherever they are.

Journal: Write about the differences between living on earth and living in heaven.

Pray: Dear Jesus, thank You for making a home for me in heaven. Help me to remember that I am here to share Your love with others! In Your name I pray. Amen. B. T.

Back to School

What new things do you purchase for your new school year? Pencils, shoes, folders? It feels good to get something new for school. It helps you make a fresh start. As you find out whom you will sit by or who has a locker next to yours, you can look for chances to make new friends.

But watch out! Satan is working so you can make new enemies! He loves all kinds of evil.

Today's verses tell us to "lift your drooping hands and strengthen your weak knees," to strive for peace with everyone and see that no "root of bitterness" causes trouble (Hebrews 12:12, 15). These verses tell us to look out for Satan's tricks. But Satan is smart. He wants only bad things for all of us. He loves to see what kinds of trouble he can cause.

How can we strengthen ourselves against that? The truth is, we can't. That kind of strength comes from God. As we read and hear His Word, He strengthens our faith. Because we are baptized, the Holy Spirit works in us as we struggle in this sinful world. Each morning, we wake to a new day rich in mercy from our everlasting God.

As you go back to school and face new challenges, remember that God's mercy and love go with you. When you fail and sin, He will forgive you and strengthen you to share His mercy and love with others.

Journal: Is there someone at school you have a difficult time getting along with? Pray for that person this week.

Pray: Heavenly Father, I am weak, but You are strong. Thank You for forgiving me and for making all things new. In Jesus' name I pray. Amen. L. H.

The Only Way

Morgan's first day in her new school had gone well. She liked her teacher. Her new classmates were friendly and helpful.

As the dismissal bell rang, she walked out with the rest of the students. Eight buses were lined up. Morgan was confused. Then she remembered that her bus driver had a red cap. Morgan peeked in the door of a bus and saw a man with a red cap. She climbed the steps and sat down.

Thirty minutes later, all the riders except Morgan had been dropped off. That's when she discovered that all the drivers wore red caps. She was on the wrong bus, far from home. The driver took her back to school, where her grandmother picked her up.

Many people don't realize that different religions are like different buses. They think that every religion worships the same God who is just called by different names. They believe that everyone will eventually end up in heaven. Nothing could be more wrong!

Only one bus would take Morgan home. Only the Christian religion will take us to our heavenly home. The true God is the triune God, Father, Son, and Holy Spirit. Only through faith in Jesus can we have the eternal life He earned for us. Jesus lived a perfect life as our substitute and then paid for our sins. Jesus is what makes Christianity different from other religions.

Journal: Jesus commanded us to take the message of salvation to all the world. How can you share your faith with someone else in your life today?

Pray: Keep me on Your path, beautiful Savior, so I may live with You in heaven forever. Give me grace to tell others about You. Amen. D. N.

Sleepless Night

Karalee was nervous. All summer, she had been eager for school. Now, she couldn't sleep.

Her clothes were ready and her backpack was ready. She had packed a lunch, even though school was only a half day and would end with a picnic. Karalee's wheat allergy meant that she needed to bring her own food. Her lunch bag was by the door.

She got ready for bed early. Her dad came in and had a devotion and prayer with her. After she was in bed, she remembered about her calculator. She was glad she did! She found it and put it into her bag.

She crawled back into bed, and her mind raced through her checklist one more time. She was nearly asleep once again when she suddenly panicked—was her alarm set right? So she turned on the light to check. Then she was wide awake. She tossed and turned, imagining all kinds of things that could go wrong. The clock kept ticking.

Karalee was worried about all the details of tomorrow. After a long time in bed, she finally noticed the moonlight shining on her picture of Jesus. She remembered what God's Word said about worrying—the same words you read today. Jesus already took care of tomorrow's big need, she thought. He died on the cross, suffering for my sin of worry and my lack of trust in my heavenly Father. "Jesus," she whispered, "will take care of tomorrow."

Journal: What kinds of things worry you?

Pray: Dear God, thanks for taking away my worries and fears and helping me trust in You. Be with me always. In Jesus' name. Amen. J. G.

AUGUST 23

Psalm 14

A Foolish Belief

Emily dropped her bag on the floor and sat on the couch.

"How was your day?" Mom asked.

"Not so great. My science teacher told us today that the world was created through a big explosion, and that anyone who thought differently was a fool."

Mom paused a moment. "And what do you think?"

"I know how the world was created, Mom, but he seems so smart."

Mom knelt down.

"Emily, how do you know how the world was created?"

"The Bible tells us in Genesis."

"That's right. And there are many scientific facts that support the creation account found in the Bible. But even if there weren't, would you still believe it?"

"I think so," said Emily.

"Why?" asked Mom.

"Because it's God's Word. And God is smarter than humans," said Emily. "Plus, I don't believe God would lie to us."

"You're right, Emily; the Bible is true from beginning to end. You know, God tells us in Psalm 14 that people who don't believe in Him, who don't think God exists, are foolish."

"I'm pretty sure my teacher doesn't believe God exists," said Emily.

"Then we'll pray for him," said Mom. "We'll pray that he's given the greatest wisdom of all, that salvation is found in Christ alone."

Journal: Write about a time when your beliefs were challenged.

Pray: Dear Holy Spirit, please work faith in the lives of unbelievers and strengthen my belief in the one true God and in Jesus Christ, our Savior. Amen. M. B.

Blog Questions

Mr. Huber set up a blog so the class could talk about events over the summer. In June, they had talked about the environment. In July, they had talked about Christians serving in government. In August, they were talking about hunger and homelessness.

Ella added to the blog each week. So did Ava, Quinn, and Hunter. In June, Ella pulled weeds instead of using the power weed trimmer. In July, she prayed for her state representative and wrote two letters to her. In August, she bagged food products for shipment to people around the world.

Next, Mr. Huber had them look up Matthew 25:34–40 and write about what Jesus meant when He said those who serve the poor also serve Him. Ella responded first. Jesus said that there would always be poor people around, but Ella thought it was a sin for people to spend too much money on themselves. She suggested that everyone give up soda and donate the money to the poor. She said that if people didn't participate, they weren't good Christians.

Mr. Huber reminded everyone that what makes us Christians is faith in God's gift of grace and forgiveness through Jesus Christ. Christians are not "good" because of what they do. They are made righteous by Jesus—through His mercy and grace. A loving response to Jesus comes through the power of the Holy Spirit. He leads us to serve others, including those who have less than we have.

Journal: What is one thing you could do to serve others in Jesus' name?

Pray: Dear God, thanks for blessing me with so many things. Give me ways to share what You have given me with others for Jesus' sake. Amen. J. G.

Deliver Us!

"Tell me a Bible story, Grandpa," Darryl begged.

"Well . . . once, a king named Nebuchadnezzar had a golden idol built. He commanded all the people to bow down and worship it."

"But Grandpa, it would be wrong to worship something besides God," Darryl protested.

"Nebuchadnezzar wasn't known for doing the right thing. He threatened to throw the people into a fiery furnace if they didn't obey," Grandpa said.

"But Grandpa, wouldn't it still be wrong?" Darryl asked.

"Yes, Darryl, it was wrong. That is why Shadrach, Meshach, and Abednego refused to bow down to it."

"Did they get into trouble?" Darryl asked.

"They knew it would cause trouble. However, they trusted God to save them. The king was angry, and he had them thrown into a fiery furnace."

"Why didn't God push the king into the furnace instead?" Darryl asked.

"God had a better plan. He protected the men while they were in the furnace. They were not burned. The king was amazed that God saved them. He commanded all the people to worship God instead of the idol."

"When we are in trouble, do you think God will help us?"

"Of course He will," Grandpa answered. "That's what we pray for when we say, 'Deliver us from evil.' We ask God to rescue us from all the evil that the devil can send our way. And we know God can do it, because He did it on the cross."

Journal: How has God delivered you from evil?

Pray: Dearest Jesus, thank You for saving me from the devil's tricks and plots. In faith, let me trust in You every day. Amen. G. G.

Overdoing It

Make a list of all the sports you play. Add to that list the clubs or groups you are in. Finish the list by adding lessons you take, special projects, and chores you do.

Whew! What a list! Do you ever feel overwhelmed with your schedule or your to-do list? Are you ever so busy that you cannot find time to relax?

When God, who commands that He be first in our lives, is not even on the list, we are overdoing it big time. When He is forgotten, our lives are out of order. When we are too tired to pray, are too busy for church and Sunday School, or forget to read our Bibles, we miss out on the nourishment of God's Word, the chance to focus on the needs of others, the support of our church family, and the time to talk to our heavenly Father in prayer.

How do we overcome overdoing it? We do it through the power of God. We can ask God to forgive us for not placing Him as the most important thing in our lives. Since God is faithful and just, He will forgive our sins. He will cleanse us from all unrighteousness.

Through His Word and Sacraments, God will strengthen our faith. Through the power of our Baptism, He will renew us daily, so we can make new lists that include Him and service to others in His name.

Journal: As a family, talk about how you use God's gift of time. What ways can your family make God number one?

Pray: Lord, forgive me when I put other things ahead of You. Help me slow down and make more time to pray and to study Your Word. Amen. C. K.

AUGUST 27

Isaiah 65:24

Faster than Fast

Did you know that races are going on inside your body? The races run along nerve cells called neurons. There are about one hundred billion neurons in your brain. They're much too small to be seen by the human eye.

Information is carried to and from the brain along neurons and their projections, called dendrites. No one knows exactly how this happens. But we do know how fast the messages travel. Information goes racing along your neurons at up to 180 miles per hour. That's a speedy delivery to and from the brain.

But there's one kind of communication that's even faster. In today's Bible reading, you discovered what it is. God says through the prophet Isaiah, "Before they call I will answer; while they are yet speaking I will hear."

God hears our prayers even faster than messages to and from our brain. He hears us even before we pray! That's because God is all-knowing. He looks into our hearts and minds and knows our inmost needs.

Prayer is a special privilege that God gives us, His children. Jesus came to earth and died on the cross to give us that privilege. Since Jesus paid for our sins, we can ask our heavenly Father anything. We know that however He answers our prayers, He has heard us. In fact, He knows what we want and need before we even ask. What a terrific Lord and Savior we have.

Journal: Why is it a comfort to know that God hears our prayers before we pray?

Pray: Dear Jesus, thank You for hearing me even before I pray and for answering me in the best way. Amen. C. A.

Rescued from a Mess

When my mom was a young girl, she lived on a farm. They did not have indoor plumbing, so her family had an outhouse behind their home. My mom also had a cat that she dearly loved.

One day, Mom's cat fell down the hole of the outhouse. That cat was in quite a mess. Mom searched for her dad and told him what had happened. He said there was only one thing to do—they had to rescue that cat!

He held my mom by the ankles and lowered her into the hole. Mom grabbed her cat, and my grandpa pulled them both back out to safety.

We are sinners. We get ourselves into some terrible messes sometimes. In fact, we may feel the situation we have gotten into is so hopeless that there is no way out.

When such times come, it's wise to remember a promise Jesus made to us: "I am with you always, to the end of the age" (Matthew 28:20). Jesus loves us and will never leave us. He rescued us from sin, death, and the power of the devil through His suffering on the cross. And He promises to help us get out of any messes we get in.

There is no sin too great for our Savior to forgive. There is no mess so big that He can't rescue us from it. He is all-loving, all-knowing, and all-powerful. Jesus is the best rescuer in the world!

Journal: What are some messes you have been in? How has Jesus rescued you from them? What does your list tell you about your future messes. Will God be there to help?

Pray: Jesus, forgive me when I don't follow You and end up in a bad situation. Help me remember the promise You made to be with me always and to rescue me. Thank You for Your great and powerful love. Amen. L. E.

AUGUST 29

James 1:15

Splinters and Sinners

Elaina loved her new play set. It had a twisty slide, a rock wall, a rope ladder leading to a lookout tower, and two big swings. The only problem was if she were not careful, she might get a splinter while playing on the wooden structure.

One day, Elaina got a small splinter in her thumb. She tried hiding it from her mom and dad. She didn't like having splinters taken out. But her thumb became tender and painful. One evening, her mother reached out to grasp her hand, and Elaina cried out in pain. That's how her mom discovered the splinter!

Then Elaina's father removed the splinter. Even though he was careful, it still hurt. Afterward, her parents explained that, if they had removed the splinter right away, the experience would not have caused her so much pain. Instead, by keeping the splinter in, the skin around it had become infected.

Elaina's splinter problem is much like our sin. When we hide or ignore our sins, they don't go away. They only get worse and end up hurting us even more. We need Jesus to remove our sins.

To get rid of them, God leads us to repent. Then we confess our sins to God. He promises to forgive our sins for Jesus' sake. He wipes them away. God accepts our repentant hearts and forgives our sins. Through Jesus, we are made new; our sins are forgiven.

So, don't be afraid!
Let Jesus take out that splinter of sin!

Journal: If you are hiding a sin, consider repenting. In your journal, write "Jesus, Savior, have mercy on me."

Pray: Dear Jesus, please forgive me for trying to hide my sins from You. Help me repent of my sins and bring them to You. Thank You for forgiving me and renewing me. Amen. C. K.

The Most Important Book

On chapel day, Pastor Jorgan asked each student to bring a book along. As the students came into church, they made a stack of all their books. Then Pastor said, "This is a pretty big stack, isn't it? If you learn everything that's in those books, you'll be pretty smart. You'll know math and science and history and lots more."

The students knew there had to be more to Pastor's chapel service than talking about their schoolwork, so they waited to hear what else he had to say.

Pastor continued, "You would have learned a lot of facts, and that will be useful later in life. They'll help you get a good job, and you will be able to do good work. But . . ." Pastor paused. "There are more important things to learn than facts. Those books will help you in your earthly life, but this will help you in your faith life."

Then he held up a Bible. "This is the book that tells you about your faith life. The Bible tells us about God's love. It tells us about God sending His Son, Jesus, to earth, and it tells us about how we will live with Him forever."

Journal: Make a list of your favorite Bible stories. Why are they favorites?

Pray: Thank You, God, for the Bible, where we can learn about Your love. Amen. P. L.

AUGUST 31

John 3:16

It's a Mystery

DO YOU LIKE TO SOLVE MYSTERIES?

Let's try a few. See if you can read this next mysterious sentence.

Ths sntnc sn't s hrd f y pt th vwls whr thy blng.

The sentence is confusing and looks strange until you see that all the vowels have been left out. Try putting in all the a, e, i, o, u's.

Well, here's another mystery. See if you can read the following:

Fr Gd s lvd th wrld, tht H gv Hs nly Sn.

Add the vowels, and you will have part of John 3:16. We read, "For God so loved the world, that He gave His only Son."

Now, let's consider something else that is a mystery to some people. How do we get to heaven?

Some people think that the way to heaven is to keep every one of the Ten Commandments. So they try very hard not to cheat or curse, to lie or covet. Some people actually think that they are doing a pretty good job. But even kids like you know that no one is perfect—not even your parents.

The way to get to heaven has nothing to do with what we do. It has everything to do with what God has done for us in sending Jesus to suffer and die for our sins. Those who believe in Jesus will be saved. And that's no mystery to those who believe the words of John 3:16.

Journal: Do you like mysteries? What's your favorite mystery book? Reading your Bible will help you solve many important mysteries.

Pray: Dear Jesus, thank You for solving the mystery of how to get to heaven. Help me to tell others how much You love them. Amen. P. L.

The State Fair

All summer long, Micah and Briana did chores for their families and neighbors. They saved their money so they could go to the state fair. When they got to the fair, they purchased tickets for rides and divided them evenly. Some rides cost more tickets than others, so the siblings had to plan how to use the tickets to the best advantage. Soon, the tickets were gone.

As they were leaving, a man handed them some tickets. He had more than he needed and wanted to know if Micah and Briana wanted them. They couldn't believe their eyes. There were enough tickets for both of them to have two more rides.

This story is a good illustration of grace. Grace is what God gives us even though we don't deserve it. The extra tickets were a gift. The children did not earn them or do anything right to get them. The tickets were a gift, a pleasant surprise.

God's grace is a gift too. We are sinners who cannot keep God's commands. We cannot earn heaven or God's love. God gives us these things because Jesus has earned them for us.

When the children were done with the rides, the tickets were gone, and their evening came to a close. But God's love and grace does not end. It continues for you in His Word, in Baptism, and in the Lord's Supper. God's grace comes to you and never ends.

Journal: Write about a time you received a surprise gift.

Pray: Dear Jesus, thank You for Your grace-filled gifts to me. Through Your Spirit, give me kindness and love to share with others. Amen. K. D. M.

Ears—
Elephant and Itchy

Here's a recipe for a gigantic treat—an elephant ear. Cut flour tortillas in half. Spread margarine on both sides of each half. Ask an adult to fry the tortillas in vegetable oil, turning the tortilla over when it puffs. Sprinkle the puffs with a mixture of cinnamon and sugar.

Another kind of ear is an itchy ear. That term refers to the desire to hear words we agree with. In other words, we keep our ears open so we can hear what we *want* to hear. We like to hear that we can skip piano practice. We like to hear the teacher announce, "No math homework!"

What is our response when our ears hear something that we *don't* want to hear? For instance, who likes to hear that he has been mean to his sister? Who is happy to be reminded that she has neglected her chores *again*? Let's not turn our ears away from truth. We need to hear about our sin and God's grace.

Through our ears, we hear God's Word, which tells us just what we need to hear: that we are sinners in need of forgiveness. He tells us that He sent Jesus to be our Savior. He tells us that our sins are forgiven, that we are free to live as His children.

While you are munching on that big elephant ear, rejoice that God sends to your ears just what they need to hear—His Word of truth.

Journal: What are some nice things you could say to people you meet today? What are some wonderful things that God says to you?

Pray: Dear Lord, help me to speak Your Word with courage. Help my ears to itch for Your truth. In Jesus' name I pray. Amen. K. D. M.

Science Fiction

"Let me get this straight," said Jason. "In this scene, I've just time-traveled from the future to the present. Future me has to get present me to visit past me. Then we defeat evil me from another dimension."

"Right," said Sean, lowering the camera. "But don't forget that evil you is really good you, and future you is evil. So the other yous have to stop future you."

Have you ever seen a TV show or movie that confused you?

There are times when God's Word seems confusing. Have you ever read a Bible passage and had no idea what it was talking about? Maybe it was crammed with big words or unfamiliar images. It's not fun to be confused.

For many people, the last book in the Bible, Revelation, is confusing. It's full of beasts and dragons and bowls and horsemen. In some ways, it sounds like a confusing science-fiction story. It's even set in the future!

There is, of course, a huge difference between science fiction and the Bible. The Bible is true. Every word in God's book is filled with truth. Even when some parts are difficult to understand, He makes one thing very clear: God loves us and wants us to know that Jesus died for our sins. Then Jesus rose again so that we may live forever with Him in heaven. That's a simple message and a simple truth.

Journal: Write about a time you were confused. How did God help?

Pray: God, though I don't always understand Your words, I thank You for understanding every one of my needs. Amen. J. S.

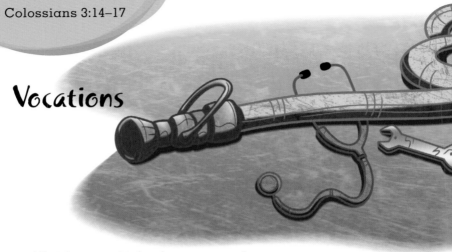

Vocations

What do you want to be when you grow up? Perhaps a doctor? a mechanic? a firefighter? a teacher? a baseball player? an artist?

Labor Day is a day set aside to remember the work people do in our communities. The jobs people do are an important part of who they are. For Christians, jobs are one way to show love for God by serving others. No wonder kids often look forward to growing up.

It can be hard to wait. You may ask, "But what can I do right now?" God has things for us to do besides jobs. He gives every one of His people something called *vocation*. A vocation is not just what you do, but what you are. You have several vocations. Are you a son or daughter? a brother or sister? a student? a friend? a neighbor? a teammate? a church member? All of these are vocations. God shows His love for all people by helping us love and serve others through our vocations.

The most important vocation you have is "Christian." God gave you that vocation when you were baptized and the forgiveness Jesus earned on the cross became yours. God put His name on you. Nothing can take this vocation away from you. It's yours forever! It's what makes you able to "do everything in the name of the Lord Jesus" (Colossians 3:17) as you serve others as a son or daughter, brother or sister, friend or neighbor.

Journal: What vocations do you have now? How can you serve others through them?

Pray: Dear God, thank You for making me one of Your people. Help me to serve others in the vocations You give me. Amen. E. G.

True and False

"Mom, how did I get this email?" Maggie asked.

Her mother looked over her shoulder. It said scholars discovered "new truth" about the Bible. They claimed to know when Jesus was going to return to earth. The message closed with these words: "If you are a real Christian, send this message on to ten friends."

Maggie's mother said, "This isn't good. You should delete it."

"Why?" Maggie asked. "What if they really know?"

Her mother explained, "Jesus told His disciples that no one knows the day or hour of His return. He warns them to avoid false teachers who claim to know."

Some people are eager to look smart. They say they are Christians, but their teachings are not Christian teachings. How can we recognize the truth from the false ideas?

Maggie's pastor explained how during confirmation class. "Our best defense against false teaching is to know God's Word."

What happened to Maggie can happen to you. You will hear false teachings that test what is said about Jesus. When you watch a movie, ask yourself if what is said agrees with God's Word. Read your Bible. Listen during Sunday School and church. Ask the Holy Spirit to enlighten you, protect you from false teaching, and lead you to God's truth.

Journal: How well do you know the Apostles' Creed? Try saying it and then write it.

Pray: Heavenly Father, protect me from false teachers. Through Your Holy Spirit, keep me trusting in my true Savior, Jesus. In His name I pray. Amen. C. O.

Examples

Susan loves music. She downloads her favorite songs onto her phone to listen to all the time. Her room and her locker at school are decorated with posters of her favorite musicians. She has even adopted the language and dressing styles of her favorite artists.

Susan is not the only young person to model her life after popular people. Young people are often looking to emulate people such as movie stars, professional athletes, musicians, and even superheroes. These are the people that some young people want to be like when they grow up.

Today's Bible reading is from a letter Paul wrote to a young man named Timothy. Paul was not only a role model to Timothy, but he was also a father figure. In this letter, Paul told Timothy that he was not too young to be a role model of purity, speech, love, faith, and conduct for other believers.

Paul reminds Timothy to devote himself "to the public reading of Scripture" (1 Timothy 4:13) as he prepares to lead God's people. Like Timothy, we grow through time spent studying God's Word with others in Church and Sunday School. God the Holy Spirit works through the Word to strengthen our faith and help us be an example of faith for others.

Journal: List some favorite Bible verses that give directions for living.

Pray: Dear God, thank You for helping me to know and understand that even though I am young, I can serve You and be an example to others. Amen. D. M.

Turtle Crossing

The box turtle had gone about twelve inches; the other side of the highway was far away. Cars whizzed past, going in both directions. Rebecca didn't see how the turtle could possibly make it all the way across.

Rebecca pulled her bicycle over to the shoulder of the road. She carefully walked back to where the turtle was trying to get across the road. She watched as it pulled its head inside its shell every time a car came speeding past.

Finally, there was a break in the traffic. Rebecca looked both ways, carefully stepped onto the road, scooped up the turtle, and hurried to the other side. Once there, she set the turtle down in the ditch.

Just like Rebecca scooped up the turtle and delivered it safely on its journey, so God did for the Israelites. While they were slaves in Egypt, God reached down and brought them out of their captivity. He protected them throughout the entire journey. He kept them safe as they traveled through other nations.

God sent His Son into the world to save us from our sin. He reaches into our lives. He gives us faith through His Word. He forgives our sins and gives us safe passage along our journey.

Journal: On what journeys are you traveling now? Where will your journey end?

Pray: Dear Father in heaven, thank You for reaching down into my life and lifting me up to safety. Through Your love, keep me safe from all harm and danger. In Jesus' name I pray. Amen. C. H.

Red Rover Strategy

Do you know how to play Red Rover?

To play, two teams stand in lines facing each other about twenty feet apart. Team members hold hands and make a chain. One team calls the name of a person from the other team. Then that person runs at the opposing team and tries to break through two clasped hands. If the runner succeeds, his or her team chooses an opponent to join their team. If the runner is unsuccessful, he or she joins the opposing team.

With these rules, it makes sense to call the name of the strongest member of the other team. If you capture that runner, you gain another strong player. Of course, you take a risk that the strongest player may break through and win one of your players.

Satan likes to use a type of Red Rover strategy against God's children. He plans to steal you away from God and destroy your life. Satan calls to those who are strong in the Lord, who love God, and who live in His freedom. Satan tempts Christians to lure them to his side.

Should we worry that Satan's temptations are too strong? Can we win against Satan? We already have! Jesus broke through Satan's line. Jesus took away Satan's strength and power through His death on the cross. In Baptism, Jesus gave you His victory. He makes us winners.

Journal: Satan wants to take you away from Jesus. Write about Jesus as your Good Shepherd.

Pray: Dear Jesus, thank You for defeating Satan and all my enemies. Make my faith strong through Your Word so that I can stay strong against him. Amen. V. S.

Get Ready to Grow!

"Okay, kids, let's get ready for church!" Dad told his children.

"It's only Saturday, and it's nighttime!" Nathan cried.

"We're watching our favorite TV show," Charles added.

"I already got my clothes out," Susie said.

"That's good, Susie, but I'm talking of a different way to prepare."

"What do you mean?" asked Charles, turning off the television.

"Well, son, how do you get ready for school?" Dad asked.

"By doing my homework," he said.

"I finished mine at school on Friday!" Nathan piped up.

"Good. Doing your lessons prepares you for class," Dad said. "We can do the same thing to get ready for church."

"Oh, I see," said Susie. "We can read the Bible!"

"Yes. We can read the Scripture lessons we'll hear in church tomorrow," Dad said.*

"Why read them now if we'll hear them tomorrow?" Susie asked.

"Because Dad can explain the parts that may be hard for us to understand," Charles answered.

"Absolutely," Dad said. "God's Word is powerful and effective. The more we hear it, the more it grows in us. Preparing causes our hearts and minds to think of God and His gift of salvation in Christ."

Right now, as you read this devotion, you are like the Thompson family. God is working in you. He is preparing your heart and mind for the gifts He has for you.

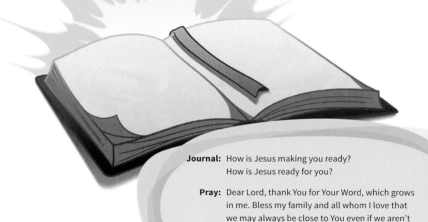

Journal: How is Jesus making you ready?
How is Jesus ready for you?

Pray: Dear Lord, thank You for Your Word, which grows in me. Bless my family and all whom I love that we may always be close to You even if we aren't like the family in this story. Amen. C. W.

SEPTEMBER 10

Matthew 14:13–14

Documentary

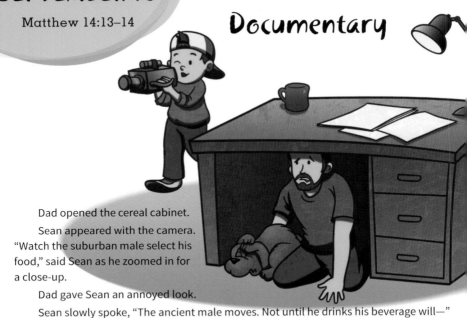

Dad opened the cereal cabinet.

Sean appeared with the camera. "Watch the suburban male select his food," said Sean as he zoomed in for a close-up.

Dad gave Sean an annoyed look.

Sean slowly spoke, "The ancient male moves. Not until he drinks his beverage will—"

"Sean," Dad interrupted, "turn the camera off."

"But I'm making a documentary," said Sean.

"Now!" commanded Dad. "You filmed me yawning, shaving, and taking out the garbage. I need a little privacy."

Documentaries are movies that show real life. If you're the subject of a documentary, you don't get a lot of privacy. That would be hard.

Jesus needed to be alone sometimes. In today's reading, Jesus is sad because He's just heard that John the Baptist has been killed. So Jesus goes off by Himself for some privacy.

But He doesn't get to be alone for long. Crowds of people find out where He is and begin following Him. Still, rather than selfishly running away, Jesus has compassion. He feels bad for the people and heals those who are sick. Jesus was happy to do this. He knew that His life was not His own. He was on earth to help and serve other people. He was on earth to do His Father's will.

We're grateful because God recorded His documentary of Jesus' life and death in the Bible. It tells us that God loves us too much to ever ignore us.

Journal: Why is it helpful to be alone?
Why is it special to be with others?

Pray: Jesus, You never stop serving or loving me. Thank You. Amen. J. S.

SEPTEMBER 11

Day after Day

Psalm 30:5

It's that day again, isn't it? September 11. On the news, on social media, on the radio, people are probably remembering the terrible tragedy that happened on this day in 2001. In a few months, some will talk about December 7, when Pearl Harbor was attacked in 1941.

But those aren't the only dates of tragedy. Other nations throughout history marked dates to remember with sadness. God's people of Nehemiah's day were still hurting from the time invaders came and took them from their Promised Land. Their unfaithfulness to God eventually led to the destruction of their homes and families. They wondered if things would ever be the same again.

In a way, no. They would always have that dark history of losing their kingdom. In another way though, things would be even better. Nehemiah was one of the leaders God chose to help His people restore their city Jerusalem and their temple hundreds of years later. But God also promised that even if things aren't as good as before, the new Jerusalem of heaven will be better than ever. Then we'll all rejoice in His kingdom.

Maybe you have some sad days that still hurt when you think about them. In a way, you may always remember those days while here on earth. But God is with you to give you healing. And someday He'll also bring you to Him for endless joyful tomorrows.

Journal: Write about an important day in your past.

Pray: Eternal God, You have seen joy and sorrow, triumph and tragedy. Thank You for being there with me in all my days—happy and sad ones. Amen. L. C.

A Bear's Advice

Two travelers strolled through the forest. They laughed at each other's jokes and enjoyed the natural beauty around them.

Suddenly, a huge bear rushed out. The first traveler saw the bear coming and quickly ran to hide. The second traveler didn't have time to hide. Instead, he fell to the ground and buried his face in the dirt.

The bear quickly spotted the traveler lying on the ground. He circled the man, eyed him carefully, and stopped to shake the man with his paw. Finally, the bear leaned over and sniffed by the man's ear. But the man didn't move. The bear, assuming he was dead, turned and ambled off into the forest.

The first traveler came out of hiding. "What did the bear whisper in your ear?"

"He told me never to trust a friend who runs off when you are in trouble."

We have a friend who never runs away. No matter how dark or dangerous or scary the situation is, Jesus stays with us. Long ago, He had a chance to desert us when crowds of people wanted to kill Him. Jesus didn't run off. He didn't hide. He knew we were doomed by our sin. Our eternal lives were at risk. He gave His life to save us so that we could be His forever. He's the best friend and Savior of all.

Journal: Read today's verses from Isaiah again. Write down all the writer's actions. What do they show you?

Pray: Dear Jesus, thank You for giving Your life so that I may have life eternal. Thank You for always being my friend and Savior. Amen. E. F.

Championship!

—TICKETS—

This is the time of year when baseball teams dream of being in the World Series. Some teams earn a chance to be in the playoffs. Finally, two teams will compete in October in the ultimate contest. Only one team wins.

Some people think that getting into heaven is like winning the championship. You have to be good enough. You have to be better than the others. Well, that's wrong.

Getting into heaven is more like going to the best concert ever in a huge stadium. All you need is a ticket. Some people try to buy that ticket or earn their ticket. Sorry! Not for sale! The tickets are free! But the only way to get a ticket to this concert is to wear the right uniform—a special robe. The Owner of the stadium had His Son make an endless supply of these robes. Ever since then, the Owner's Special Helper has offered the free robes to everyone in every place.

Getting into heaven isn't something we earn; it is the free gift of God. He sent His only Son, Jesus, to win the ultimate contest between sin, death, and the devil for us. Now He sends His Holy Spirit to offer you and me the "ticket" into heaven. As believers in Jesus, we wear His robe of righteousness, and we receive our "ticket" into heaven.

Journal: Think of other events where you need a ticket to get in. Have you ever been given a free ticket for anything? What was it?

Pray: Dear God, thank You for sending Jesus to make my ticket to heaven free! Help me to share this great news with others. Amen. P. L.

SEPTEMBER 14

Ephesians 3:17–19

Rooted in the Cross

Jorge's dad is an agricultural agent. His job is to help farmers with problems and answer their questions. One afternoon, Jorge went with his dad to make some calls at nearby farms.

Jorge's dad looked at the first field. The corn was short and spindly. Most of it had an unhealthy yellow color.

"This land is worn out," Dad said. "The soil doesn't have what the corn needs to grow well."

Dad and the farmer talked about what could be done to help the soil. While the two were talking, Jorge noticed that the corn across the road was tall and strong and dark green in color.

After they got back in the car, Jorge pointed to the field he had noticed. "That corn has lots of what it needs!"

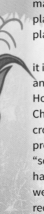

"Yes," Dad agreed, "the soil makes all the difference. If the plant's roots can get good food, the plant thrives."

Just as a plant's roots anchor it in soil, God's people have an anchor in their Savior. On this day, Holy Cross Day, those who believe in Christ as their Savior remember the cross. Christ's sacrifice on the cross provided us with fixed "roots." His "soil" is rich in nutrients. His "soil" has an endless supply of grace. When we hear God's Word proclaimed and receive His gifts in the Sacraments, our "roots" drink in that Gospel. God makes us grow steadfast and strong so that we, rooted in the cross, can serve others.

Journal: We are rooted in love. We are rooted in God. How are these two statements really the same?

Pray: Father, help me to grow in the ways that You want. Keep me rooted in the nutrients of Your love. In Jesus' name. Amen. G. S.

How Will You Spend Your Weekend?

Think about how you feel on Fridays. You made it through another week at school—a week of classes, activities, cafeteria lunches, and much more. Now it's time for the weekend! But how will you spend your time?

It seems everyone has a list of things they want to accomplish over a weekend, but weekends are also a great time to rest and recharge after a long week. Rest is a necessary part of our lives on earth. It helps us regain our energy and prepare for the work God has in store for us. It's a natural part of our lives as created beings—in fact, in the Book of Genesis, we see God model the practice of rest, taking time on the seventh day of creation to rest from His work (Genesis 2:1–2).

Another part of our weekend rest is joining with other believers to hear God's Word and celebrate the gifts God gives us in Baptism and Holy Communion. This rest is so important that God even gave us the Third Commandment to remind us about this great gift.

Ultimately, true rest is found in Christ alone! Jesus invites us to come to Him in faith, knowing that we will find peace. We trust that Christ has indeed overcome the world (John 16:33) and that He came to save us out of His abundant grace and love.

Journal: How can you rest in Jesus this weekend?

Pray: Dear God, please help me to rest in Your promises rather than the things of this world. Amen. H. L.

Defeating Evil

Some days, the world can be a scary place. The evening news and Internet make it feel like the news is all bad. Often, we don't even need to look far to see all the bad—a family member might be sick or maybe a parent lost his or her job. We can easily be discouraged by all the evil and trouble we see.

In the Garden of Eden, sin and evil first came into the world when Adam and Eve disobeyed God. We have continued the cycle of sin ever since. The good news is that Jesus came into the world to overcome sin and evil. By His death and resurrection from the dead, Jesus put our relationship with God back to good.

Many times when we see or experience the bad and evil, we want to repay it with more evil. But there is no need for that. Jesus' defeat of the devil calls us to a new life, a life that even repays evil with good.

When you see something evil or bad going on around the world, or even close by, overcome it with good. It doesn't have to be huge. You can help your parents clean the house. You can collect food for the local food pantry. You can visit your elderly neighbors. There are many ways you can share the Good News about Jesus and spread the good.

Journal: List some ways you and your friends could overcome evil with good in your community.

Pray: Dear Jesus, thank You for defeating all evil for us. Help us overcome evil with good. Amen. A. B.

God's Extreme Provision

There was an old TV show in which deserving families were chosen to have a new home. Usually, the crew came in and demolished the existing home. Then they had five days to build a new house from the ground up—and not only to build it but also to completely furnish it.

This is how the show went. When the big day comes for the family to return, a giant bus blocks the view of the new house. The family is nervous and excited. They don't know what to expect, but they know it will be so much better and more beautiful than what they had.

When the bus is moved and they see their house, the reaction is always one of amazement. Is this really their home? It's so much more than they expected. As the family goes inside, their excitement grows. Each room is grander than the next, exceeding anything they could have imagined.

Wouldn't it be nice to have someone give you a gift like that? You know what? Someone already has.

Through Baptism, God has given you a new life. It's full of plans and opportunities, greater than you can imagine. It may be too good to believe because sin causes us to doubt that God knows or cares what we do. But He knows exactly who you are, who you will grow into, and what you need to get there.

And when your life here on earth is done, He has something else amazing planned: an eternity with Him in the most magnificent home ever.

Journal: Think about your future. What's the most exciting thing you think could happen to you? When you have finished, ask several people to share how God has worked in their lives.

Pray: Dear God, thank You for the amazing things You have given me through Jesus Christ—forgiveness, life, and salvation—and for all You have in store for me. Keep my love for You strong. Amen. J. A.

The Best Start

"Mom! Where's my permission slip?"

Logan ran through the house, trying not to forget anything. It was a big day at school—tests, assignments, and the permission slip to turn in.

"If I don't find it, I can't go on the field trip tomorrow!"

He turned a corner and ran right into his mother. "Is this what you're looking for?" She held up a piece of paper.

"Yes," he said with a sigh. "Thanks."

She put her hand on his shoulder. "Logan, wait."

"But Mom, I've got so much to do."

"I know. But I think you need to do one more thing."

He rolled his eyes. "What?"

"Pray," she said.

"I don't have time."

Mom smiled. "Trust me, Logan, you don't have time *not* to pray. Sometimes our lives get so busy that it's easy to think it isn't important to stop and talk to God. I try to start my day with prayer. I give the day to God, even days I'm not looking forward to. It makes a big difference.

"Prayer is an acknowledgment of God's power to bless our day," she continued. "He is willing to do this because He loves us so much that He sacrificed His Son, Jesus, to pay for our sins."

It made sense. Logan looked at his watch and then looked up at Mom with a smile. "Would you make me breakfast while I pray?"

She ruffled his hair. "You bet."

Journal: Learn Luther's Morning Prayer. Use it along with your personal prayers. Write down something about your day.

Pray: Thank You, God, for the privilege and the command that I can pray to You. Help me remember to talk to You no matter what good or bad stuff is going on in my life. In Jesus' name I pray. Amen. J. A.

Pray for Him?

Jason greeted his mom at the door when she got home from work. "Mr. Greenwood made a bunch of kids stay in during lunch for no reason."

"Surely there was a reason," said Mom.

Jason explained. "At our assembly," he said, "one kid burped real loud and then others did too. Since no one would confess, Mr. Greenwood made that whole section stay in."

"I suppose some of your friends had to stay in," said Mom, "and you thought that was unfair. You know, Jason, it isn't easy being a leader. We should pray for Mr. Greenwood and your friends."

Jason's eyes popped wide open. "Pray? For *him*?"

"Yes. For *him*. The Bible tells us to pray for those in authority. That includes Mr. Greenwood." Jason's mom got out her Bible. She showed him the verses in 1 Timothy 2. "God invites us to pray and give thanks for *all people*. It even says 'all who are in high positions.'"

That day, Jason learned that God wants us to pray for all people who hold power over us, even if we don't like their decisions. This makes for peace, and living in peace is a great blessing. When we live in peace, God's Church has a better chance to grow so that all people can come to know the true peacemaker between God and man—Jesus Christ, the Savior of all.

Journal: Write how Jesus brought peace between God and man.

Pray: Dear God, grant grace and guidance to all who people who are in authority over me. When I disagree with them, give me wisdom to know how to handle the problem. In Jesus' name I pray. Amen. J. H.

What and When

"I'm really angry with God," announced Sam, slamming the door.

"My goodness," Mom said. "Sit down and tell me about it while I fix you a sandwich."

"Well, okay, but a sandwich isn't going to help," Sam protested. "Mr. Hart told us the Bible says we can ask God for anything in prayer."

"That's what the Bible says," Mom responded.

"Well, God might have heard my prayers, but He sure didn't answer any of them. I prayed for lots of things last night, but God didn't listen to me," Sam said. "I asked for a football like Jason's and for sugar cookies in my lunch, and I asked for—"

"Whoa," Mom said. "I know God heard those prayers. But that doesn't mean He gives us everything we want. He gives us what we need. Did you really need those things you asked for?"

Sam stammered, "N-no, not really, but I wanted them."

"I'm sure you did," Mom continued. "God knows what's best for us and when it's best for us. The Bible records many times people prayed. God heard, but He didn't always answer exactly the way they wanted. Sometimes He said no; sometimes it was best for people to wait. Abraham and Sarah waited for a child. God waited thousands of years before He sent His Son to be the Savior of the world."

Journal: Make a list of times when God answered your prayers with a yes.

Pray: Dear God, thank You for hearing and answering my prayers. Give me a trusting heart. In Jesus' name. Amen. P. L.

Growing!

"I'm an inch taller than I was last school year!" exploded David.

"That's great," Dad replied. "I notice, David, that you are growing in lots of ways. You need a bigger pair of shoes, and you have outgrown some of your clothes."

"Yeah, Dad, and I can do more in school."

"David, let me ask, how have you grown with God? Are you praying more? Are you reading your devotions and Bible every day now? Are you listening and learning in Sunday School?"

"Well, yes, sort of. But how does that help me grow?"

"As you read or listen to God's Word, the Bible, and pray about it, God gives you many blessings. He gives you faith to believe in Him as your only way to heaven. He helps you to say kind things and to be helpful to other people. He even helps you to share the love of Jesus that you have with other people in your life," Dad explained.

"I get it! Just like when I eat food, my body grows, when I read the Bible and study it and pray about it, I grow in godly things through the power of the Holy Spirit."

Journal: How tall are you? How are you growing? What are you doing to grow closer to God?

Pray: Dear God, thank You for creating me and growing me every day. Help me to feed on Your words of love and forgiveness, that each day I might grow in my faith. Amen. P. L.

Everyone Is Useful

Juan liked to spend time with his grandfather, Señor Martinez. His grandfather was a carpenter and had a workshop where he built lots of things. Juan watched Abuelo as he carefully measured, sawed, and hammered. Juan said, "Abuelo, God wants everyone to do things for Him. What can I do? I'm just a skinny little kid."

Abuelo said, "Look around my workshop. I have all sizes of saws, screwdrivers, and hammers. I can't use a big saw to make a birdhouse. But I can use this small one. Every tool is useful.

"God can use you too. You can help out at home or help your elderly neighbor Mrs. Farley. You can invite your friends to Sunday School or church."

Many Bible-times people were not considered very important, but they did great things for God. Find out who they are and write their names on the lines.

A slave saved thousands—Genesis 41:57 _____

A shepherd became king—1 Samuel 16:1, 13 _____

A herdsman became a prophet—Amos 7:14–15 _____

A tax collector became a disciple—Luke 5:27 _____

A tentmaker became a missionary—Acts 18:1–3 _____

_____

A seamstress helped the poor—Acts 9:36–40 _____

We may not think we are important. But God sends the Holy Spirit to us and helps us do great things for Him. God's Son, Jesus, has given us new life by dying for our sins and rising again. God will help us live this new life for Him.

Journal: What are some things that you can do to help others?

Pray: Dear God, please help me as I do something for You each day. Amen. J. D.

Answers: Joseph, David, Amos, Levi (Matthew), Paul, Dorcas.

A Communion Blessing

The wedding was beautiful. After the bride and groom spoke their vows to each other, the pastor said, "I now pronounce you to be husband and wife. What God has joined together, let no one put asunder [separate]."

These are important words! God is offering His blessing to two people who have faith in Him. God will show mercy and help them throughout their married life.

He calls them to repent daily of sins, pray to Him for guidance, and receive Christ's good gifts in the Divine Service. As they have been forgiven and blessed, they are to be a forgiving couple who bless others!

A similar thing happens when people come to Communion. Christians stand before the altar and hear God's blessing. The pastor speaks Jesus' words: "This is My body, which is given for you. . . . This cup is the new testament in My blood."

Jesus, the Son of God, allowed His body to be given over to death when He was crucified. He let His blood flow as an atoning sacrifice for our sins. He gave His true body and blood to pay for the guilt of every person.

In Holy Communion, God offers forgiveness and eternal life to people who have faith in Him. He calls us to repent of selfish ways, pray for guidance, and show a forgiving heart to others. God's altar is a place of blessing!

Journal: Write down the good things God promises the person who receives Holy Communion.

Pray: Lord, prepare my heart to receive Your love and forgiveness. I need to hear Your promises again and again. Amen. C. O.

SEPTEMBER 24

1 Corinthians 12:12–13

Joined Giants

Along the northwest coast of California grow the largest and oldest trees on earth. Some redwood trees are as tall as skyscrapers and may reach over 350 feet in height. It's hard to understand how huge they are. These amazing giants can live two thousand years and can weigh more than five hundred tons!

An unusual thing about redwoods is that their root systems are shallow, especially for such tall trees. They have no large tap root to anchor them in the ground. Most of the roots are only an inch thick and grow less than twenty inches deep.

So how do these mighty trees remain standing upright? By growing close together with other redwood trees and intermingling root systems. The roots form a thick underground network that is nearly impossible to pull apart. Redwood trees illustrate the importance of close relationships between Christians. We do not need others in order to be saved. Jesus earned our salvation. However, God tells us to gather with other believers. In the church service, we remember what God has done for us and celebrate the Sacraments. We learn about God's love and work in our lives when we study His Word with others.

Praying together gives us strength and encouragement. Jesus tells us, "For where two or three are gathered in My name, there am I among them" (Matthew 18:20). Like the roots of redwood trees woven together, Christian friendships support us and add God's glory to our lives.

Journal: Write your name in the center of a circle. Around the circle, write the names of others who support you (and those you support) in your faith.

Pray: Guiding God, thank You for all You have done for us and the ways You strengthen us in Word and Sacrament. Open my eyes to opportunities to grow in my faith and to support others. Amen. D. N.

Robbie's Mistake

Robbie was invited to spend the night at Chris's house. Chris's father grilled hamburgers, and his mother prepared corn on the cob.

After dinner, they played street tennis. Robbie ran into the garage to retrieve some tennis balls. Do you know what he did? He hid one of the balls. Later, when no one was looking, he got the hidden tennis ball and put it in his duffel bag.

Soon Robbie felt awful. He worried that Chris would find out he was stealing a tennis ball. Robbie knew he had broken one of God's Commandments. He felt guilty about stealing the ball! When he found a moment alone, he placed the ball with the other ones. He confessed his sin to Chris. Now he wasn't hiding a secret anymore, and he could have fun the rest of the night.

Are you ever tempted to take something that doesn't belong to you? This is known as "coveting." Just *thinking* about stealing is a sin!

When you have stolen something, God wants you to repent. You can give back what you took, apologize to the person, and ask for his or her forgiveness and also for God's forgiveness.

The Bible promises, "If we confess our sins, [God] is faithful and just to forgive us our sins" (1 John 1:9). Jesus has taken our guilt upon Himself, and on the cross He was punished for sins such as stealing. He is a true friend who rescues us from the punishment we deserve.

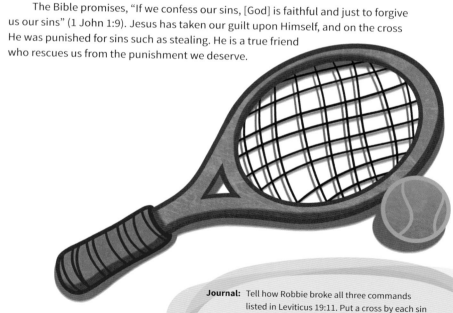

Journal: Tell how Robbie broke all three commands listed in Leviticus 19:11. Put a cross by each sin God can forgive.

Pray: Dear heavenly Father, help me to be content with the things I have. For Jesus' sake, forgive me when I covet, steal, or lie. In His name I pray. Amen. C. O.

Toss It or Keep It?

Jon's class studied the First Commandment: "You shall have no other gods." Then Pastor asked the class to read a Bible passage in Joshua that described how people threw away their false gods. That's when Jon decided he had things to throw away too.

He had a few CDs with songs bad words. When he got home, he threw out the CDs. Jon also had a poster of his favorite baseball player over his bed. He took that down too. He wondered if he was worshiping this hero.

Later, Jon told his father what he was doing and asked if there was anything else he should give up as a "false god." His father was wise. He helped Jon see that it isn't wrong to own something. It doesn't mean that each thing is a false god. But he also helped Jon realize that he does sin against this and every commandment.

What do you think? Can you keep the First Commandment by getting rid of posters and CDs? What if you cleared your room of electronic games?

The truth is we can't keep the First Commandment or *any* of God's Commandments. We are sinful, and by breaking one of God's commands, we have broken the entire Law. That's w we need Jesus. He kept all the Commandments perfectly for us. Now we are free to live our lives so that others can know that Jesus is the only Savior from sin.

Journal: Write out Mark 12:30 in your journal.

Pray: Dear God, I am so blessed to be a Christian, forgiven of my sins and guided by Your Holy Spirit. In Jesus' name I thank You for all these gifts. Amen. C. O

Karma? Really?

Have you ever heard someone say something like this? "Albert was being so mean to Rasheed at recess. But karma came around later. Albert fell down in PE and twisted his ankle." Or, "I held the door open for an elderly couple, and then I found a dollar bill lying on the ground. That's karma for ya!"

The word *karma* comes from the Hindu and Buddhist religions. The basic idea is that people earn positive or negative outcomes based on their own actions. Doing good brings good karma. Evil actions bring bad karma. Either way, you get what you deserve.

Instead of karma, God offers grace and mercy. Here are some simple definitions:

GRACE — Getting something that *is not* deserved

MERCY — Not getting something that *is* deserved

The writer of the New Testament Book of Hebrews wrote that we can approach our holy God without being afraid. Through our Savior Jesus, God does not punish us with death—even though we deserve it. Instead, God forgives all of our sins and saves us—even though we don't deserve it. We can be confident in our salvation. God grants us grace and mercy. So much better than karma, don't you agree?

Journal: Why should Christians not believe in the idea of karma?

Pray: Thank You, God, for Your endless grace and mercy through Jesus Christ. Amen. K. S.

Remain in the Faith

Pastor was teaching confirmation class. The topic was "What happens when we die?" Tiana was really surprised when Ryan asked, "Do we believe in reincarnation?"

"No," Pastor replied, "that is not the teaching of the Christian faith. We believe we are born once of our mother and father, and we face judgment when we die. We who are baptized and believe in Jesus as our Savior will go to heaven on that day."

Tiana learned the truth of God's Word from her parents, personal reading, confirmation class, and attending church and Sunday School. But she heard false teachings about God from her friends, from television, and from websites on the Internet. Sometimes it was very confusing! She was grateful that her mom and dad were always ready and happy to answer her questions.

All of us who are baptized in the name of the triune God will be tested. We will hear ideas and teachings that don't sound right. As Paul wrote in 2 Corinthians, we must "examine" ourselves. We rejoice in knowing that Jesus redeemed us from the curse of sin, offering the forgiveness of our sins. We rejoice that He rose from the grave, assuring us that we will be raised from the dead on the Last Day.

Knowing the clear teachings of Scripture enables us to recognize and avoid false teachings. When others challenge our beliefs, we will be prepared to give a gentle witness to the truth.

Journal: Use your catechism to see how Scripture does not teach reincarnation. Hint: See the Third Article of the Apostles' Creed, "the resurrection of the body."

Pray: Lord Jesus, You are the way, the truth, and the life. Amen. C. O.

Which Path?

Anh and Thanh went bike riding with their mom on the rail trail near their house. The trail wandered through the woods. On the edge of the trail were wildflowers, bushes, and trees. In the woods were squirrels, raccoons, and deer.

Anh and Thanh wanted to explore the woods, but Mom said, "Stay on the path, girls." Even though the woods looked like fun, Mom knew they were dangerous. On one side of the path was a high cliff with thorn bushes and sharp rocks. On the other side was a steep hill with vines and poison ivy.

You travel many paths. Some might be bike paths, but most are different kinds of paths, like becoming better at something. Maybe you practice to improve as a clarinet player or be a more skilled soccer player. Some paths are investigations. They help you find out more about Jesus. The Bible is the path for that journey.

Have you ever read a book in which the characters didn't believe in God? Have you read a book in which someone said he could get to heaven by being good? That doesn't sound like the words of today's Bible passage. All those trails lead away from Jesus. God's people believe God's Word when it says Jesus is the way, the only path to eternal life! And God's Holy Spirit is at work, keeping you on that faith trail and away from the evil one. God wants you with Him forever.

Journal: Do you know someone who does not know that Jesus is the only way to heaven? Write a prayer to God for that person.

Pray: Dear Jesus, when I hear people talking about other ways to heaven, give me words to say to them. In Your name I pray. Amen. N. D.

Honoring God in All Things

Let's start today's devotion with some questions:

Do your parents ever ask you to help out around the house?

What are some of the things they ask you to do?

Do you like all of the chores they ask you to help with?

One last question—and be honest: how do you respond when you are asked to do something you don't enjoy?

Growing up, my family ate dinner together at the kitchen table. One of my responsibilities was to set the table each night. It was a simple task, but I never enjoyed it. After all, I thought, there were far better options for how I could spend that time! Have you ever had an experience like mine?

Sometimes we are asked to do things we don't enjoy doing—such as our chores. When that happens, it is very easy to grumble and complain. But God's Word reminds us that no matter what we do, we can give God glory . . . even when we are doing things we don't like!

And if we fail to honor God through our everyday tasks, we know God will forgive us. Jesus died on the cross to take away our shame and guilt. He rose from the dead, lives, and reigns to all eternity—definitely worthy of our glory, honor, and praise!

Journal: What are some areas of your life in which you struggle to honor God? How can you show God honor through those activities?

Pray: Dear God, forgive me for the times I have not honored You with my life. Thank You for the forgiveness that is mine in Jesus. Help me honor You in my thoughts, words, and deeds. Amen. H. L.

Give Thanks for Jesus

It's Sunday. It's time for war. Look out! The "big three" are attacking.

"What?" you ask. You don't see enemies knocking down the door. You don't see them climbing through your window.

But it's true. The big three are tricky. You can count on having the devil, his angels, and the world as your enemies today. The devil, the world, and your own sinfulness are at war against you. It's scary, isn't it?

It's even scarier to think that there is no way you can win. You can be the wisest person, the most athletic person, the tallest person, the most talented person, the kindest person, or the richest person, and you will never win against the big three. It is impossible.

But it's Sunday. It's time for rejoicing. Look in God's Word. It's in your Bible. It is read, taught, and proclaimed in your church service. Jesus won the victory without us. He won the victory in us. Do you know how He did it? Do you know how much it cost?

Through His death and resurrection, Jesus fought and won. The daily battles continue, but through faith in Jesus, God gives us His gracious victory. He crowns us with forgiveness, life, and salvation. So go ahead and say with Paul that Jesus brought you to God, gave you life, and declared you sinless. "Thanks be to God, who gives us the victory through our Lord Jesus Christ" (1 Corinthians 15:57).

HAVE A GREAT SUNDAY!

Journal: Draw around your hand. In it, draw a victory flag for Jesus.

Pray: Lord Jesus, thank You for giving me the victory over sin, death, and the devil through Your death and resurrection. Amen. M. W.

Forgiving When It's Hard

Alexandra had created the perfect duct-tape pencil case. She had snipped, torn, and stuck something perfect. Then, in a moment, her hard work was ruined when Ian cut through it with scissors.

Alexandra was angry. She'd spent a long time on the project, and now it was ruined. Worse yet, Ian wasn't even sorry.

Sometimes it's hard to forgive people who hurt us. And it's especially hard when we think they're not even sorry. At times like that, it's important to remember what God has done for us. You see, we've offended Him by our sinful nature and by the things we've done against His Law. He tells us not to murder, but then we hate someone. He tells us we should have no other gods, but then we make friendships or possessions more important than Him.

We often sin against God in the things we do, say, and think. We don't even say we're sorry.

Living the life of a Christian is not easy. God holds us to a high standard, to forgive even when we don't feel like it. But what He has given is far more important than getting an apology from someone who has hurt us. He's given complete forgiveness and the promise of eternal life. In Christ's death on the cross, God has secured forgiveness for our sins, and for that we can be truly thankful.

Journal: Write about a sin someone committed against you and your feelings. Then, with a big brown marker, draw a cross over what you wrote.

Pray: Dear Jesus, it is often hard to forgive others. Please help me remember the kindness You have shown to me and so to be kind and forgiving. In Your name I pray. Amen. J. S.

Middle School Jitters

In two years, Paul would move up to middle school, but he was already worrying about what it would be like. He'd heard that the eighth graders were bullies, the lunch ladies were grouchy, and the homework was difficult. He had been looking forward to more sports in middle school, but from everything he heard, those were a challenge too.

At times, the hardest thing about life is knowing what to expect and not being afraid. When we don't know what to expect or when we expect the worst, life can seem like one scary episode after another. Maybe we dread going to the dentist, taking a difficult test, or playing in a piano recital. But the truth is that often our *anticipation* for such an event is much worse than the actual event itself.

Worry is not just a bad idea; it's a sin. God expressly tells us to avoid worry, just as we should avoid other sins. Why? Worry makes us doubt God's care. Worry makes us think of only the worst, when God promises to give us good things.

After all of Paul's worrying, he is enjoying middle school. He is on the track team and in the drama club. And the homework isn't so bad. Even the lunch ladies are nice.

So put your worries on a shelf, and place each day in our Savior's loving hands. Your Lord Jesus, who died to save you, will certainly carry you through all the difficulties in life.

Journal: Write a prayer asking God to help you with something you've been worrying about. Imagine placing that worry into God's strong hands.

Pray: Dear Jesus, thank You for always caring for me. Help me trust in You and give You all of my worries. In Your name I pray. Amen. J. S.

When God Shows Up

Where I live in Taiwan, it's a big deal when a god comes. Last year, people brought a new idol to my town. Everyone was very excited. Men carried idols from other temples in a big parade. People played music and set off fireworks. They had a stage with bright lights and set a big table of food for the gods.

But guess what! The Taiwanese gods didn't eat the food on the table. They never moved after people set them on the stage, and these gods never told the people they loved them. These "gods" were made by people. They weren't alive.

Do you remember when our God came to earth?

There was no parade or fireworks. Jesus came as a little baby. He was born in a simple stable and spent His life serving other people. He died for us and rose again to save us from our sins. Our God is able to answer our prayers and save us.

We don't have to make a god out of wood or gold and carry it on our shoulders. Our God made us and cares for us. *He* provides food for *us*. God tells us that He loves us and gives us everything we need from the time we are babies until we are old and gray.

And like when Jesus came, God still comes to us in simple ways when we read the Bible, go to church, and pray to Him.

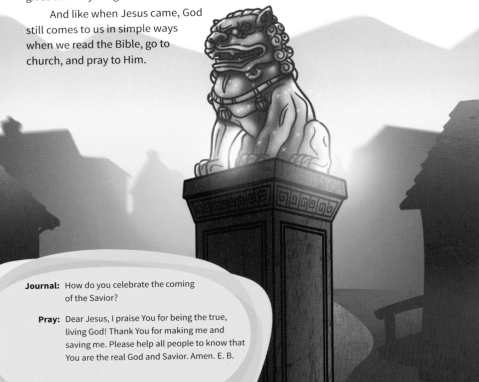

Journal: How do you celebrate the coming of the Savior?

Pray: Dear Jesus, I praise You for being the true, living God! Thank You for making me and saving me. Please help all people to know that You are the real God and Savior. Amen. E. B.

Overcome

Boy, it's a good thing you're a Christian. Your life is perfect, isn't it? Nothing ever goes wrong! Ever!

Wait a minute. That's not true, is it? Being a Christian doesn't mean that life will always be happy and worry-free. (After all, look at the life of Jesus. Not exactly smooth sailing all the time!)

No, Jesus tells us that we will have troubles in our lifetime. Friends will hurt us. Responsibilities will stress us out. Family members will die. Sometimes we might even feel overcome with sorrow, as if there is no way out of the pain we feel.

But even when our feelings overwhelm us, our faith tells us something different. Even through our tears, we have hope. Jesus tells us to take heart. The world will be a difficult place to live in sometimes, but Jesus assures us that He has overcome the world. When we feel overcome, we know Jesus has overcome it all. For us. We know this because He took our sins to the cross and overcame death three days later. Jesus won the victory.

No, life isn't always easy. But we don't have to worry about the outcome: Jesus won the ultimate victory, and He's right beside us every day.

Journal: Write down one struggle you're going through. Cross it out! Right next to it, write "Jesus won the victory!"

Pray: Dear Jesus, You know what it's like to suffer. You know what it's like to go through trouble. Thank You for promising to be with me every day. Thank You for overcoming the greatest enemies: sin, death, and the devil! In Your name I pray. Amen. L. C.

OCTOBER 6

Isaiah 53:2–3

Grapefruit

Do you like grapefruit? Some people say that the ugliest grapefruit are the sweetest and juiciest ones.

What about people? Are the ugliest people the sweetest? Are the pretty ones the most sour? Often we check out people the same way we check out fruit. Do you or your friends value how people look more than any other quality?

No matter what we look like on the outside, we don't look good on the inside. From the time we were conceived inside our mothers, we have had original sin. Original sin is inherited from Adam and Eve. It is a condition that makes us imperfect—ugly on the inside.

Do you think Jesus was ugly or fair? We don't know how He looked. Isaiah foretold that Jesus would not be beautiful (53:2). But what Jesus did for us was sweet and full of love. He came so that by faith in Him, all people might be saved from the ugliness of sin.

As a child of God, you received forgiveness, life, and salvation at Baptism. Now Jesus dwells with you and forgives your sins—those things you think, do, and say and those things that are a result of original sin.

Jesus came to save those who are sick and ugly in spirit. He lives in us. Because we are God's dear children, the Holy Spirit gives us the power to do sweet and wonderful things for others—no matter how we look.

Journal: What sweet and wonderful things is the Holy Spirit working in you?

Pray: Dear Jesus, I am sinfully ugly because I judge others by the way they look. Forgive me and lead me to value others as Your children. Amen. S. H.

Goldfish or Koi Fish?

"Look what I won at the school carnival!" Shaun said, excitedly showing Dad his new pet fish. "I named him Little Goldy."

"Hmm," Dad said as he studied Shaun's fish, "I wonder if it is a koi fish or a goldfish."

"What's the difference?" Shaun asked.

"Well, for one thing," Dad explained, "goldfish are from China and koi fish from Japan. Also, goldfish live only up to thirty years and grow around a foot in length. But koi fish can live forty years and longer, and they can grow to three feet or more!"

"Jeepers, Dad, I thought Little Goldy was just a tiny fish. I never dreamed he could get to be gigantic and cool!"

"You know, Shaun, what you thought about Little Goldy is a good example of what many Christians think about themselves. They think, 'Oh, I'm just a little fish. I could never be anything big or wonderful for God.' They forget that at their Baptism, the Holy Spirit brought the immeasurable greatness of God's power into their life. The same power that raised Jesus from the dead lives inside of *you*!"

"Wow, that's some superpower, Dad! I'll pray that I can do great things through Christ's power at work in me!"

Journal: Write a prayer thanking God for the gifts He has given you.

Pray: Thank You, God, for raising Jesus from the dead so we can live with Him forever and for giving us Your superpower to boldly share that message with others. In Jesus' name we pray. Amen. M. P.

Time to Relax!

ALL STAR

Do you know someone who has a collection? Maybe it is fossils, baseball cards, teddy bears, or comic books.

Do you have a hobby? Maybe you take part in Scouts, music, or sports. Maybe you like to read, draw, or take care of your pet. It's important that people have the chance to do something they enjoy. Why? People who have a hobby or take part in a relaxing activity are usually healthier. They fight off disease better, are sharper mentally, and will likely live longer than people who work hard all the time and never relax. God created people to work and to rest.

When God created the world, He worked for six days. Then, on the seventh day, He rested. In the Old Testament, God also commanded His people to rest on the seventh day so they could be refreshed. God's example and commands are also good for us. When we rest, we get recharged rather than worn out.

We sin when we think that we don't need to rest our bodies or when we don't rest our souls by receiving the refreshment of God's Word and Sacraments. We can read or study God's Word each day, but we can do it in a special way when we spend time in church and Sunday School. There we hear the reviving words of God's love and forgiveness for all our sins, because of Jesus' death and resurrection.

May God bless the relaxation time of your body and soul.

Journal: List the ways you relax your body and your soul.

Pray: Dear Father, thank You for time to relax and meet You in church. Forgive me when I do not take time to enjoy Your blessings. In Jesus' name. Amen. S. R.

Discover the Good News

"Yeah! No school!" exclaimed Rachel as she helped her mom get breakfast ready. "I *love* Columbus Day!"

"What do you know about Columbus Day, Rachel?"

"It's the day we remember that Columbus discovered America!" Rachel replied.

"Well, you're on the right track. Actually, he thought he had reached Asia. It was only then that he realized he had actually found a new land," Mom explained. "And the date of that first journey was October 12. In 1937, it was declared a national holiday by President Franklin D. Roosevelt. Later, in 1971, President Nixon moved the celebration day to the second Monday of the month."

"Thanks for the lesson, Mom. But I thought I had the day off from school," laughed Rachel.

Our reading today tells of another person on a voyage: the apostle Paul. He was not sent by the queen. He wasn't seeking a treasure or a new land. Paul was sent by God to proclaim the Good News of Jesus Christ and salvation to Gentile nations. Paul was giving others the treasures of God. He preached the greatest news of all: salvation won through Jesus Christ! God wanted people to know they could not be saved by keeping the Law. They needed faith in Jesus.

God has chosen you too, but not because of what you have done. You have been chosen by God's grace in Christ Jesus because of what He has done. That is God's Good News to share.

Journal: Do you know a rhyme about Columbus? Write a rhyme to remind you of Paul and the Good News he shared with all.

Pray: Heavenly Father, send Your Spirit to help me explore Your Word. I want to grow in the faith and knowledge of Jesus, my Savior. Thank You for the grace and peace You have given me. I am grateful for the Good News of the salvation Jesus won for me. In His name I pray. Amen. B. J. S.

OCTOBER 10

John 6:1–15

The Wrong Idea

Miriam was good at spelling, so the girls in her class thought she would win the geography bee. Wrong. She didn't even know where to find Kathmandu.

Kirby did amazing stunts on his bike, so the boys thought he was also a gymnast. Wrong. Kirby couldn't stand on his head.

Connor was a great soccer goalie, so his classmates thought he would be a good center in basketball. No way. He had trouble dribbling.

Clara played the clarinet without squeaking, so her friends thought she should try out to be the lead singer in the school musical. Wrong again. Clara was strictly an instrumentalist.

One day, Jesus did a miracle and turned five loaves of barley bread and two fish into enough food to feed five thousand people. There were even leftovers—twelve baskets of leftovers!

But some people in the crowd on the edge of the Sea of Galilee had a wrong idea about Jesus. They wanted Jesus to fix all their earthly problems and be their earthly king. Jesus knew what they were planning, and He went away from them.

That day, Jesus' miracle was a sign that He is the Christ, the Son of the living God. He had come to earth to be our Savior, to die for our sins and rise again.

Jesus is our heavenly King. He feeds us in spiritual ways. He forgives our sins and gives us eternal life. Now that's the *right* idea.

Journal: Miracles were signs that pointed to Jesus as God's Son. Write about your favorite miracle.

Pray: Dear Jesus, please take care of my need for food, a place to live, good friends, and a loving family. More important, take care of me so that I will always be Your child and live forever with You. Amen. G. P.

Foreigner!

As a blond American living in Taiwan, I stick out a lot. Many times when I'm in a store, a child will point at me and tell his mom, "Foreigner!" Other times when I'm biking, old men on their motorcycles slow down to stare at me and yell, "Hello!" I'm sure going to cause a traffic accident someday!

Have you ever felt like a foreigner? Maybe you play sports and you felt out of place at your sister's band concert. Or maybe you went to someone's house and were the only kid with all the adults. Did you ever get your face painted at the zoo and then have people stare at you when you drove home with zebra stripes?

Jesus says we are "not of the world" (John 15:19)—like foreigners—because we're Christians. We often look different from other people because we know Jesus. Sometimes people stare at us when we don't do what everyone else is doing. Sometimes we feel out of place going to church when everyone else is sleeping in. Sometimes people even laugh when we tell them what we believe.

Jesus understands. Jesus was mocked, spit on, and killed because others didn't understand who He was. Even though we may feel like foreigners here, we belong to a different country—God's kingdom. We are part of God's family, and our real home is in heaven. We will always be welcome there because of God's grace through Christ.

Journal: When is a time you have felt out of place in the world?

Pray: Dear Father, thank You for making me part of Your family and Your kingdom. Comfort me when I feel like a foreigner because I'm a Christian. Give me courage to live as Your child. Amen. E. B.

The Spirit Is with You

Have you ever seen the Holy Spirit? That's a silly question; if He's invisible, how could we see Him? You may not see the Holy Spirit, but you can know He is with you wherever you go.

God reminds us in His Word that "the Spirit helps us in our weakness" (Romans 8:26). Even when we can't see the Spirit, He is there to comfort us when we are sad, give us hope when we are afraid, and point us to our Savior, Jesus, who forgives our sins.

It's easy to get confused. We might ask, does God or anybody really love me? And why do I still sin? Jesus' disciples were human, just like us, and they were amazed that our Lord would forgive sin and promise people they would be in heaven. But that's just what grace is all about. God promises to pardon our sin and give us eternal life because of Jesus' perfect life and death in our place.

Jesus told His disciples, "I will send [the Helper] to you. . . . When the Spirit of truth comes, He will guide you into all the truth" (John 16:7, 13). The Holy Spirit has come upon us through the water of Holy Baptism and in God's Word.

He will guide you to trust that your salvation is secure through faith in Jesus. He will encourage you to trust God when you suffer or are sad or discouraged, even when you can't see Him.

Journal: Look up John 3:8. What does it mean to be "born of the Spirit"?

Pray: Dear Lord, through my problems, give me perseverance, character, hope, and most of all, faith that You are guiding me. In Jesus' name I pray. Amen. C. O.

Scared to Death?

The month of October is perhaps the scariest of the year. All month long, you might experience haunted houses, fright fests, and scary movies. Some people love the thrill of a haunted house.

A lot of the creepy-crawly activities in October are fun. There's no harm involved, and some spine-tingles are no big deal. But other things can be dangerous, and as Christians, we need to know the difference.

It's not okay, for example, to play with Ouija boards or to try to communicate with the dead. God says in the Bible that these activities are dangerous. We should not consult fortune-tellers or horoscopes or other things that try to tell the future. We can trust that our days are in the mighty and powerful hands of God. We don't need to fear what may come. In His perfect timing, God will reveal His plans to us.

We should also be careful about movies, TV shows, books, and music. We want our thoughts, words, and deeds to reflect the love of God in our lives. Sometimes, if we have too much "junk" in our minds, thoughts of God and His Word get shoved to the side. Instead, we should reflect on the things of God.

As baptized children of God, we have forgiveness through Christ for the times we fail to trust God, times we disobey His will. He is with us in all trials to strengthen our faith and guide us through His Word.

Journal: Think about some of your fears. Write a prayer to God beginning this way: "Dear God, I fear, love, and trust in You. These are the things I bring before You today . . ."

Pray: Dear Lord, thank You for not leaving me in my fears but instead saving and loving me with an eternal love. Help me fear, love, and trust only in You. Amen. J. S.

What Now?

"Hey, sis, how was the sleepover at Natalie's?" Annalise asked.

"It was okay," Olivia said. She didn't feel like talking about it.

"You don't seem happy. Did you have a fight or something?" Annalise asked.

"No," Olivia answered. "It just didn't turn out the way I had hoped. Natalie is my friend, but she doesn't go to church or Sunday School. I've been praying that I would have a chance to talk to her about Jesus. The sleepover seemed like the perfect time."

"Go on," Annalise said. "What happened?"

Olivia shook her head. "Nothing. Well, I did talk to Natalie, but she didn't care about what I was saying. She even joked about it," Olivia said.

Annalise put her arm around her sister. "I'm sorry Natalie didn't seem to care. Remember, God gives us opportunities, but it is the Holy Spirit who gives people faith.

"In our Bible study, we are reading about Paul," Annalise continued. "He traveled a lot of places to tell others about Jesus. Paul knew that the message of Jesus dying for all people's sins was super important. Some people didn't want to hear Paul's message though. They even tried to kill him. But Paul never gave up. And many people became believers because of his preaching."

"Thanks," Olivia said. "It's good to remember that the Holy Spirit, not me, gives people faith. I'll keep praying for Natalie, and I will invite her to church."

Journal: What did you learn from reading this devotion?

Pray: Dear Jesus, thank You for being my Savior. When I am able, give me words to tell others—especially my friends—about You. Amen. J. D.

The "No Sin" Day

Jack was quiet on the ride home from Sunday School. Finally, he said, "Mom, I think Mrs. Fisher was wrong. She said everyone sins, every day. I don't think I sin every day. In fact, I'm going to work *really* hard. Tomorrow will be my 'No Sin' day."

All the next day, Jack tried to be as good as possible. He didn't argue with his sister, he didn't talk back, and he didn't take anything that wasn't his. When recess was over, he even went to the end of the line.

At bedtime, Jack told his mom, "I was perfect today, Mom. I knew Mrs. Fisher was wrong."

"You did many good things today," his mom said, "but you weren't perfect. In fact, you are sinning right now. You were not humble, and your thoughts about Mrs. Fisher weren't kind."

Jack thought about what his mom said. "I guess Mrs. Fisher was right," he admitted. "Now I'm going to ask God to forgive *all* my sins, even the ones I didn't know I was doing."

Even when we try hard not to sin, we do. Because we are all sinners, we need God's forgiveness. That's why He sent Jesus to earth. When Jesus died on the cross, He paid the price for the sins of the whole world. God doesn't want us to sin, but because of His love for us, He does not hold our sins against us.

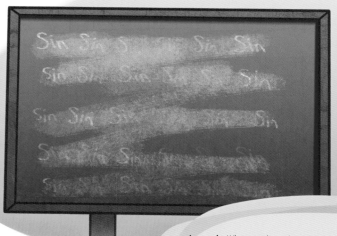

Journal: Who was the only sinless person who ever lived? (Hint: See 2 Corinthians 5:21.)

Pray: Dear Jesus, sometimes I am so proud that I think I don't need Your forgiveness. But I am wrong. I need You every day. Amen. P. L.

Trust Only Jesus

Who is a false teacher? They are ones who tell false or imaginary things about God. One way to recognize a false teacher is if he or she claims to know the date when Jesus will return. Jesus said, "And then if anyone says to you, 'Look, here is the Christ!' or 'Look, there He is!' do not believe it" (Mark 13:21). Jesus also said, "Concerning that day or that hour, no one knows" (Mark 13:32).

Many people have claimed to know when Jesus will return. But Jesus encouraged people to trust the Scriptures, which clearly teach the truth about Him and about the Last Day. Pastors, teachers, missionaries, and parents are given the responsibility of teaching God's Word to others. The Holy Spirit, working through the Word, creates faith in the hearts of those who hear.

Through that faith, Christians wait eagerly for the return of Christ. On that day (which the Bible says only God knows), there will be a final judgment against sin. But it will also be a day of joy and thanksgiving, as Christians who remain steadfast in the true faith see the one true God to whom they have prayed.

There will always be false teachers. But take heart—our Lord and Savior, Jesus, will come on the day appointed, and all of us who are baptized and believe in Him will live with Him forever in heaven.

Journal: Read Revelation 22:12–13. How does Jesus describe Himself?

Pray: Come, Lord Jesus, and take me and those I love to be with You. Amen. C. O.

Anytime, Anywhere

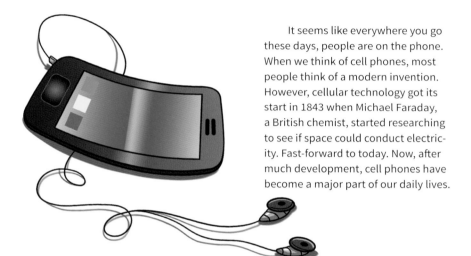

It seems like everywhere you go these days, people are on the phone. When we think of cell phones, most people think of a modern invention. However, cellular technology got its start in 1843 when Michael Faraday, a British chemist, started researching to see if space could conduct electricity. Fast-forward to today. Now, after much development, cell phones have become a major part of our daily lives.

Why do people love their cell phones so much? The phones can go almost anywhere, giving instant connection to friends and family anytime, from any place. Plus, today's cell phones can do more than just make phone calls. Many people use their phones for texting, email, games, taking pictures, telling time, and more. No wonder people love their cell phones!

In prayer, we have an instant connection to God Himself! There are no boundaries to where or when we can talk with God in prayer. Just like cell phones can do more than one thing, we can pray about more than one thing. There is no limit to the prayers we can bring to God!

As great as cell phones are, they can break, run out of battery, or be lost. With prayer, we never have to worry about those things. God invites us to "pray without ceasing," and He promises always to hear and answer our prayers!

Journal: Keep a list of special prayer requests for this week.

Pray: Thank You, God, for hearing and answering my prayers. Help me to use this gift to talk with You anytime, anywhere. Amen. H. L.

OCTOBER 18

John 14:28–31

Surprised by Joy

When Emmalynn came home from school, her mother was waiting to tell her important news. "Grandpa Bill died. It was very sudden. It's a surprise to all of us!"

Emmalynn burst out crying and went into her room. Her mother sat on the bed with her, and they talked about memories of Grandpa.

Two days later, when they arrived at her grandparents' house many miles away, Emmalynn was afraid everyone would be sad. She was in for a surprise. Grandma greeted them in the driveway. She was smiling and even laughed when the family dog jumped out of the car.

Grandma hugged Emmalynn and said, "It's so good to see you! Come in for some cookies."

"Grandma," said Emmalynn, "I thought you would be crying today. Don't you miss Grandpa?"

"Of course I do," Grandma replied, "but I know Grandpa's in heaven with Jesus. God always keeps His promises."

When someone we love dies, we feel lost and afraid at first. But we take comfort in knowing Jesus promised that there is a place for all believers. He promised to take us to be with Him!

Jesus died on the cross to pay for the sins of the world. After three days, Jesus rose again to assure us that truly there is life after death. He offers eternal life to all who have faith in Him as the Son of God.

Believing in Him as our Savior, we have the assurance that we are forgiven. We are "heaven bound" because we are baptized into His death and His resurrection. We can have joy in our hearts knowing that our loved ones live with Jesus forever and that someday we will see them again.

Journal: Think of someone you know who does not believe in Jesus. How can you be a good witness about the hope we have?

Pray: Christ, our Savior, risen from the dead, grant me joy in knowing there is truly life after death. In Your name I pray. Amen. C. O.

God's Wonderful Love

Kelly brought her friend Ellen home with her after school. As they walked to the front door, they heard a crying sound. "It's a kitten!" Kelly said.

They walked toward the sound. "It's in the shrubs," Ellen whispered. The orange kitten was too miserable to notice them. Its eyes looked glazed. Kelly spoke softly as she scooped it up in one hand.

"Yuck, Kelly, put it down!" Ellen said. "It has bugs all over it!"

She was right. The kitten was covered with fleas and tiny crawling bugs. Its eyes were swollen, and its fur was matted.

"Put it back!" Ellen said. "How can you stand to touch it?"

"I think it's beautiful," Kelly said. "It needs help."

"You think *all* cats are beautiful," Ellen responded.

"I'm going to give this kitten a bath," Kelly said. "Then I'm going to feed and brush it. Do you want to help or not?"

Imagine the ugliest thing you can think of. To God, sin is even uglier than that. Sin bothers God much more than fleas and bugs ever bother us. God is pure goodness, the very opposite of evil.

Sinners are a real mess. But when God looks at us, He doesn't see things such as our disobedience or selfishness as reasons to leave us alone. He sees us as His baptized children—marked with the cross of Christ, all our sins washed away. He scoops us up and says, "You're beautiful. I'm keeping you as Mine forever."

Journal: Some people think they are too bad for God to love. They think He would never want to come close to them. What could you tell those people?

Pray: Father in heaven, thank You for loving me. Forgive me when I do wrong, and keep me always close to You. In the name of Jesus. Amen. G. S.

OCTOBER 20

Psalm 51:1–2

Consequences

Jeffrey yelled, "Touchdown!" and got up from the ground. Out of the corner of his eye, he saw one of his mother's flowers. "Looks like I landed on the mum."

Later that afternoon, his mother came into his room. "I just noticed my bronze mum is in pretty bad shape, Jeff. Know anything about that?"

"Uh, which one?" Jeffrey asked.

"The one way in the back."

"What's wrong with it?"

"Looks like a first-down tackle."

Jeffrey paused. "Sorry, Mom," he finally said. "My friends came over. It was an accident. I'm really sorry."

"Thank you for being honest and for apologizing. I forgive you. We can get another bronze mum. I'll take the cost of it out of your allowance."

"Wait, Mom! I said I was sorry," Jeffrey protested. "Why do I have to pay for a new one?"

"Actions, even accidents, have consequences," Mom explained. "When you've done something wrong, it's important to confess it to the person you've offended and to God. I know you've done that. Have confidence that God forgives you. Jesus paid the consequences for all sin when He died on the cross."

Jeffrey stomped his foot and walked away. He needed time to think. Slowly, his resentment turned to sorrow and then to thanks. He considered the consequences Jesus had suffered and the price Jesus paid. Then he walked back to his mom. What do you think he said?

Journal: Write the word *consequences* in your journal. How can consequences be a good thing?

Pray: Thank You, Lord, for Jesus. You took the consequences of my sin and offer me forgiveness. Give me courage to accept the consequences of my actions without complaining. In Jesus' name I pray. Amen. V. S

Peace and Protection

After many months at sea, the submarine came into port. Within days, however, there came an urgent weather warning. A large storm was coming. Preparations were made to secure buildings and evacuate people. Ships were sent out to sea, away from the storm's path. The submarine went down below the surface. There, she rested in the safety of calm water while the storm raged above her.

Twenty-five feet or more below the surface, the water is always calm, no matter what is happening above. Fish swim lazily, and plant life is undisturbed as boats, human activity, and bad weather stir the water above them. The depth of the water protects and sustains them.

Like the vast sea He created, God's loving care is deep and wide. Sometimes life gets stormy, like when the high winds of family problems, illness, accidents, and losses blow into our lives. It may seem like the trouble will wash over us.

In His Word and Sacraments, our powerful and loving God promises to be with us and protect us during those times. No matter what is going on, His love holds us and never changes. God the Father loved us enough to send His only Son to die for our sins. Since He cared enough to solve our biggest problem, sin, we can trust Him with everything else. The depth of His love will help us ride out the storms, knowing He is always near.

Journal: How can God's peace help you right now, today?

Pray: Father, I thank You for the care You give me. When storms come into my life, give me Your peace, and help me trust You. For Jesus' sake I pray. Amen. D. N.

On the Clouds

On this date in 1797, a Frenchman named André-Jacques Garnerin made the first parachute jump from a high altitude. He made a big parachute and attached it to a basket. He went up about 3,200 feet with a hydrogen balloon and jumped over Paris, France. People were amazed to see him coming from the sky.

One day, we will look up at the clouds and see someone else coming down—Jesus! He promised His disciples that He would return on the Last Day, though we don't know when that day will be. The Lord will come down from heaven. Those Christians who have already died will rise first. Then those who are alive will go up in the clouds. We will be with the Lord forever. All this is explained in today's reading.

What a wonderful day that will be! We won't have any more problems like sickness or pain. We won't ever get mad and say things we shouldn't. We won't be tempted to disobey. And we'll never have a bad day! Imagine always being with Jesus in heaven!

Christians gather to worship and to learn more about Jesus and His forgiveness. They gather to pray and give Him thanks and praise. We don't deserve His love, but He loves us anyway. Yes, He will return for all those who trust Him to save them. Maybe He'll come back today!

Journal: Draw a picture of Jesus returning on the clouds. Be sure to include Christians who will join Him there.

Pray: Jesus, help us to watch and be ready for Your return, maybe even today! Keep us faithful, that we may live forever with You. Amen. R. G.

God Formed You

Has anyone ever told you, "You sure are growing fast." But did you know that you grew much faster *before* you were born? Babies grow faster before birth than at any other time in their lives!

Inside your mom, God formed you smaller than the period at the end of this sentence. Just eighteen days later, your heart began to beat. The next day, your eyes formed. A week later, your arms and legs began to grow; so did your nose and mouth. Your brain was working.

At two months, you had every organ in your body. At three months, you could breathe and swallow, sleep and stay awake. At four months, you could swim, turn somersaults, kick, and suck your thumb. All this was before you were even born!

God had a great plan to make each of us as a baby in our mom's womb. The Bible says He knew us and loved us way back then. But do you know how He loved us the best? He sent His Jesus as a baby inside His mother, Mary. Jesus grew just like we do. Then He was born in Bethlehem and grew up so He could die on the cross to save us. He rose on Easter, and someday we also will rise and live with Him forever in heaven.

When you see a pregnant woman, remember that babies are special because God forms them and sent Jesus for them.

Journal: Look at one of your baby pictures. Write about how you looked.

Pray: God, You formed us in our mothers. Thank You for sending Jesus as a baby to save us. Amen. R. G.

The Eight-Year-Old King

How did Josiah, only eight years old, know how to be a king?

For the first few years, he just studied about being a king. His advisers did most of the ruling. Then, when he was in his twenties, Josiah gave an order to repair the temple. In the temple, a high priest found a long-lost book. King Josiah was so excited that he ordered the elders of Judah to come to Jerusalem. Josiah read to them all the words of the Book of the Covenant. The people once again became faithful to the Lord and promised to follow His will.

It's okay to be young. When Mozart was only eight years old, he composed music that's still played today. When Jesus was twelve, He spent time in the temple, carrying out God's plan to save the world. When Julie was ten, she walked twenty miles in a marathon to raise money to send a missionary to a foreign country. Later, she became a missionary. When Aaron was eleven, he volunteered to tutor a third grader who was having trouble with math. Now Aaron is a math teacher.

You are probably not a king or even a prince, but you are God's child through Baptism and an heir of God's kingdom. You are free to use the gifts and talents God has given you for a meaningful today and for as many tomorrows as God gives you.

Journal: What are some things you can do now that will help you to be faithful to God's will when you are older?

Pray: Dear God, thank You for making me Your child in Baptism and for blessing me with a future with You forever. In Jesus' name I pray. Amen. D. S.

His Plans for You

Ever feel like nothing was going according to plan? Maybe you were all packed up and ready to go on vacation when an emergency stopped your family from getting in the car. Maybe you were looking forward to seeing a longtime friend when a fight early on ruined the rest of the day.

Sin gets in the way of things. Things like sickness and tragedy exist because we live in a fallen world. Nothing is perfect like it should be. And sometimes, bad things that happen are even our fault. We don't listen, and we break something. We get angry at school, and we hurt our friend's feelings.

For the kingdom of Judah, things went very wrong, and it *was* their fault. They didn't listen to God, and they wound up in the hands of the enemy, their homes and families lost.

But whether or not things go our way and whether or not it's our fault, God still loves us. He loved the people of Judah, and He told them that He had plans—good plans—for their future. God knew what was best for them. He says the same to us. You can trust in the plans He has for you.

God sent His Son, Jesus, to make all things right again. Because of Jesus, sin won't change our plans for eternity. We have the certain hope of a perfect life in heaven with God.

Journal: Name the best plan God has for you—because of Jesus, you know what that is!

Pray: Dear God, I don't always trust in You or Your plans. Forgive me for the times I think my plans are better than Yours. Thank You for the best plan of all—my forgiveness and eternal life because of Jesus Christ. Amen. L. C.

What Makes a Person Rich?

Jason looked at the Monopoly board. His cousin Susan owned lots of hotels, and his game piece was getting close to them.

"You're in trouble now," Susan said.

Jason's stack of money was almost gone. He'd lose the game for sure if he landed on a hotel. Jason rolled the dice then let out a groan.

Susan's fists shot up into the air. "Yes! I own Park Place. Hand over all your cash. I win!"

In the game of Monopoly, the point is to accumulate as much property and money as you can. Unfortunately, a lot of people treat real life like a game of Monopoly. They think the more money they have, the happier they will be.

God tells us something different. He says that the more we give, the happier we'll be. There's nothing wrong with making money and having nice things. But when those things become more important than God or other people, our life is out of balance.

When Jesus came to earth, He could have done anything He wanted. But instead of accumulating money, He gathered people to Him. He served them and showed them the love of His Father. Then He made the ultimate sacrifice, paying for our sins with His death on the cross. A lot of people thought Jesus lost that day, but they were wrong. He rose from the dead and now waits for us in His heavenly. No hotel on Park Place can compare to that!

Journal: Can you think of ways that people make possessions more important than God? Who has shown God's love to you today?

Pray: Dear Jesus, thank You for giving Your life to pay the debt for my sin. Please help me to give my time and attention to others today. Amen. J. A.

Psalm 27:1

Stronger Than the Evening News

Jana pushed her food around on her dinner plate as her parents and older brother, Matt, talked about a story they'd heard on the evening news. When the conversation died down, Dad put his hand on her shoulder.

"What's wrong, Jana?" he asked. "It's not like you to be so quiet."

She shrugged. "I hate the news. It's always so depressing."

"Not always," Matt said.

"Just about," she shot back. "They hardly ever talk about anything good. It's always about politicians fighting, wars, and people dying."

Mom put down her fork. "It's not very nice to hear about, is it?"

"No. And it scares me."

Jana expected her brother to make fun of her, but instead, he nodded his head. "When I was your age, it used to scare me too."

"But it doesn't anymore?" Jana asked.

"Nope."

"Why not?"

Matt smiled. "Because God is stronger than all that. He loves me, and He saved me from my sins. So I believe He's going to save me from all evil, all that depressing stuff on the news. If it doesn't happen now, it will happen in heaven."

"Well put," Dad said. Then he looked at the chicken on Jana's plate. "Hmm, I'm still hungry. Are you going to eat that?"

"You bet," she said, spearing the piece of chicken with her fork. "I'm starving!"

Journal: Is there anything going on in the world today that scares you? Talk to your parents or a trusted grown-up about it.

Pray: Dear God, I know You are stronger than all the evil in the world. Help me to remember Your protection and safety when I'm scared. Amen. J. A.

OCTOBER 28

Romans 8:1–2

No Condemnation

Laurie's conscience was bothering her. Yesterday at lunch she did something she now regrets. She said something mean about Jenny, a girl in her class who has a disability. She called her a really hurtful name. Later she found out Jenny had heard her, and so had Miss Jones, their teacher.

Of course, Laurie got in trouble, and she was sorry for what she had done. It was hard, but with tears in her eyes, she apologized to Jenny and Miss Jones. Jenny forgave her, but Laurie couldn't forget the sad, hurt look in her eyes.

Even though Laurie knew that Jesus had forgiven her, she still felt guilty. It was hard for her to sleep and hard for her to eat. Finally, Laurie decided to talk to Miss Jones again about her guilt.

Miss Jones was very understanding. She knew Laurie was sorry. Miss Jones read a Bible verse from Romans 8. She reminded Laurie that when we trust in Jesus as our Savior, we can be certain that all of our sins are forgiven. We do not have to feel guilty anymore. God's Word says there is no condemnation for those who trust in Jesus as their Savior. The devil tries to make us feel guilty, but we are not guilty. Jesus paid for our sins once and for all when He died on the cross. We are forgiven!

Journal: Romans 8:1 says, "There is therefore now no condemnation for those who are in Christ Jesus." What does that mean? Do we still need to say we are sorry when we hurt someone?

Pray: Heavenly Father, thank You for sending Jesus to die for my sins. Help me to leave my sin, shame, and condemnation at the foot of the cross as I trust in You, my Savior and Lord. Amen. J. D.

Pumpkins Everywhere

Quick—what's the first fall food that comes to mind? Many people would say pumpkins. You can do a lot with pumpkins. You can make pies and bread. You can make muffins and soup. Some families use pumpkins to decorate their home. You might scoop out the inside and carve a silly face on one. Pumpkins are a versatile food.

But what if pumpkins were the *only* kind of food? What if there were no other fruits or vegetables? Can you imagine how boring it would be? Pumpkin pancakes, pumpkin ice cream, pumpkin frozen yogurt, pumpkin turnovers, pumpkin ravioli . . . too much pumpkin would get very old, very fast.

When God created the world, He could have taken a shortcut. He could have decided to make only one kind of tree, one kind of flower, one kind of bird. Imagine a world with only pine trees, sunflowers, and doves. Each one is beautiful, but without variety, you'd get tired of seeing them all the time.

God created a world full of unique and different things. He knows everything we need and everything that makes us happy. We may not require a world of variety, but He knows we enjoy it more.

Because of the faith God gives us in Jesus Christ, we are free to enjoy the world He made for us. And because of our faith, we look forward to the day when we'll live in the perfect home He's prepared for us in heaven.

Journal: List five things you are especially thankful to God for creating.

Pray: Thank You, God, for all the wonderful things You've created. Be with me today, and help me notice the variety of all things around me. In Jesus' name I pray. Amen. J. A.

OCTOBER 30

Romans 1:16–17

Luther's Great Discovery

Martin Luther was born in Eisleben (ICE lay ben), Germany, on November 10, 1483. When he was growing up, he thought of God as a harsh judge who would punish him. He thought that if he'd done too many wrong things, he'd go to hell.

One day, Martin was caught in a terrible thunderstorm. He prayed for protection and promised to become a monk if he was saved from the storm. When the storm passed, Martin was safe. He kept his promise and entered a monastery at age 21.

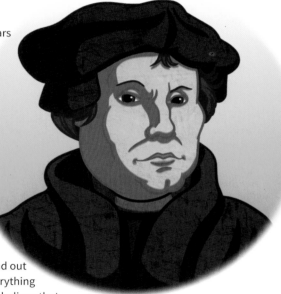

While in the monastery, Martin had many doubts and fears about salvation. He felt that he must *earn* his way into heaven. So Luther often starved himself and beat himself, trying to please God.

Martin Luther became a priest. He enjoyed reading and studying the Bible and then teaching and preaching about what he had learned. He eventually discovered God's truth about salvation in Romans 1:16–17.

After years of trying to earn his way into heaven, Luther found out that Jesus had already done everything for him! All he needed to do was believe that Jesus had suffered and died for him, and he would receive God's gift of salvation. And he learned that even this faith was a gift to him through the power of the Holy Spirit.

How relieved and happy Luther was to learn that God is not only a judge; He is also and especially a God of grace who saved us through His Son.

Journal: What gifts does God give to those who read His Word?

Pray: Dear God, thank You for bringing us to faith in Jesus. Please give us Your Spirit's guidance as we read and study the Bible. In Jesus' name I pray. Amen. A. B. W.

No More Indulgences

At the time of Martin Luther, the Christian Church in Europe had something called "indulgences." These were pieces of paper that people bought, believing that they brought forgiveness of sins.

As for those who had died, a priest named John Tetzel used this slogan: "As soon as the coin in the coffer rings, the soul from purgatory springs." Many people believed wrongly in a place called purgatory. Christians were said to go there after death to be purged, or cleansed. Tetzel asked people to give money so that their loved ones would get out of purgatory.

Martin Luther believed selling indulgences was wrong. On October 31, 1517, he nailed the Ninety-Five Theses, or statements, on a church door in Wittenberg, Germany. These statements said that we should rely on the forgiveness of God and not on indulgences. Luther believed that the Bible teaches we are justified (or saved) by God's grace, through faith alone. People cannot buy or earn their way to heaven. Heaven is a gift from God through Jesus.

When Luther was asked to take all this back, he said:

"Here I stand. I can do no other. God help me. Amen."

He had to stick to what the Bible taught, not what sinful people decided to teach.

Remember this great Reformation theme from Romans 5:1: "Since we have been justified by faith, we have peace with God through our Lord Jesus Christ." Praise God that Christians believe this today.

Journal: What does the Reformation begun by Martin Luther mean in your life? Why do we still need the Bible truths that Luther taught?

Pray: Lord God, I love You so much. I pray that You will forgive my sin and reform me every day to be more like You. Make me strong in what I believe, and comfort me with Your love. In Jesus' name I pray. Amen. D. P.

Who Is a Saint?

Today is All Saints' Day, a day when we think of Christians who once lived on earth but now live with God in heaven.

The Bible doesn't tell much about what heaven is like. On the cross, Jesus told the thief next to Him that he would be in paradise. Passages in the Bible say that in heaven no one will be hungry or sad.

Some TV shows and movies pretend that those who have died become angels. They sit on puffy clouds or fly around, trying to help humans still on earth. That is not true. It is just someone's imagination. We know that whoever believes in Christ as his or her Savior from sin lives forever in the presence of God after dying on earth.

Does a person have to die to become a saint? No. You became a saint when God gave you a new life and made you His child. For most of us, that happened when we were baptized. In Baptism, God gave you a new identity as His child. Even though you live as a sinner in this world, you are a saint.

Therefore, on All Saints' Day we thank God for His grace. We thank Him for the millions of saints who have already died in Christ. We also thank Him that He has made us saints who will someday join them.

Journal: In your journal, write the names of some saints you know.

Pray: Thank You, God, for the faithful witness of all the saints who have ever lived. Keep my faith in Jesus strong so that someday I will be a heavenly saint. In Jesus' name I pray. Amen. D. N.

Reach Out to Others

He dyed his hair red and wore overalls. Trace was a funny boy who didn't mind being different. Some students made comments, but his friends knew him as a nice person.

When Jesus was in Capernaum, He asked Matthew to follow Him. Matthew's job was to collect taxes for the government. Some tax collectors were dishonest. When some religious leaders saw Jesus with Matthew, they said it was wrong for Jesus to be his friend.

Jesus disagreed. He said, "Those who are well have no need of a physician, but those who are sick. . . . I came not to call the righteous, but sinners" (Matthew 9:12–13).

Jesus taught them that everyone is a sinner who needs to repent and seek first the kingdom of God. He commanded His disciples to baptize people so they would receive forgiveness of sins and the promise of eternal life. Jesus told the Matthew about God, who freely offers grace to all who have faith in Him, and Matthew believed!

This is how the Church grows! When we make friends with others who don't know Jesus, we can tell them about our faith in the triune God—Father, Son, and Holy Spirit.

As we treat them with respect, we often discover they are willing to listen to us. Trace was open to talking about many things, including God. Perhaps his Christian friends were part of God's plan for helping him hear the Good News!

Journal: Think of people from the Bible who were different but who believed in Jesus as the Son of God.

Pray: Father in heaven, open my eyes to those who need to be loved. In Jesus' name. Amen. C. O.

NOVEMBER 3

Ephesians 5:1–2

A Look at Differences

My brother and I have the same parents but we have different hair colors and eyes. We aren't the same height or size. Perhaps you have a sister or brother who looks a little different from you.

God made us and formed us, but each one of us is unique. We each have fingerprints that are entirely our own. We have different personalities and even different laughs.

Sometimes we have trouble loving people who are different from us. When the difference is the color of skin, we may become suspicious. When people from another country or culture approach us, we may try to avoid them.

Jesus loves us all. During His earthly ministry, Jesus reached out to those whom others feared or despised. Jesus didn't say, "I came to save those who are nice looking and don't get into trouble." He came to seek and rescue all who were lost. His death and resurrection are for all. He saw no differences among those He came to save. They were all considered lost and in need of redemption.

When God's children imitate Christ's love, we reflect His grace and live for the sake of others—no matter the color of their skin or what their culture is or what language they speak. When we sin toward others, we need not be discouraged, for God's forgiving grace is waiting for us in abundance.

Journal: How does Jesus treat differences among people? What does Jesus say to you when you realize that you have been unkind to someone who is different from you?

Pray: Dear Lord, thank You for making each of us unique. Help us to look at others with Your eyes of love. In Jesus' name I pray. Amen. C. W.

S'more of God's Word

If you want to make s'mores but don't have a campfire, try a solar oven. Line a small box with foil. Place your stack of graham crackers, chocolate, and marshmallow inside the box. Take the box outside and point it toward the sun. In a few minutes, the chocolate should be soft. The sun makes the chocolate melt. This snack is called a "s'more" because when you eat one, you want *some more.*

David wanted to hear more about God. In fact, the reading for today tells us that David couldn't get enough of hearing God's Word. He rejoiced at the opportunity to worship God in His temple. Of course, David had it easy, right? God made him king and helped him kill Goliath. David had real reasons to want to go to the temple to worship.

But wait a minute. David knew that worship was itself a blessing. We, too, have much to be thankful for in our lives. Maybe we haven't slain a giant, but we have benefited from so many blessings from God. One of those blessings is God's love. He sent His Son to suffer and die for our sin. The Son's sacrifice is how we are saved. Indeed, when we go to church, several things happen. We receive God's power though His Word and Sacraments. We also pray and thank God for His blessings. We sing and present our offerings.

As we gather with other Christians, God's sweet gifts pour out more and more.

Journal: Make it a point to learn three new things about your church's worship service. What would you like to know?

Pray: Dear Lord, thank You for the blessing of worship. Create in me a desire to worship You and learn Your Word. In Jesus' name I pray. Amen. K. D. M.

NOVEMBER 5

Hebrews 13:15–16

A Majestic Place and More!

When everyone in church stood up, Jordan couldn't see the pastor. But he heard his voice: "In the name of the Father and of the Son and of the Holy Spirit." The people said, "Amen," and turned to face the back of the sanctuary. Jordan heard organ music. A boy Jordan knew from Sunday School carried the processional cross.

After the opening part of worship, Jordan followed along. He heard the pastor read a Bible passage from Hebrews: "Let us continually offer up a sacrifice of praise to God" and "Do not neglect to do good and to share what you have."

Yes, Lord, Jordan thought, I'm here with all these people to hear Your Word.

Isn't it amazing how we learn about the church service? We watch others, listen to their words, and pray along with the pastor as he speaks to God. The Lord comes to us in worship—through His Word, the Scripture-based hymns, the words of pastors, and the Sacraments. We receive God's gifts, His divine gifts.

Jordan doesn't understand everything he sees, but that doesn't matter. In the church service, people of all ages experience the same thing. What Jordan does understand is this: God is holy and has offered everyone forgiveness through His Son.

Jordan is God's child. Each week, he offers a sacrifice of praise in a majestic place. He receives God's gifts. He knows that he belongs in God's house.

Journal: Describe the altar in your church and its furnishings.

Pray: Dear Lord, forgive me when I do not see the wonderful gifts in Your house. Give me a childlike wonder that I might hear and receive Your forgiveness, life, and salvation. In Jesus' name I pray. Amen. C. O.

No Comparison

Becky stomped into the kitchen and dropped her books. "I'm guessing you didn't have a great day," her mother said.

Becky sighed. "It was the worst day ever!"

"You were in such a good mood this morning." Mom and Becky sat at the kitchen table. "What happened?"

"Well, last week, all the girls at school were wearing those flared-leg jeans—you know, like the pair you bought for me on Saturday."

Her mom nodded.

"I was so excited that I'd finally be like everyone else. But today, skinny jeans are in. It's like the girls got together over the weekend and decided to change the style!" Becky laid her forehead on the table.

"Honey, that's a problem you'll have your entire life. There's only one solution."

Becky looked up. "What?"

"Stop comparing yourself to other people. Instead, be content. God wants us to be content with what He has given us. That isn't easy. We can become jealous if we don't have what other people have. God wants you to be content and know that He will never leave you, no matter what clothes you have. God gives you all you need for your earthly life. More important, He gives you what you need for your salvation! After all, He sent His Son to die for you and give you eternal life."

Becky shrugged. "I'm sorry. You're right, Mom." Then she smiled. "And I know God loves me no matter what jeans I wear."

Journal: If God gives the gift of contentment, how can you get it?

Pray: Dear heavenly Father, forgive me when I compare myself to others. Give me contentment through Jesus, my Savior. Amen. J. A.

God's in Charge!

"There are too many laws to remember," John remarked to his dad

"Are you studying our government in school right now?" Dad asked.

"Yes, and it seems there are so many rules we have to follow," John said.

"Why do you think that is?" Dad asked.

"I think it's because somebody just wants to be in charge and make us do what they want," replied John.

Dad said, "Being in charge can be tough at times. The people in our government work hard to lead us well. Sometimes things work okay for them, but sometimes they don't. Do you remember who always leads us and takes care of us the right way?"

John brightened up. "Jesus, of course."

"That's right," Dad affirmed. "Jesus did what His Father in heaven wanted. The biggest thing our Father wanted is to have us in His family. That's why Jesus died on the cross for us. He was punished for our sins. Since Jesus rose from the dead, we get to live in His family forever."

"So God's in charge?" John asked.

"He's the King. It's great to have our Father be our King. We know He will always lead well. That's such great news!" Dad shared.

"It sure is," John said.

Journal: Write a list of people who are in charge. Pray for each of these people this week.

Pray: Father in heaven, You are the King of all! Thank You for bringing me into Your family. I praise Your name! Amen. S. R.

Light That Can't Be Hidden

NOVEMBER 8

Matthew 5:14–15

Lighthouses serve two main purposes: to guide ships to the harbor and to keep ships from crashing against the rocks. Just imagine being on a ship in the middle of the night, surrounded by darkness and fog. It would be nearly impossible to navigate safely if you could not see where you were going. But then a light cuts through the fog. Now you know in what direction to go.

As Christians, we are called to be a light to the world. The love of Christ and the hope we have in Him shines through us. People see there's something different, and they want to know more.

Think of what your faith means to you. Does it bring you joy to know you have a loving heavenly Father who watches over everything you do? Does it give you peace to know that you have a Savior who died in your place so that you can have forgiveness and eternal life?

Now think of the people who don't know Jesus or who have turned away from their faith. They are like sailors in a dark ocean. They have no direction. They don't know which way to turn. But then they see the light.

God wants to use us as beacons of hope in a hurting world. He wants the light of His love to shine through us so brightly that it draws people out of the darkness and back to Him.

Journal: Do you know someone who seems lost in the darkness? How can you be God's light for that person?

Pray: Dear heavenly Father, thank You for filling me with the light of Your love. Help me to share that light with others. Amen. J. A.

Spiritual Nutrition

In eighteenth-century England, John Montagu, the Fourth Earl of Sandwich, began asking his valet to bring him meat tucked between two pieces of bread. People had eaten this type of food before, but there wasn't a name for it. The earl's friends started ordering "the same as Sandwich." Eventually, the word *sandwich* stuck.

Some people like their sandwiches cut in half to form two rectangles. Some like them whole. Others want the crusts cut off. But one thing everyone agrees on—you need bread to make a sandwich.

But can you imagine if there was nothing else in the sandwich? What if it were just two pieces of bread stuck together? It would be unsatisfying.

Jesus told His disciples that no man can live by bread alone. But He wasn't talking about actual bread. He was referring to people who take care of their body's physical needs only. Jesus was speaking about people who worry about what they'll eat and drink. They worry about their clothes and their homes. But they ignore their spiritual needs.

What is spiritual food? Taking part in worship and Sunday School, remembering your Baptism, reading your Bible, and praying all feed your soul. Sharing the love of Jesus with a friend feeds your soul, as does telling others how Jesus sacrificed Himself and paid the price for all people's sins. As you feed your body with nutritious food, ask the Holy Spirit to do the same for your soul.

Journal: Have you been getting enough spiritual nutrition? In what ways have you done so? What else might you try?

Pray: Dear Lord, feed my soul today, and show me ways to bless others. Amen. J. A.

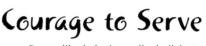

Courage to Serve

Danae liked playing volleyball, but it was stressful. She worked hard, but she still felt like the worst player on the team. One day during practice, the stress got to Danae. She slipped out to use the restroom and didn't go back to the gym. An assistant coach found her sitting on some stairs. "What's up?" Coach Anita asked.

"Nobody wants me on the team," Danae said. "I should just quit."

Coach Anita listened and gently encouraged her. "Oh, I'm not so sure you have your facts right," she said. "We need a player like you on our team. When I watch you, I see a girl who wants to do her best and is learning new skills, even though it takes work.

"Doing new things is hard," Coach Anita continued. "Did you know that God promised Joshua that He would go before him as he did something hard? God will also go before you. He goes ahead of you to school. Even before our games, He is on the court. Before you go home, God's already there to help you and your mom."

"I figured you'd try to make me feel better," Danae said. "I guess I should believe Jesus is my strength, even if I've been frustrated." Then Danae smiled and asked, "Do you really think I can play this game?"

"I can't promise you'll be a star," said her coach, "but I know you can honor God by doing your best."

Journal: Name some athletes you know who are Christians. Do you see Christlike qualities in anyone on a team at your school?

Pray: Dear God, please give me strength to learn new things and to do my best, even when something is hard. Thank You for assuring me in Your Word and in my Baptism that You are with me every day. In Jesus' name I pray. Amen. C. O.

Bumps on a Log

Here's a recipe for you to make and enjoy. Wash a celery stick and cut it into pieces four inches long. Spread each piece with peanut butter and top it with sunflower seeds.

While munching on your celery, think about being a "bump on a log" and about today's Bible reading. What was so wrong about what the third servant did? After all, he kept the money safe until the master returned.

His sin was that he didn't trust God enough to use the gift. He sat around like a bump on a log. He took no risks with his talent, and he did no good. God doesn't give us blessings so that we might guard and hide them. He gives them to us for a purpose. His gifts of food, clothes, family, and money are for us to use. Through them we can learn more about God; we can also use them to spread the Good News of Jesus. Any talents or abilities God has given you are also for this purpose.

God has a plan for you, and His plan for you includes the use of your gifts and talents. Through Jesus' death and resurrection, Jesus forgives you. He gives you purpose and courage. His plan shows up as you play in band, rake leaves, shop with a friend, serve as an acolyte, or visit your grandmother! So have some more celery, and enjoy using your gifts in God's plan.

Journal: Make a list of five blessings you have received from God. Write down one way to use or share each blessing.

Pray: Dear Lord, thank You for loving me. Thank You for the many blessings in my life. Keep me from sitting on a log. Help me to share Your love and my blessings with others. In Jesus' name I pray. Amen. K. D. M.

A Nest by Your Altar

One Sunday, I was sitting in Trinity Lutheran Church, El Reno, Oklahoma, listening to Pastor Phillip's message. Behind the altar, sunshine was sparkling rainbows through the colorful stained glass window. Suddenly I noticed a flicker behind the glass. As I watched, I saw tiny birds fluttering behind the corner of the window. I smiled as I thought how sweet that the little birds built their nest near God's altar.

I leaned over to whisper to my daughter, Lisa, "Look, honey, even the birds want to be at God's house!" I had to quickly shush her as she started to squeal and point with excitement.

Later that week, Psalm 84:3–4 was a part of my devotion, so I just had to share it with Lisa.

Some people may ask, "Why do we have to go to church?" But at our house, everyone knows that we don't *have* to go to church . . . we *get* to go to God's house! How blessed we are to have the freedom and joy of being able sit in God's house, hearing His message of salvation—that Jesus Christ has given us forgiveness of sins and eternal life through His death and resurrection! It is our privilege to show our thanks and sing praises to the Lord of the universe, our Father, our friend.

Journal: Draw a picture of the altar in your church.

Pray: How lovely is Your dwelling place, O Lord Almighty! Amen. M. P.

Don't Worry . . . Be Happy!

Some people love Mondays. They look at them as a time to start fresh. But for other people, Mondays cause worry. They think about all the things they need to do.

Which kind of person are you? Is Monday a chance to learn new things at school and catch up with friends? Or do you worry about homework, tests, sports practice, and chores at home?

Jesus tells us not to worry. In today's Scripture reading, He tells us to seek first the kingdom of God (Matthew 6:33). God is to be the top priority in our lives.

Jesus says that the birds never worry about where their next meal is coming from. God takes care of them. And if He takes care of them, He will surely take care of us, the children He loves.

Sometimes it's hard not to worry. If your family is having financial problems or someone you love is sick, it might not seem like God is taking care of you, but He is.

God gave us His Word, the Bible, to remind us of His love. And He took care of our most important need: salvation from our sins. He showed us just how much He loves us by sending His Son to die for us and win victory over death.

Try beginning each day by spending time with God. You can pray or read the Bible or do both. Putting God first is the best way to start your day!

Journal: Write down one thing you want to accomplish this week. How can spending time with God each day help you reach your goal?

Pray: Heavenly Father, thank You for seeing my needs and taking care of them. Help me not to worry, and help me to put You first. Amen. J. A.

Harvesttime

My grandfather was a cotton farmer. Late in February, Grandpa would use his tractor to plant the cotton seeds. Then over the next months, he would pray for just the right amount of rain and sunshine. He would pray that bugs would not eat his plants. But mostly, he would wait until the plants flowered and opened up to show the cotton "boll." When he saw the white field of bolls, he knew it was harvesttime.

Harvesting cotton was a family affair. Everyone was needed. My grandma and mom and all her siblings would help in the fields and drive the machinery that picked the cotton.

Jesus tells us that the harvest is ready today, but He isn't talking about cotton or corn. Jesus means that there are many people in our world who are ripe and ready to hear about God's love and believe in Jesus as their Savior. But He says there aren't enough workers.

Tractors and machines can't do this kind of work. Jesus says we need people to preach and teach about the love of God. Church workers in our congregations can do this in our neighborhood. Missionaries can do it around the world. With God's help, we can do it with our family and friends. Because the harvest is ripe, we want workers in the kingdom. We want everyone to know about Jesus' love. We want everyone to receive Jesus' gifts of forgiveness, life, and salvation.

Journal: Jesus sent someone to tell you about His love. Who are those workers?

Pray: Heavenly Father, You say the harvest is plentiful and people are ready to hear the Good News. Help me pray for those who preach and teach about You. Help me share this news too. In Jesus' name I pray. Amen. A. B.

Up and Over

The mother duck was frantic. She was in the middle of a four-lane street with her seven ducklings. Cars was screeching and swerving around her. She couldn't get those babies safely across the street.

A car suddenly came to a stop by the frightened duck family. A man and woman jumped out of the car. The woman stopped traffic while the man lifted each duckling to safety. All the mother duck saw was someone messing with her babies. She snapped, quacked, and hissed at the man. But the man just kept helping the ducks until they were on the other side of the street.

Do you have any obstacles in your life? Some obstacles are small, but some may seem impossible to overcome.

The ducks didn't make it over the obstacle alone. They had rescuers. God puts people in your life who love you and want to help you when things get tough. The mother duck didn't want to let the people help her, but they did, and it all worked out.

God loves you and wants to give you strength and guidance to make it through all the hardships and obstacles in front of you. God never said our days would be easy. After all, we live in a sin-filled world with all kinds of difficulties. That's why God sent Jesus to be our rescuer. He died to save us from Satan, death, and sin. He will help us through any other obstacles that come along. Just ask Him.

Journal: What obstacles are you facing right now? Write a note to Jesus, asking Him to send helpers to get you over them. Use the note as a prayer.

Pray: Dear Jesus, I need You to lift me over my problems. Thank You for being my rescuer, Savior, and forever friend. Amen. V. S.

Back When I Was a Kid . . .

"Kids today have it so good." Have you heard that before? Maybe a grandparent or other relative likes to talk about how many advantages kids today have that they didn't have.

For example, when your grandparents were your age, they may have had one television for the entire family. That television may have had only a black-and-white picture and only three channels available to watch.

When your grandparents were your age, there was probably only one telephone in the house, and it was attached to the wall. They had to sit or stand next to it to use it. They didn't dream of having a phone so small it would fit in a pocket.

When your grandparents or great-grandparents were your age, there were no cell phones, microwaves, home computers, video games, DVDs, or space shuttles.

Things have changed a lot since then.

One thing has not changed since even before your grandparents were born—God's Word. The Bible reading for today tells us that God's Word is eternal. That means it has always been and it will never end. God's faithfulness to us will continue through all generations. God's Word speaks of God's love for us. He showed us this love in many ways and most perfectly through His Son, Jesus. God's love, with His Word, has been there for all people and will continue for all people to come.

Journal: Ask your grandparents how life was different when they were children. Write down two things in your journal.

Pray: Dear Lord, thank You that You will never change and that Your love will last forever. Amen. V. S.

Strength for New Things

Twelve-year-old Jasmine watched from the window as her mother backed the van out of the driveway. She walked to the door of her sister's room and looked in on the sleeping toddler. Jasmine was both nervous and proud of the new responsibility—staying alone with Molly for the next two hours. Mom had given her good instructions and phone numbers and assured Jasmine she would do a good job.

"You are growing up," Mom told her, "and you are able to do new things. Some of those things are easy, and some are hard. If something hard comes along, phone me. I'll help."

What are some new things you are learning to do? God's children learn new things all the time. Some are easy, and some are hard. You may have to move to a new house in a new neighborhood. You may have to take care of younger children. You may have to wear glasses or braces. You may have to live through life being made fun of by your peers or not having things you really want.

God's children have access to their heavenly Father. He's closer than a phone call. God invites you to pray to Him any time, especially if you feel nervous or worried.

If something new comes along for you today, talk to God about it. He will give you strength and power through His Word. In all things, good and bad, you have God's strength to grow and thrive!

Journal: Make a timeline of your life. Include at least three dates that identify when you did new things or grew in new ways.

Pray: Lord, thank You for the ways I am growing! Help me recognize those things You have for me to do today. Thank You for Your Holy Spirit, who keeps my faith in Jesus strong. In Jesus' name I pray. Amen. D. N.

Peanut Butterscotch Trouble

Make this sweet, lumpy treat to help you think about troubles: In a large saucepan over low heat, melt a 12-ounce package of butterscotch chips and ¼ cup of crunchy peanut butter. Stir in 3 cups of square rice cereal. Mix with a large spoon until the cereal is covered with the butterscotch and peanut butter. Drop by the spoonful onto waxed paper.

The bumps and lumps in this treat are covered with a sweet mix of butterscotch and peanut butter. Troubles are kind of like bumps and lumps. Jesus tells us that we will have troubles in our lives. We have sad days when we are angry with others and days when we are disappointed with ourselves. We have frustrating days when we annoy our friends or mess up an assignment. But just as this cereal treat comes coated with butterscotch and peanut butter, our troubles come wrapped in God's love and care.

Because of Jesus' death and resurrection, we can go directly to our heavenly Father in confession and with requests. He loves us no matter what happens to us. He loves us no matter how we feel. He loves us unconditionally.

God uses our troubles to lead us closer to Him. In His Word, we find the sweet news that we are forgiven. We know that we have a Father who cares for us, a Savior who died for us, and a Spirit who comforts us.

Journal: Think of three ways you can show God's love to others who are sad. (Why not make a batch of peanut butterscotch treats?)

Pray: Dear Lord, thank You for Your love and care when I am sad. Thank You for loving me no matter what. In Jesus' name I pray. Amen. K. D. M.

The Gift of Seconds

Pretend that a bank has just informed you that you will receive $86,400 each day for a year. At the end of every day, you will lose any money you haven't spent. How would you spend your money? Would you give some away? What would you buy for yourself? How much would you give to your church?

Although it is fun to think about, it is not likely to happen. But God gives each of us 86,400 seconds per day. What a gift to spend!

You spend a lot of your seconds sleeping. You might have done homework or spent time eating or going places. You might have spent some of your seconds in Sunday School and church. Maybe you spent time with friends.

We don't always think of time as a gift. If we did, we might use it better. We might realize that someday, all our time will be gone. In fact, someday, all time will end. What will be important then? It will be important that as many people as possible believe that Jesus i their Savior from sin.

When we think about our use of time, we might be sorry. But we can ask God to forgive us for Jesus' sake and to help us use time differently. We know God forgives our sin and gives us another day of opportuni ties to share His love through the things we say and do

Journal: How can you spend seconds with Jesus? How can those "Jesus seconds" benefit you and others?

Pray: Dear God, I confess that I don't always think about time as a gift or as having an end. Thank You for the time You give me each day. In Jesus' name I pray. Amen. J. H.

A Case of the Mondays

Many different words jump into people's minds when they hear the word *Monday*—very few are good. In fact, most people think Mondays are terrible, awful, boring, back-to-routine kind of days.

Weekends are fun. Weekends are sleeping in, going shopping, watching television, hanging out with friends kind of days. Mondays . . . well, Mondays are nothing like that.

Monday means your friend's visit is over, you have to get up early, and you have long, hard hours ahead at school . . . that test is just one day away! No one looks forward to Monday!

But Mondays are actually very, very special. You see, God has redeemed us, His children, through the sacrifice of His Son, and He gives each person unique things to do today and every day, even Mondays! He gives those things only, uniquely, to you, along with the strength and ability to do them. No one else can do your special jobs from God. They are your difficult tasks, your exciting adventures, your new discoveries. Don't waste your Monday wishing it were a Friday instead. You might miss an opportunity! Here's a fun way to remember that every day is a gift from God that He gives you to serve Him, because a

MULTITUDE

OF

NEW

DISCOVERIES

AWAIT

YOU!

Journal: Make your own word list from your favorite day of the week.

Pray: Dear Lord, show me the special things You want me to accomplish today. Thank You for the gift of every new day and for the faith to live it as Your child. Amen. J. D.

Give Thanks in Everything

I give thanks for many things, especially my family, tortillas, flip-flops, camping, and the library. Think about what things you are especially thankful for and write them on the line below:

_____

I am not thankful for other things, like not being able to have a puppy and having to wear boots in the winter. Maybe you can think of some things that you aren't very thankful for.

In today's Bible reading from 1 Thessalonians, we are told to

"give thanks in all circumstances" (5:18).

It is hard to be thankful for everything, especially the things we don't like. But these Bible words remind us to think about what might be good in each situation. For instance, I don't like that we can't have a puppy in our apartment, but I am thankful God has provided us with a great place to live. And even though I'd much rather wear sandals all year long, I'm thankful that I have warm clothes and boots in the cold months. Years ago, my brother and I argued, but I'm thankful I have a brother and parents who loved me.

God has given us so much to be thankful for every day. Most important, He has given His Son, Jesus, to take away our sin and die on the cross, so that we can spend eternity with Him. For this, we can definitely "rejoice always, pray without ceasing, [and] give thanks in all circumstances."

Journal: Think about one thing for which you are not thankful. Turn it into a prayer of thanks to God.

Pray: Heavenly Father, You give me all things, the things I see as good and not so good. Thank You for providing it all for me. Help me to be thankful in all things. Amen. A. B.

What Are You Eating?

Everybody's Thanksgiving traditions are a little different, but most include one very important activity—eating. Do you eat way too much or do you only nibble so that there is plenty of room in your stomach for the treats of the day?

Have you ever heard the expression "You are what you eat"? If that's true, you had better stay away from ice cream unless you want to be propylene glycol monoesters! Corn chips will turn you into disodium phosphate.

Of course, that isn't really what the saying means. It pretty much means that if you eat healthy, you'll be healthy. If you don't eat healthy, you may not be able to do some of the things you want to do. The foods we put into our bodies don't really determine what we are, but putting other things in does.

Today's Bible reading tells us to fill our minds with things that are true, honorable, just, pure, lovely, commendable, excellent, and worthy of praise. Where do we find such things? Maybe not in the shows we watch on TV. Not always in the music we listen to. Never when gossiping about others.

We find these things in God's Word—the Bible. The Bible gives us words that we can use to guide our lives, as we bring glory to God. God's Word leads us to the truth of our praiseworthy Savior, Jesus.

Journal: Is there something in your day that doesn't fill your mind with God-pleasing things?

Pray: Dear Lord, thank You for giving me Your Word to fill my mind and my heart. Amen. V. S.

Clouds Rain Fatness

Ellie left the Thanksgiving service still singing part of the last hymn:

"God makes the clouds rain goodness, The deserts bloom and spring,
The hills leap up in gladness, The valleys laugh and sing.
God fills them with His fullness, All things with large increase;
He crowns the year with blessing, With plenty and with peace." (*LSB* 893:2)

Grandma walked back to the car with Ellie. "I remember that hymn from when I was little," she remarked, "but I sang it a little differently: 'God makes the clouds rain fatness!' "

"That's funny! Clouds can't rain fatness," Ellie laughed.

"Actually, think about the rest of the hymn," her grandma said. "It describes how God fills the entire world with blessings and goodness. When it rains, the grass gets fatter."

"But it's not just the grass that gets fatter, right?" Ellie asked.

"You're right," Grandma said. "Animals eat grass and grow fatter too! All the blessings God gives lead to a life full of good gifts. Most important, the forgiveness God gives you every second because of Jesus makes you fatter with His grace and love! Every time I hear that song, I think of the fat forgiveness God pours down on me each day."

"I don't mind being fat on forgiveness! Now we can eat Thanksgiving dinner and get fatter on yummy food!" Ellie grinned as she hopped into the car.

Journal: Draw some "fat" raindrops in your journal. Fill each drop with the name of something God gives you.

Pray: Heavenly Father, thank You for raining fatness on the earth every day. Thank You for forgiving each one of my sins. Amen. J. D.

Thanksgiving to Christmas

The doorbell rang. "I've got it!" Rachel shouted as she opened the door for Aunt Jen. "Good morning, Rachel. Are you ready?"

Aunt Jen usually did all her Christmas shopping the day after Thanksgiving. She says, "With my shopping out of the way, I can think about the real preparations for Christmas."

Rachel agreed and had planned for this shopping trip for weeks. She'd saved her allowance and made her list.

Then one last time, Rachel and her aunt studied the newspaper ads. "How can you two rush into Christmas so soon?" Rachel's mom asked. "I can't imagine shopping yet. It's still Thanksgiving."

Not all of us can switch from Thanksgiving to Christmas in one day. Sometimes we get so caught up in November and December activities that the real reason we celebrate Thanksgiving, Christmas, or any holiday can get lost.

Many years ago, God used a star to lead some Wise Men to Jesus. They didn't know where the star would lead them. They even stopped off in Jerusalem for a while. Still, they never lost sight of the star. God continued to lead them to Bethlehem, where they worshiped the Savior, Jesus.

When you flip your calendar to December, draw a star on December 25. This star can help you remember that the heavenly Father lovingly gave up His Son, Jesus. Ask God to lead you through the weeks of Advent so you can see God's greatest gift in the manger.

Journal: Does your church have Advent services? How do these prepare you for the coming of Christ?

Pray: Dear Jesus, sometimes I get so busy, I forget to think about what I am doing. Lead me to see You as the Christmas gift God promised for my salvation. Amen. A. S.

The End

Some people make up scary stories and movies about how the world will end. Maybe you've seen movies with zombies or robots or you've read books about computers that take over the world. You know that won't happen. There is a lot of false teaching out there.

In his Second Letter to the Thessalonians, the apostle Paul says Christians should not be afraid by the thought of Jesus returning on the Last Day.

Instead, we are to avoid godless people and false teaching. We can love all that Jesus has taught and take His Word of salvation to all nations. We can remember that we are not alone. Jesus promises that He will be with us to the end of the age (Matthew 28:20).

No one knows when Christ will return. It will be unexpected when it happens, and it will be wonderful for us who believe in Him. On that day, the Lord Jesus will come from heaven. Won't that be exciting! He will give a commanding cry, and an archangel will shout. (Don't you wonder what that will be like?) There will be the sound of the trumpet. And all who believe in Jesus and have died will rise. Then we will see God with our own eyes and enter life everlasting. Amen!

Journal: When you rise from the dead, what does the Bible tell you will happen?

Pray: Dear Jesus, thank You for making it possible for me to be with You on the Last Day and every day after that. Help me to live as Your child and tell others about Your salvation. In Your name I pray. Amen. S. H.

Time

Anna watched the clock anxiously. Her aunt Jo was coming at two o'clock to take her shopping for her birthday. She loved spending time with her aunt.

Anna had gotten up early, even though it was Saturday. She had gotten all of her chores done without being asked. She carefully picked out what she would wear. And now all that was left was the waiting. Twenty more minutes. Ten more minutes—would the time ever come?

It seems that when we are waiting for something fun or exciting, time moves very slowly, like it did for Anna.

The early disciples had a similar experience. When Jesus returned to heaven after His death and resurrection, the disciples thought He was coming back right away. They were in a hurry to tell others about Jesus so they believed in Him before He came back to get them.

God is waiting for just the right time for Jesus to return to earth and take all believers to heaven. It seems as if it has been a very long time since Jesus ascended to heaven after Easter. In God's time, it has been the time it takes to blink your eyes.

We want to be ready for Jesus' return. While we wait, we can tell others about their loving Savior so they are ready to go to heaven with Jesus too. God doesn't tell us when Jesus will return, but we know for sure that it will be at just the right time.

Journal: Think about friends who might not know Jesus. Ask your parents if you can invite them to go to church and Sunday School with you.

Pray: Dear Jesus, it's hard to wait for things we really want to happen. Help me to use my time well by telling others about You. Amen. V. S.

Your Footprint

Carbon footprint is a term that refers to how much impact is made on the environment. If a factory burns fuel that sends smoke into the air, it has a large carbon footprint. But if a factory uses clean-burning fuel, it has a smaller carbon footprint.

When it comes to the environment, the idea is to leave a small footprint that isn't noticed.

When it comes to being a Christian, we want a big spiritual footprint. We want people to see it and to know we're around. And the best way to do that is to love one another.

Acts of love come in all sizes. When you're kind to a stranger, when you let someone go in front of you, or when you compliment a friend, you're showing love.

When Jesus came to earth as a human, He showed His love. When He took our place on the cross and died for our sins and then rose again from the dead, He showed love. Now He wants us to show that love to others.

The Bible tells us to share our faith with all people. Sometimes it's hard to know how to do that. The best way to share your faith is to ask the Holy Spirit to let the love of Christ live in and through you. When people see your spiritual footprint, they will want to know how to walk the same path: the path of faith in Jesus.

Journal: Think of older Christians you respect. How do they display the love of Christ? How can you leave your spiritual footprint on the world?

Pray: Lord, thank You for loving me so much. Fill me with Your love, and help me share it with others. Amen. J. A.

Proverbs or Fortunes?

Read these sentences. Pick out the three biblical proverbs (wise sayings).

1. "Like a madman who throws fire-brands, arrows, and death is the man who deceives his neighbor and says, 'I am only joking!'"

2. "You will receive a present from a mysterious stranger."

3. "Like a dancing monkey are your basketball skills."

4. "A word fitly spoken is like apples of gold in a setting of silver."

5. "Surely, good fortune will follow you until Saturday, and a thousand strangers will eat your dust."

6. "Like clouds and wind without rain is a man who boasts of a gift he does not give."

Did you figure it out? Wisdom and foolishness may look alike. When the foolishness sounds clever, it can be hard to tell the difference. A great way to tell wisdom from foolishness is to ask if it comes from someone you trust. If it's from God, you know it's wise. True wisdom always lines up with God's Word.

Some people thought it was foolish of God to sacrifice His own Son to die for us. Since our sin was our own fault, wasn't it silly that Jesus took our place? Of course not. It was the wisdom of God to send His sinless Son to forgive sinners. It was God's wisdom that allowed that faith to be planted in your heart. God works wisely in our lives and for our eternity. He knows that's exactly what we need—the power of God.

Journal: Write about a time when you felt foolish.

Pray: God of wisdom, give me grace to avoid foolish thoughts and wants. Thank You for leading me in Your ways. Amen.   J. S.

Answers: Statements 1, 4, and 6 are from Proverbs 26:18–19; 25:11; and 25:14, respectively.

The Colin Chronicles

Colin looked into the camera on the tablet and said, "These are the Colin Chronicles: the record of one boy's attempts to find excitement in a boring family. Next stop—the Dungeon of Despair."

Colin walked into his sister's room. "As you can see, the vicious Della likes her dungeon cluttered." He zoomed in on a plate of buffalo wing bones. "This strange beast tries to scare away visitors by surrounding its treasures with the bones of its victims."

"Colin!" Debbie screamed from the doorway. "Get out!"

Colin pointed his camera at her. "You can see its razor-sharp teeth and its . . ."

Just then, Mom came in. She reached for the tablet. "Colin, your chronicle is done for today."

A chronicle is a long record of historical events. There are a number of Bible books that are chronicles, including two books in the Old Testament actually named Chronicles.

In many ways, the whole Bible is one huge chronicle. It tells the events of the world's fall into sin and of God's actions to save us. It chronicles how Jesus lived, died, and rose again to save us from sin and death. It does this so we know what happened. But it's also so we believe what God did and is still doing for us daily. He will record our names in His chronicle, the Book of Life, that contains the names of all who will live eternally in heaven!

Journal: Ask a relative about your family's faith history. Write a short chronicle about it.

Pray: Almighty God, You have known every moment of my life before I was even born. For Jesus' sake, record my name in Your eternal Book of Life. Amen. J. S.

NOVEMBER 30

Psalm 118:24

Some Days Are like That

Reid woke up with a smile. Today was going to be a good day. She jumped out of bed—and right onto the tail of her dog, who was lying next to her bed. The dog barked, which woke Reid's baby brother. The baby cried, which sent a groggy mom to calm him.

It was still going to be a good day, she thought as she dressed for school. Her family had been too busy to get the laundry done. The only thing in her closet was her old red shirt. And her hair had its own plan and would not lie down.

At breakfast, Reid dribbled syrup on her shirt. And then her dad said she should practice her smile. It was picture day at school! So much for having a good day.

Some days are like that. It seems nothing goes right, and no matter how hard you try to have a good day, it just does *not* happen.

When nothing is going right, we can turn to God's Word, where we are reminded that God is always faithful to us. He always knows what is going on in our day, and He cares. He will never forget His children. He knew that because of our sin, we needed a Savior, and He sent Jesus, His only Son, to rescue us from sin and give us eternal life. Even on the worst of days, that is reason to smile.

Journal: Make a list of the good things that happened in your day. Thank God for those blessings.

Pray: Dear Jesus, thank You for loving me so much that You came to be my Savior. Thank You for caring about everything in my day. Amen. V. S.

Creation Set Free

As Mom and Juan shared an after-school snack, they talked about what Juan had learned that day.

"In science, we studied acts of nature," said Juan. "A few years ago, an earthquake damaged Haiti. Then a tsunami wiped out parts of Japan, sending ships up on shore. We also talked about tornadoes that destroyed everything in sight. Oh, and we discussed droughts, major forest fires, and snowstorms. And do you remember Hurricane Sandy? It poured lots of water into New York City."

"I remember all those tragic events," said Mom. "Do you know why those things happened?"

"Don't they just . . . well, happen?" Juan replied. "Aren't they natural?"

"Actually, they aren't natural," Mom replied. "God did not create the world that way. In the beginning, all creation ran perfectly. But when Adam and Eve sinned, that perfection was lost. And since then, the Bible says 'the whole creation has been groaning together'" (Romans 8:22).

"Those bad things we talked about at school must be that groaning," said Juan.

"But creation won't always be groaning," Mom said. "Someday, it will be free of sin."

"And when will that be?" asked Juan.

"Everything will be perfect on the Last Day, when our Savior, Jesus, comes back for all those who trust in Him," explained Mom. "When Jesus returns, He will put all things right again. All believers will live in a perfectly new creation."

"Whoa!" said Juan. "That will be an awesome day."

Journal: What are your favorite parts of the creation?

Pray: Dear Jesus, thank You for healing the brokenness of my sin and sinfulness. Come soon to set me and all Your creation free. Amen. R. G.

The Temple of God

Do you notice how beautiful churches are? Some have tall, graceful steeples you can see from afar. Others have enormous stained glass windows that come alive when the light shines through them. In some, pews of dark wood shine with polish. Linens adorned with symbols cover the altar. Ornate candlesticks stand, waiting to be used.

A church building is called the house of God. That's why so much care goes into how the church looks. Out of love and respect for God, we want everything to be clean and beautiful. We work hard to keep the church in good repair. It's a way to show reverence, or respect, for God.

The Bible says that our body is the temple of God. God's Spirit lives in each of us, giving us faith in Jesus' saving sacrifice.

There are some people who say, "It's okay if I smoke or drink too much or take illegal drugs—I'm not hurting anybody but myself." But that's not true. By hurting themselves, they hurt God's temple. When we do anything wrong, it's like painting graffiti on the walls of a church. When we swear or gossip, cheat or watch bad television, we pollute the place where God lives.

We are all guilty of sin. We need God's forgiveness, bought with the perfect life and blood of Jesus. His sacrifice covers our sins better than a fresh coat of paint. The Holy Spirit lives in us so we are the temple of God.

Journal: Describe your church home. Describe yourself. How are these both temples of God?

Pray: Dear heavenly Father, thank You for loving me so much and sending Your Spirit to live in me. Forgive me when I have not treated my body as Your temple. Help me remember that You are always with me. Amen. J. A.

DECEMBER 3

Psalm 98:4–9

Joy to the World

What do you hear almost everywhere you go at this time of the year? If you said Christmas songs, you're right. Some of these songs are about snowmen, Santa, or reindeer. They can be fun to sing, but the best and most important songs of Christmas are about the birth of Jesus.

A favorite Christmas carol for many is "Joy to the World" (*LSB* 387). It was written almost three hundred years ago by Isaac Watts, an English hymnwriter.

Few people who sing "Joy to the World" know that they are singing a psalm. Isaac Watts wanted the psalms to bring a message of God's love to His people. He thought singing the words of some of the psalms would make it easier for people to understand them. The words of this carol are based on Psalm 98:4–9.

Isaac Watts died before "Joy to the World" was used as a Christmas carol. In 1837, Lowell Mason set the words to a tune that already existed. It certainly remains one of the most well-loved Christmas songs of all time and has been recorded by many singers and choirs.

The words of this carol tell about Jesus' love and how He died on the cross for our sins. Someday we will live in heaven with Jesus forever. Jesus truly brought joy to the world!

Journal: What is your favorite Christmas carol? Try to find out something about when and how the carol was written. Or draw a picture to go with the words.

Pray: Dear God, thank You for sending Your Son into the world as a human baby. Give me the true joy of Christmas. In Jesus' name I pray. Amen. J. D.

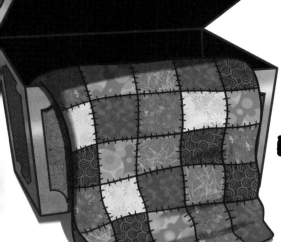

Every Piece Is Important

When I was growing up, my mom used to make quilts. She took all kinds of fabric in different colors, patterns, and textures and cut them into small pieces. Some pieces were decorated with polka dots, some with stripes. The fabrics looked so different that I thought there was no way to put all the things together to make something beautiful! But I was wrong. With love, Mom sewed the pieces and shapes of fabric together. Little by little, they went together and became a beautiful quilt.

God, who made the world, also made different kinds of people—men and women, old and young, short and tall, with different colors of hair, eyes, and skin. People are different on the inside too. Some are funny; others are serious. Some like to read; others prefer sports. People like different kinds of food, music, and games. Sometimes it seems like there's no way that so many types of people can work together!

But we do have something in common with others. Every person on the face of the earth is sinful and needs the Savior. This life-saving Gospel message is important.

Long ago, Jesus told His disciples to go into the world and teach the Gospel to everyone. It is still true today. The Gospel is for all people everywhere—all shapes, sizes, and looks.

Journal: Draw a quilt with pieces of different shapes. In the shapes, write the names of people you know.

Pray: Dear Lord, thank You for all the different types of people You made. Give me time and ways to show Your love to others today. In Jesus' name I pray. Amen. J. A.

Light of the World

You know that Jesus is the light of the world, but did you know *we* are lights too? No, we aren't the Savior God sent to save our fallen world. Only Jesus could do that through His suffering and death.

Yet Jesus says, "You are the light of the world. . . . Let your light shine before others, so that they may see your good works and give glory to your Father who is in heaven" (Matthew 5:14, 16). God uses us to show and tell the world about Him. Sometimes we use words, but often it is our good works that point people to our heavenly Father.

My neighbor and her children are trying something new for Advent. Instead of buying presents for one another, they are serving others. Each day before Christmas, they do an "act of kindness" for somebody else. Here are some of the things on their list.

✱ Visit older people in a nursing home

✱ Take care of the little boy next door so his mom can shop

✱ Tape change to a vending machine

✱ Pay for a stranger's meal at a restaurant

✱ Take baked goods to the police station and fire station to thank them for serving

✱ Grocery shop and put it in the "Food for Families" box

Your list might be different. Because Jesus has redeemed us, we are free to light up every place we go, with everything we do. And we do it all to the glory of God.

Journal: Make up your own list for letting your light shine.

Pray: Jesus, help me to shine Your light for others this Advent and always. Amen. R. G.

A Day for Giving

On this day, December 6, we celebrate the life of St. Nicholas. No, not Santa Claus, but the real St. Nicholas, who lived in the fourth century in a place called Myra, which is in the country we now call Turkey.

Many legends and stories have surrounded Nicholas, and some are true. Nicholas was a bishop, a pastor in charge of many churches. Many people looked up to him as their spiritual leader. He even was at the meeting that produced the Nicene Creed, which Christians confess on Sunday!

What we remember best about St. Nicholas is that he was a giver. The best-known story about him is that he gave a family three bags of gold. The family needed money for the daughters in the family to marry, but they were very poor. So Nicholas, in the dark of night, sneaked to their home and dropped three bags of gold through the open window.

More important than giving money, though, is what Nicholas gave to those who came to church. He preached about Jesus. He gave them the Lord's Supper. He baptized babies. Jesus is the best gift of all.

Last night, all around the world, children set out their shoes, hoping for a St. Nicholas Day treat. And when they woke up, they found gold coins and candies! Why don't you celebrate St. Nicholas Day by surprising someone with gold-wrapped chocolate candy—and a reminder that Jesus loves him or her? He's the best gift of all.

Journal: Instead of making out a Christmas list today, think of items for a different list. List five ways you can tell about or show Jesus' love.

Pray: Lord Jesus, You love to give Your children gifts. Thank You for giving me Your salvation and love. Thank You for being the best gift of all. Amen. J. S.

All Good Gifts

Kyle and Matias were on their way to basketball practice. Matias said, "That's an old shirt. Man, look at the holes and tears in it!"

"It is pretty ragged," Kyle admitted. "But it's my lucky shirt. I need it. That's why I wear it under my good shirt."

"What do you mean, you *need* it?"

"When I wear this shirt, I make almost all of my free throws," Kyle said.

Matias was surprised. "Really? And that's because of that old shirt?"

"What else could it be? It's my lucky shirt," said Kyle. "Besides, today is the seventh day of the month."

"What does that have to do with basketball?" Matias asked.

Kyle responded, "Seven is a lucky number."

Matias sighed. "Kyle, there's no such thing as lucky charms. That would mean things happen by chance. I just don't believe it."

"Well, then, what do you believe?" asked Kyle.

"I believe God's Word," said Matias. "It tells us God created this world and everything in it and still cares for it. I believe *every* blessing comes from Him—every good and perfect gift. When it comes to being good at basketball, Kyle, it's about practice."

Like Matias, we may hear people talk about lucky charms as if they were real, but they are not. God provides everything we need, including a new life in Christ. Thankfully, God provided the blessed Savior to die for our sins, and now He blesses others through us.

Journal: What "lucky" items have you heard about? How does relying on something like that prevent you from relying on your heavenly Father?

Pray: Father, I know You love me, and You know everything that happens in my life. Forgive me for not relying on Your promises and care. Thank You for Your good and perfect gifts. In Jesus' name I pray. Amen. H. W.

For Us

About seven hundred years before the birth of Christ, the Old Testament prophet Isaiah told of God's plan for the salvation of sinners.

	A	B	C
1.	Surely He has	borne our griefs	and
2.	carried	our sorrows;	yet we esteemed Him
3.	stricken,	smitten by God,	and afflicted.
4.	But He was pierced	for our transgressions;	He was crushed for our iniquities;
5.	upon Him was the	chastisement	that brought us
6.	peace,	and with His wounds	we are healed.

Isaiah's words (53:4–5) paint a picture. Let's find out what that picture looks like. The prophecy tells us Jesus has borne our griefs and carried our sorrows. All our griefs and sorrows are caused by sin. Our sin hurts us and others. Color boxes 1B and 2B.

The prophecy tells us that Jesus was stricken, smitten by God, and afflicted. *Stricken* means wounded. *Smitten* means killed by striking. *Afflicted* means tormented or tortured. God laid on Jesus the sins of the entire world and punished Jesus for all those sins. He was indeed stricken, smitten, and afflicted. Color 3A, 3B, and 3C.

The prophecy then says Jesus was pierced and crushed for *our* transgressions (or sins), for *our* iniquities. It is *our* fault, *our* sin. Color 4A, 4B, and 4C. Jesus took our chastisement, our punishment. Color 5B. With Jesus' wounds, we are healed from sin, death, and eternal condemnation. Color 6B.

Where was this prophecy fulfilled? What do your colored spaces show? What powerful love that Jesus would suffer so greatly! For us!

Journal: Use joyful, peaceful colors to shade the remaining boxes.

Pray: Dear Jesus, we praise and thank You that Your sacrificial death and resurrection brought us peace and healing. Amen.   S. S.

DECEMBER 9

2 Corinthians 5:17–19

Before and After

Do you like to look at before-and-after pictures? They show us how something originally looked and how it looks after it's been changed.

Decorating magazines show how rooms or even whole houses have been done over. Places go from looking shabby or run-down to beautiful. All the details are explained so the reader can understand how the changes were made. There are even TV shows where old houses are redone. You can watch each week as the makeover is done step-by-step.

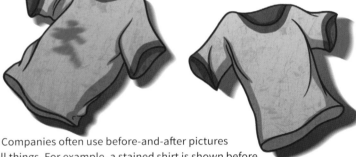

Companies often use before-and-after pictures to sell things. For example, a stained shirt is shown before it was washed in Brand X soap. Then it's shown to be super clean after washing.

You can also read before-and-after stories about people. These people want to change something about themselves. Maybe they want to look different or be stronger or be healthier.

Paul talks about a before-and-after makeover in the Bible too. "If anyone is in Christ, he is a new creation. The old has passed away; behold, the new has come" (2 Corinthians 5:17). Now that's really a makeover! And it happened to you!

Even though we look the same on the outside, we have been changed. We become new creations in Baptism. God's Spirit gives us faith to believe that Jesus is our Savior from sin. Each day, that same Spirit works in us. Our sins are forgiven, and we continue our life as children of God. What a marvelous after picture that is!

Journal: Think of yourself as a before-and-after person. How does believing in Jesus as your Savior change your life?

Pray: Dearest Jesus, thank You for loving me so much that You died for my sins. Through Your Spirit, help me to will and to do what You would have me do. Amen. J. D.

Look Carefully

You might call the nativity scene a manger scene (American English); *crèche* (French); *krippe* (German); *praesepio* (Italian); *nacimiento* or *pesebre* (Spanish); *svokka* (Polish); *steaua* (Romanian); or *putz* (Moravian).

No matter what you call it, which pieces tell the story? There are the manger, Mary, Joseph, and baby Jesus. Sometimes there are animals. Often there are shepherds and angels. Sometimes, you will find Wise Men. Where are they looking? Each piece is looking at the baby in the manger. Imagine it. There, in the place where animals eat their food, they saw a baby—the Savior.

Where are *you* focused this season? Maybe you are looking in stores or on the Internet for Christmas presents. Maybe you are looking through boxes of ornaments for the tree. Maybe you are looking at a tray of cookies for one with red sprinkles. Maybe you are planning to watch your favorite Christmas movie. Are you looking the right way? Will you find Jesus?

The angel got the shepherds looking in the right direction—toward the baby wrapped in swaddling cloths, lying in a manger. Who is that baby? He is Christ the Lord.

Go ahead—look for presents, decorations, cookies, and movies. But to find the real message of Christmas, look to Jesus. He came to be our Savior, to live and die for your sins and mine. He came to give us life eternal. When you see who Jesus is, you will probably join the figures at the manger in wonder and awe.

Journal: What joyful news about Jesus coming to save sinners could you share on a Christmas card? Design one.

Pray: Heavenly Father, so often I look for You in the wrong places. Fix my eyes on the Savior, Christ the Lord. In His name I pray. Amen. R. M.

Numbered Hairs

Jayden's little brother had never gotten a haircut—and he was almost two years old. His curly red hair bounced when he ran or played. It was his most distinguishing characteristic. People often asked Jayden, "Are you the brother of the redhead?"

Jayden wished he had something that made him stand out. His hair and eyes were brown, the most common colors in the world. He was of average height and weight. He was an ordinary student, always chosen somewhere in the middle of the selection for athletic teams. His next-door neighbor never got his name right, always calling him Jared. Even his mom and dad sometimes called him by the wrong name.

In Sunday School, Jayden heard a comforting Bible verse from the Gospel of Matthew: "But even the hairs of your head are all numbered." God knew everything about him, right down to knowing the exact number of hairs on his head at any given moment. And those hairs were brown, not noteworthy red! It made Jayden feel good to know that even if he was forgettable to others, God still loved him.

This Bible verse said more about God than it did about Jayden. Jayden didn't feel he was extraordinary, but God chose to love him anyway. God loves ordinary people with His extraordinary, forgiving love. He sent His only Son, Jesus, to be an ordinary, but not-so-ordinary human being, to live, die, and rise for the salvation of all people, regardless of their physical features.

Journal: What do you like least and best about yourself? How do you compare yourself to others? How does God see you?

Pray: Dear God, thank You for knowing everything about me and for loving me with a powerful, eternal love in Jesus. Amen. J. G.

Dust Bunnies

Chloe's family was expecting a new baby. They washed and folded baby clothes. They set up the crib.

Today, they were cleaning. Chloe and her family wanted a spotless house. "When we bring home your new brother or sister," Mom said, "we don't want dust bunnies anywhere."

"Where do all these dust bunnies come from?" asked Chloe.

Good question. Where do dust bunnies come from? No matter how often you clean, they gather again. Mom was right. The room really isn't clean until the dust bunnies are gone.

We aren't really clean, either, until our sin is gone, all gone. So we need to begin with cleaning our hearts, because there we will find evil thoughts, mean words, rebellion, and unkind actions.

Like Chloe's family, we are expecting someone. We are expecting Jesus. How can we clean up our hearts for Him? That's a hard question, isn't it? The Holy Spirit begins the cleaning. He leads God's people to confess their sins.

When we confess our sins, we plead guilty to saying, doing, and thinking bad things. We plead guilty to the sins we don't even realize we have done. When we confess our sins, we receive God's forgiveness. God forgives us for Jesus' sake—Jesus, the baby who came at Christmas, died and rose to take away our sins. His blood cleanses us from all sin.

May God's Spirit work in you a new and right spirit as you prepare for the coming of the Savior.

Journal: How do families prepare for the birth of a child? How do God's people prepare for Jesus' coming?

Pray: Dear God, I confess to You that I sin daily. Cleanse me through the blood of Jesus Christ. Create in me a clean heart, O God. Give me a new spirit to love and serve others. In Jesus' name I pray. Amen. P. L.

DECEMBER 13

Isaiah 9:6–7

Great News!

Some people claim they can tell what's going to happen next month or next year. They use some silly objects to help them do that—tea leaves, glass balls, even the palm of someone's hand.

Only God knows the future. Long ago, He chose prophets to tell His message to His people, regarding both the present and the future. He sent these prophets to warn His chosen people about their sinfulness and to promise them God's mercy and pardon.

A prophet named Isaiah carried a special message from God to His people. In Isaiah 9, we read that message: God said He was going to send someone to set up a kingdom that would last forever.

Do you know whom Isaiah was talking about? Who could that be? It was to be a newborn baby boy, a human descendant of King David. He would also be true God.

The prophet was talking about the baby Jesus. We read about Him in the four Gospels—Matthew, Mark, Luke, and John. What God had said hundreds of years before, through Isaiah, finally came true. God sent His Son to save us from eternal punishment for our sins.

God told us through His prophets that He really loves us. He showed us this through the gift of His only Son. We don't know why God loves us so much. We only know He does. He said so and proved it by sending Jesus to die for our sins. What great news to share!

Journal: Why is God's good news the best message we can receive? What do you think Jesus' four names in Isaiah 9:6 mean? Choose two of the names and write about them in your journal.

Pray: Dear God, thank You for Your Word, which tells of Your love. And thanks for sending Jesus to be my Savior and the Savior of the world. Amen. L. B.

Swimming Lessons

Madeleine didn't like swimming at all. She couldn't breathe right, sucking in water instead of air. Even though Madeleine was dreading her swimming lessons, the coach had helped her learn to roll to her side to breathe. She'd improved her freestyle, but she knew she had more work to do.

The same thing happens sometimes when we read the Bible. We try to do what our pastors suggest and read the Scriptures every day. But we get confused about what it all means and want to give up. Like Madeleine and her swimming lessons, we need a teacher to help us along the way. That's what our pastors and Sunday School teachers can do for us. They help us see how the Bible accounts fit together. They help us understand how to interpret God's Word.

In today's psalm, we learn that the Bible is "a lamp to [our] feet and a light for [our] path" (119:105). This means that God speaks to us, giving us the faith to trust in Him. Even when we feel we are making a mess of our lives, God's Word shows us that Jesus is our Savior, who loves us and cares for us. That's great news!

Journal: Write about a Bible story that helps you understand God and His love for you.

Pray: Lord, we thank You for the Scriptures and for our teachers who explain Your Word to us. Amen. J. S.

In the Dark

These days of December, near the winter solstice, are some of the darkest of the year. In some places, the sun shines only a few hours a day.

The season of Advent, which comes before Christmas, is a season "in the dark." It's a season of hope as we wait for the Lord's coming, but we spend a lot of time in darkness, waiting for daylight. As we wait in the dark, we can't see what's coming, but we know that eventually the new day will dawn.

In some ways, this is like the Christian life. In our sin-darkened world, we wait, trusting with firm faith that our Lord is taking care of us, that He loves us, and that He will come again for us. Though we can't see with our human eyes what is to come, our eyes of faith reassure us.

What is promised to us, and what we cling to by faith, we know because of God's Word. In His Word, God reveals to us truths about our Lord's first coming, predicted throughout the Old Testament and shown throughout the New Testament. The promised Savior is revealed. We cling to Jesus in the "darkness" as we struggle against the world, our flesh, and the devil. We cling to the promises of our Lord to forgive us, save us, and help us.

And soon, very soon, Jesus will come again in His glory, and we'll be with Him forever in light that will never end.

Journal: What can reassure you about God's presence in the night?

Pray: Lord Jesus, thank You for coming as a baby into the world to save me. Thank You for dying on the cross and rising again so that I can be forgiven and live with You forever. Even in my sin-darkened world, help me trust You with firm faith until You come again. Amen. J. S.

Signs of Christmas

"Name something associated with Christmas." This sounds like a line from the *Family Feud* game show on TV. In this show, family teams compete to name the most popular answers. What would immediately spring to mind if you were given that challenge? Typical responses might be carols, presents, snow, or cookies. Obvious signs, right?

While our answers may score high on *Family Feud*, our thoughts and actions often reveal hearts far away from Jesus. There's nothing wrong with cookies and presents, but they can easily take our focus away from the birth of the Christ Child. Whether or not we pay attention, our celebration of Jesus' coming is drawing near speedily. Our lack of attention does nothing to slow it down or stop it.

Were Jesus coming as a judge to punish us for our sins, we might want to slow His coming. But Jesus comes as our Savior to take on Himself the punishment we deserve. He came at just the right time. He didn't delay, even though He was to die in our place on the cross. Because He did, we are forgiven for all our sins!

Jesus and His mission are important to God. They are so important, in fact, that He gives us faith in Him through Baptism and His Word. As Christians, we want everyone to immediately see the importance of Jesus in our lives. Let's find ways to tell and show others—Christmas is almost here!

Journal: Which outward signs of Christmas could motivate you to thank God for His gift of Jesus? What could you do to show your thankfulness?

Pray: Heavenly Father, I am eager for Christmas to come. Forgive me when I dwell on the trappings of Christmas without pausing to thank You for the greatest gift—Jesus. Help me take time to thank and praise You for all the blessings of Christmas. Amen. J. H.

Firstfruits

It's almost Christmas, but have you thought about Easter? That's why Jesus came in the first place. Without Easter, Christmas really doesn't matter. Because of our sinfulness, we needed a Savior. Baby Jesus was laid in a wooden manger. Grown-up Jesus was nailed to a wooden cross and put into a tomb. But on Easter morning, He rose from the dead.

The Bible says that Jesus rose as the "firstfruits of those who have fallen asleep [died]. For as by a man came death, by a man has come also the resurrection of the dead. For as in Adam all die, so also in Christ shall all be made alive. But each in his own order: Christ the firstfruits, then at His coming those who belong to Christ" (1 Corinthians 15:20–23).

What a contrast! Through Adam, sin and death entered the world. But through Christ, forgiveness and resurrection entered. Christ gives us life and forgiveness. Christ died and rose from the grave, and when He comes again, we will rise too, because we belong to Him.

Jesus will destroy all the evil forces in the world. No more murders, sickness, hatred, or sin. He will crush all His enemies. Satan will be sent to hell forever. "The last enemy to be destroyed is death" (v. 26). All those who have died will rise; believers will live with Christ forever.

Christmas is a great time to tell why Jesus came for us. So maybe we should say, "Merry Christmas and Happy Easter!"

Journal: Write "Merry Christmas and Happy Easter!" in your journal.

Pray: Risen Lord, thank You for rising first so I can rise too. I won't stay dead, but I'll live with You forever. Amen. R. G.

No Matter What

Professionals who work with troubled people know that feeling depressed or stressed out is common in the weeks before Christmas. Surprising? Maybe not. Right now, your family might be dealing with divorce, unemployment, illness, or even death.

When this happens, you feel out of sync with others. Everyone is giggling about the presents under the Christmas tree, but you feel sad and anxious. Or numb. What do you do?

First, remember that God understands how complex or frightening our emotions can be. Also know that you are not alone. Hundreds of years before Jesus was born, a prophet named Habakkuk was discouraged. His country, Judah, was filled with sin and injustice. He thought God was letting evil go unpunished. But God saw what was going on. He allowed the Babylonians to invade Judah so they would remember that they needed God. The Holy Spirit strengthened Habakkuk and reminded him how God had delivered Judah from its enemies in the past. In spite of this awful prediction, he chose to trust God.

Although Christmas is usually a festive season, have you been feeling down? You can always talk to God—and a trusted adult—about how you feel. God, who has loved you all your life, will not abandon you. You can trust Him, no matter what.

Journal: Write about a time when you felt sad, even though everyone else seemed happy. What could you say to God?

Pray: Almighty God, sometimes I don't feel the joy of Christmas. Help me to trust that while feelings are temporary, Your love and protection will always be there. In Jesus' name I pray. Amen. J. H.

God in Control

A town was hit by a tornado. Many homes were completely destroyed, while others were just slightly damaged. Some businesses closed because tree branches broke their windows. Emergency crews helped, and total strangers came to see how they could rescue suffering people.

Some people just stood on the sidelines and looked. One man said, "What did those people do wrong that God punished them?"

Another man quickly answered, "God isn't punishing them by destroying their homes. We don't know why God allows bad things to happen, but we do know that He is in control. Maybe He is teaching us to help them."

How can we say that God is in control when bad things happen to good people? When God made the world, it was without sin. Because Adam and Eve disobeyed God, sin came into the world. All people are born sinful. Because of our daily sins, the world is different from what God designed. To rescue us, God sent Jesus to make things right. God sent Jesus to die on the cross to pay for our sins.

Bad things do not come from God. They come because of sin. Instead of sending bad things to us, our forgiving and loving God promises to be with us in all things.

Through each bad and good thing, God is seeking the lost. He wants all people to be saved, and He uses us in bad situations to let others know about Jesus.

Journal: Write how you would respond if someone asked, "Is God in control?"

Pray: Dear heavenly Father, I know You are in control. Help me remember that and share that good news with others. Amen. P. L.

Christmas Is Mine

Lindsay smiled at the little Christmas tree on her night table. For years, Lindsay had envied her friend Anne's home at Christmastime. Anne's parents were rich, and the Christmas tree in their living room was decorated with hundreds of twinkling lights and huge golden balls. But that wasn't the tree that made Lindsay jealous.

Every year, Anne got a Christmas tree to put in her bedroom. Lindsay thought that such a luxury was glorious. Yet this year, Lindsay's dad had surprised her. He brought home a simple little tree and said, "Hey, Lindsay, I think this tree needs some love."

Dad made her dream come true. Lindsay laughed at the paper chain she'd wound around her tree. She added a paper star and set up the little cardboard figures of baby Jesus in the manger, Mary, and Joseph that she'd made in first grade. Christmas isn't about fancy decorations, she thought. It's about baby Jesus being born to suffer and die for my sins.

Mary thought quietly too, after the excitement of the first Christmas. After the shepherds burst excitedly into the stable to worship her little Son and told stories of angels, she treasured these memories in her heart.

We, too, can look at the decorations and presents in our homes and say, "Jesus was born to fulfill God's plan. He came to suffer and die for my sins. He came to be my Savior." Jesus is a treasure who lives forever, and that's long after all the decorations are put away.

Journal: Look around your home. Which decoration reminds you most that Jesus was born to be your Savior? Describe it in your journal.

Pray: Jesus, thank You for leaving Your glorious home in heaven to be my Savior. Help me to treasure Your loving gifts of forgiveness and life eternal all year long. Amen. R. G.

DECEMBER 21

Looking for Angels

Have you noticed how busy the angels were in the Christmas story? Gabriel told Zechariah and his wife they would have a son named John, who would prepare people for Jesus' coming. Gabriel told Mary that she, too, would have a son and should name Him Jesus. An angel told Joseph not to be afraid to take Mary for his wife.

An angel told the shepherds where to find baby Jesus. Then a sky full of angels praised God. After the Wise Men visited young Jesus, an angel warned them not to go back to King Herod. An angel told Joseph to hide Jesus in Egypt so Herod's soldiers could not kill him.

Wouldn't it be great if angels could let us know everything that will happen to us and just what we ought to do in every situation? Life would be pretty easy with all that angel help.

In the Old Testament, long before Jesus was born on earth, Elisha's servant worried when he saw that the city where they were staying was surrounded by enemy horses and chariots. Elisha asked God to open his servant's eyes. Then the servant could see hills full of horses and chariots of fire—angels—surrounding the enemy soldiers.

Many years after Zechariah, King Herod, and Elisha, God's angels are still working. God's angels are still busy. They are circled around you right now, ready to serve God!

Journal: Write about a time when you were worried or injured or afraid. How did God's angels keep you safe?

Pray: Father, thank You for keeping Your angels working overtime to watch over me. Thank You for the salvation You give to me. In Jesus' name I pray. Amen. R. G.

It's a Gift!

Idriz and his family had come from Bosnia, a country that was in a terrible war. Idriz's family had left everything behind in Bosnia—their relatives, their home, and almost all their possessions.

Idriz was glad to make a friend at his new school. His name was Stan. One day, as Idriz and Stan were having lunch together, Idriz talked about how hard it was for him to live in a new country. "I knew it would be hard," Idriz said, "but one thing I've learned is that nothing in life is easy and nothing is free!"

Stan remembered something his Sunday School teacher had taught him. Then he said, "I know something that's free! A gift you and I have been given. To us, it was absolutely free, but it cost someone else His life. Idriz, you and I sin every day. We do things we shouldn't and don't do things we should—we sin."

"I know," said Idriz, "but I'm trying to do better."

"That's the problem," Stan said. "You can't live without sinning, and I can't either. Only God is perfect. God took all the sins that we've ever done and ever will do and put them on His Son, Jesus. Jesus suffered and died for our sins. That's God's gift to you and me!"

"That's the best gift I could ever have," Idriz smiled as a tear ran down his cheek.

Journal: What is the best gift someone has ever given you?

Pray: Thank You, Father, for sending Your Son, Jesus, to give me the free gift of salvation. In Jesus' name I pray. Amen. S. H.

The Perfect Gift

At this time of year, people receive more gifts than at any other time. Sometimes they are great gifts—the toy you wanted, a special game or book.

But sometimes the gift isn't right. Maybe you already have that DVD or someone gives you a shirt that doesn't fit. What do you do then?

There is one Christmas gift that is perfect—Jesus, our Savior. The Bible tells us that at just the right time, God sent His Son into the world. He sent His best gift, Jesus, because He knew that each of us needed a Savior.

We need a Savior because we break God's Law. Sometimes those sins are things we say or do; sometimes they are things we think. And sometimes they are things we fail to do or say. We can be thankful that God sent Jesus to keep the Law. Everything He said, did, and thought was perfect. He took our punishment. He paid the price for our sin.

The next time you get a gift, whether it's a great gift or one that isn't exactly what you wanted, remember that Jesus is the perfect gift.

In just a few days, we will exchange gifts and celebrate Jesus' birthday. And when Christmas over, we can continue to rejoice each day in Jesus' gifts of life and salvation.

Journal: What great gifts has Jesus given to you?

Pray: Dear Jesus, You are my perfect gift. Thank You for keeping the Law in my place and then suffering for my sin. Thank You for making me an heir of heaven and for giving me other wonderful treasures. Amen. P. L.

A Bed for a King

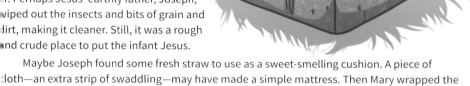

A newborn baby needs a place to sleep that is sturdy, comfortable, and safe. So what do you use if the baby's first home is a stable, a "bedroom" for livestock? The object most like a bed probably would be a manger, a stone or wooden trough from which animals eat.

But a manger is not a clean container. Perhaps Jesus' earthly father, Joseph, wiped out the insects and bits of grain and dirt, making it cleaner. Still, it was a rough and crude place to put the infant Jesus.

Maybe Joseph found some fresh straw to use as a sweet-smelling cushion. A piece of cloth—an extra strip of swaddling—may have made a simple mattress. Then Mary wrapped the baby in swaddling strips, perhaps specially woven and decorated—a birthday gift to the Savior.

The fact that baby Jesus was in a manger was said by the angel to be a sign that He was indeed the one of whom the heavenly host had sung to the shepherds. What a different sign than might have been expected to point to the Savior King—a stable instead of a palace, a feed trough rather than a throne. But this manger held the one promised in Isaiah 7:14: "Therefore the Lord Himself will give you a sign. Behold, the virgin shall conceive and bear a son, and shall call His name Immanuel."

Our heavenly Father had kept His promise. **"And this is the promise that He made to us—eternal life"** (1 John 2:25).

Journal: As a baby, Jesus slept in an ordinary feed trough. Name some ordinary things in your life that God might use in a new way.

Pray: Dear Jesus, help me to see the places in my life where I can make room for You. Be with me, Lord Jesus, forever. Amen. H. W.

DECEMBER 25

Luke 2:8–20

Trust a Shepherd

Shepherds didn't have a good reputation in Bible times. They were rough, smelly men who often spent all day and night in the fields with their sheep. Shepherds weren't allowed to be witnesses in a courtroom. People thought they were dishonest men who would not tell the truth.

How interesting that God chose poor, lowly shepherds to be the first witnesses to see His newborn Son. A bright light woke the shepherds while they were dozing, keeping watch over their sheep. They sat up, shaking with fear, but God's angel told them not to be afraid. God had sent His own Son, Jesus, to be born on earth as a baby so He could be our Savior. Then the shepherds got to hear a host of angels. We can imagine that Satan and his wicked angels shook with fear. Their downfall had begun.

The shepherds ran to Bethlehem and found baby Jesus just as the angel had said. They fell on their knees and worshiped their Savior. Then these rugged, scruffy men, whom nobody trusted, became the world's first missionaries. They hurried through the streets of Bethlehem telling everybody what they had seen and heard. God's Word tells us they got it just right too.

God's Good News of the Savior is also for us. As we gaze into the manger, we remember the great need we sinners have for a Savior. We thank God that He sent His one and only Son to rescue us.

Journal: Pretend you are a shepherd. Write down what you think and experience as you gaze at your newborn Savior.

Pray: Father, thank You for sending baby Jesus to be my Savior. Through Him, You have saved me. Like the shepherds, You have given me Good News to tell. Help me to tell about Jesus' saving work on the cross as I do my everyday tasks. In Jesus' name I pray. Amen. R. G.

The Day after Christmas

The celebrating, gift giving, special foods, family gatherings, and Christmas worship service are over for another year. Done. Gone. It will be 364 days before you can celebrate Christmas again.

At least that's what the calendar says. But is there another way to think about Christmas?

Perhaps that first day after Jesus' birthday was the day the shepherds visited Him. They had been spending a peaceful night with their flocks when an angel appeared to tell the news of the Savior's birth. They had been "filled with great fear" (Luke 2:9). But reassured by the angel, they rushed to find what the angel said they would see.

What did they do next? Feel disappointment that they had missed the birth? Feel sorry they had to go back to their routine life caring for sheep? None of that! They immediately spread the news, telling everyone who would listen the angel's astonishing announcement. They were excited, like sports fans describing the home team's victory in the big game. In awe, they told what they had seen. And what was the result? Those who heard the shepherds passed on the news.

Christmas wasn't "over" at all! The celebrating had just begun!

Each year, it begins anew for us. Now we are ready to go and tell others the amazing Good News: Jesus, the Son of God, came to live among us and save us from our sins, that all who believe in Him may have eternal life!

Journal: What are some ways you can celebrate Christmas all year?

Pray: Jesus, give me energy, enthusiasm, and a thankful heart to celebrate Your amazing birth all year long. Amen. H. W.

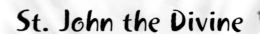

St. John the Divine

On December 27, many Christians around the world give thanks to God for St. John the Divine. God inspired this man to write the Book of Revelation.

John was an apostle of Jesus, the author of the Gospel of John and the three letters from John in the New Testament. He is thought to have been the "disciple whom Jesus loved" mentioned in John's Gospel.

In those days, people were required to worship the Roman emperor. People who refused were punished. Because John would not give up believing in Jesus Christ, he was banished to the small Greek island of Patmos. There, God had plans for John. While John was on that island, the Holy Spirit inspired him to write the Book of Revelation to encourage other Christians. Through John's writings, God declared that no power on earth would ever conquer the kingship of the true Messiah. The events described in the first part of Revelation may make us think that evil is winning the battle in this world. It may look like the devil and all his evil plans are winning the struggle, but they cannot and will not.

Instead, each baptized person who believes in Jesus is more than a conqueror. We conquerors have the assurance of God's promises to live in us and to forgive our sins, to save us from Satan, and to deliver us from evil.

Journal: What Bible verses do you remember that remind you that Jesus has already won the victory?

Pray: Dear God, I praise You for inspiring John with Your vision in the Book of Revelation. Give me power to remain faithful to You and Your promise of salvation, through Jesus. In His name I pray. Amen. D. N.

The Perfect Time

Have you ever heard a person talk about time as though it were a clock? They might say "time is ticking away." What do they mean? They mean the time is getting closer and closer to an event. Right now, the hours are "ticking away" toward New Year's Eve.

In the Old Testament, minutes, days, months, years, and generations were ticking away while God's people waited for the Savior to be born. When God decided it was the right time, He sent His Son, Jesus, to redeem the world.

The first advent was a time of waiting for Jesus' birth; the second advent is a time of waiting for Jesus to come again at the end of time. For now, God is letting minutes, hours, years, and generations tick away while His people look forward to His second coming. Jesus' birth, life, death, and resurrection were a climax in God's story of salvation, but we know there is more that will happen in God's salvation story. It isn't over yet.

We don't know when the end of time will happen. But we do know that it will happen. We do know that Jesus, who came to rescue us from sin, will come again to take us to Himself in heaven. Then sin and sadness, suffering and death will end. Then fights between friends and spats between brothers and sisters will stop. Wars and crime, disasters and sickness will be over forever. Then our heavenly life with God will be full of more riches than we can imagine.

While you are waiting for God's second coming, rejoice that He has called you in Baptism and that He strengthens you through His Word. Your minutes this year and the next can be filled with words and deeds that show others your Lord and Savior Jesus Christ.

Journal: For whom were God's people waiting the first time? When will Jesus come again? Why do we look forward to His return?

Pray: Lord of time, I praise You for Jesus, who offers me forgiveness and life forever. Fill my minutes with opportunities to serve others. Amen. K. M.

DECEMBER 29

Isaiah 1:18–19

Pure Snow

"Daddy, wake up!" urged Megan. "It snowed last night!"

Dad looked out the window. "Wow, we must have gotten a foot of snow!" he said.

"Yeah, look how perfect it is. There isn't a footprint anywhere," replied Megan.

"It won't be long before that changes."

"I know. Can I go out to play? I want to build a snowman!"

A few hours later, Megan came inside and stood with Dad at the window again. Dad said, "Megan, look at the snow now. It's all messed up with footprints. Remember how perfect it was earlier?"

"Yes, I do. It did look perfect."

"You know, that's the way God made the world. He made it perfect. When He created Adam and Eve, they were perfect. But then they sinned—they disobeyed God by eating fruit from the one tree He said not to eat from. It's like they left footprints all over creation."

"That's sad," replied Megan, pondering.

"Yes, but the good news is that God sent His Son, Jesus, to make everything perfect again," said Dad. "When He rose from the dead on Easter, it was like God put a whole new blanket of snow on the world. We are made perfect because of Jesus, our perfect Savior."

"But I know I'm not perfect, Dad. I'm selfish and mean sometimes."

"Me too. We are all sinful. But when God looks at us, all He sees is sparkling snow. With Jesus' forgiveness, it's like it snows every morning!"

Journal: Have you ever seen a fresh, perfect snowfall? How can you thank God for making your sins white as snow?

Pray: Dear God, thanks for snow. More important, thank You for forgiving my sins, making them "as white as snow" through Jesus. Amen. P. L.

New Year's Resolutions

Paul and Paula sat at the table. Each had a piece of paper and a pencil. The twins had challenged each other to see who could be first to write ten New Year's resolutions.

"Ten seconds . . . five seconds . . . two seconds . . . go!" they called out together. Ten minutes later, they both stopped writing and began to laugh. The contest ended in a tie!

When they read their resolutions aloud, they laughed some more. Several were the same! Both said they would do their homework as soon as they got home from school. Both wanted to be more cheerful when Mom or Dad asked them to do a chore. And they both wanted to try harder to get along with each other.

Making resolutions can be a good way to improve our habits and behaviors. Resolutions help us consider our actions. New Year's is a good time to think about our actions. The end of one year lets us start another, filled with opportunity to do things differently.

That's the way it is with forgiveness too. Through God's work in Baptism, we are led to repent of wrongdoing and are given the promise of God's help. We have forgiveness and are adopted as God's sons and daughters. We are changed and can live as God leads us.

Jesus has already overcome all sin and evil. In this new year, remember that you have God's help and forgiveness every day.

Journal: How do you think about the coming of a new year?

Pray: Be with me, Lord Jesus, and help me live in a way that points others to You. Help me forgive others for Your sake. Amen. D. N.

My Favorite Night

When I was a child, New Year's Eve was my favorite night of the year. It was the only time my parents let my sisters, my brothers, and me stay up until after midnight.

During the day, we took a nap so we wouldn't be too sleepy. After supper, we went to church for a service thanking God for the year that was ending and asking His blessing for the new year ahead.

After church, we went home, made popcorn, cleared the table, and began to work. Our job for the night was to put together a huge jigsaw puzzle! We worked until nearly midnight, and then we went back to church. My dad was the pastor of an old church with a high bell tower. We climbed up in the tower and at *exactly* midnight, we all pulled on the rope to ring the bell, announcing that the new year had arrived.

Today my family has happy memories of December 31, and we still like puzzles. But from our New Year's Eve celebrations, I learned an even better lesson: God is in charge of each year—the old ones *and* the new ones.

The new year reminds us that although we don't know what lies ahead, we need not worry. For the sake of Jesus, our Savior from sin, God has promised to be with His children in His Word and Sacraments every step of the way.

Journal: What are your hopes and dreams for the new year that begins tomorrow?

Pray: Thank You, dear God, for Your tender care for me and all Your children. Thank You for our Brother, Jesus, who showed us what Your love means. Amen. D. N.

> Ring around a rosie,
> A pocket full of posies.
> Ashes, ashes,
> We all fall down.

All Fall Down

Children have recited this verse for perhaps two hundred years. Who first spoke these words and exactly what they mean is not known. There are several versions that are quite different. In any case, the words in this version don't seem to be about happy thoughts and times.

"Ashes" and "all fall down" seem to mean something about burning and destruction. This may remind us of Genesis 3:19, where God says to sinful Adam, "You return to the ground, for out of it you were taken; for you are dust, and to dust you shall return."

Today is Ash Wednesday, the first day of Lent. In some worship services today, the pastor may place a smear of ash on worshipers' foreheads. This is a reminder that their bodies will someday "all fall down" to the ground in death. In the coming weeks, we will think about our sinfulness, which can lead only to the dust and ashes of death. We will think about our need to be saved from such destruction.

The amazing news is that God looks right through the ashes and dust of our sins to see us washed clean in the blood of Jesus. The apostle Paul tells us, "If the Spirit of Him who raised Jesus from the dead dwells in you, He who raised Christ Jesus from the dead will also give life to your mortal bodies through His Spirit who dwells in you" (Romans 8:11).

Journal: What difference does it make for living your life knowing that, through Jesus, you will not end up as dust and ashes?

Pray: Father, I thank You that I will not fall down in eternal death, but will be raised to eternal life because of Jesus' death and resurrection. Amen. H. W.

Palm Sunday

Danger!

There it was! Sam's favorite section of the zoo—the dangerous animals. Sam loved the crocodiles, jellyfish, and poisonous snakes. It was a thrill to be inches from something so deadly, yet safe behind a thick glass window!

"Dad," said Sam, "what would you do if the glass broke?"

"I'd grab your hand and run!" Dad replied.

We humans have a built-in survival system. When we are in danger, something inside tells us to run. If something looks harmful, we stay away.

Jesus is God, and He was human. While on earth, His hand would have jerked away from hot pans. He would have stayed away from lightning storms. He would have been cautious near dangerous animals.

Yet, when He faced the greatest danger of all, He didn't run or hide. Instead, He sat on a donkey and rode right into Jerusalem. He knew the people there hated Him. He knew His friends would abandon Him, the soldiers would beat Him, and He would hang on a cross. He knew God would forsake Him because of our sin.

Even so, Jesus chose to face danger and enter Jerusalem on Palm Sunday. He loves us that much. He was brave so He could forgive us. He died to save us from the dangers of sin and the devil. He rescued us from hell.

Through this Holy Week, may God direct us to learn more about the great love God has for us in Christ, our Savior.

Journal: Write down some ways God shows His love to you.

Pray: Jesus, You faced so much pain and suffering for my sins. Thank You for Your love and determination to save me. Bless me this Holy Week. Amen. L. H.

Watch and Pray

"Ugh! There's just too much church this week!" Addyson was struggling with her socks while getting dressed. "Why do we even have so many services during such a busy time of the year? I'm tired of it."

Kristen, Addyson's teenage sister, was reading on the couch. "That sounds a little like this devotion," Kristen mentioned while turning a page. Addyson sidled up to her big sister.

"Oh, I remember that Bible passage," Addyson said. "The disciples kept falling asleep while Jesus was praying. If only they knew what was about to happen! If I was spending the evening with Jesus, I would definitely want to stay awake."

Kristen tried not to roll her eyes and smiled. "But that's exactly what we're doing tonight. Jesus promises to be with us when we gather in His name. We're hearing God's Word. And this is Holy Thursday, when Jesus began the Lord's Supper. Jesus is present with us there too."

Addyson slipped on her shoe. "That's a good point. But I still have questions about Communion and how that works."

"Well," said Kristen as she closed her book, "it's a bit of a mystery for all of us, but I'm sure we'll learn more tonight. I'm just glad I can trust in Jesus' promises—like when He promises to be with us."

"Okay, I'll watch and pray tonight and learn more about Jesus and about Holy Thursday," said Addyson. She added with a laugh, "It would be a shame to fall asleep!"

Journal: Does spending time with Jesus sometimes seem tiring? What is helpful to remember when this happens?

Pray: Lord, I'm sorry for not always paying attention to You and for "getting sleepy" when Your Word is near. Please forgive me and give me strength to learn more about You every day. Amen. L. C.

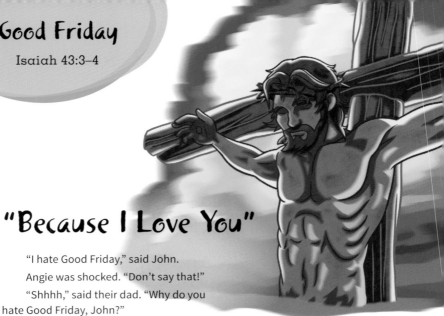

Good Friday
Isaiah 43:3–4

"Because I Love You"

"I hate Good Friday," said John.

Angie was shocked. "Don't say that!"

"Shhhh," said their dad. "Why do you hate Good Friday, John?"

"Because it always makes me feel so guilty," he answered. "We always hear about how Jesus died for us and all these terrible things happened to Him, and it's all our fault because we sinned."

His father sat next to him. Rolling up his sleeve, he said, "Do you see that scar?"

Both children looked. There was an ugly pink scar running all the way up his arm.

"Sure, Dad. You've had that as long as I can remember. Why?"

"Well, when the two of you were tiny, we had a fire in our old house. Your mom and I had to go through the fire to get you out of your beds. That's how I got this scar, and a few others too."

Angie was horrified. "You mean it's our fault? You got hurt because of us?"

Their dad answered, "I was so happy when we got you out, I didn't even think about the fire. And the scars don't bother me at all. Every time I see them, they remind me that you both are alive. Looking at them makes me happy, because I love you."

John wrinkled his brow. "So you think Jesus feels the same way about dying on the cross? And He's okay having those scars, because it means we're alive and safe?"

"I'm sure of it," their dad said.

Journal: Think of one object, picture, or letter that you keep because it reminds you of someone you love. Describe it or draw it in your journal.

Pray: Lord, I'm glad You love me. I love You. Amen. K. V.

Happy Day!

Alleluia! Christ is risen! He is risen indeed! Alleluia! Happy Easter! This is a day for exclamation points, isn't it? It's such a fun, joyful day. Different from Lent, right? Did Lent seem long to you? There are forty days in the Lenten season, but have you ever counted the days from Ash Wednesday to now? Here's an Easter surprise: there are more than forty days.

Don't worry; this isn't a math mistake. Christians view every single Sunday as a "little Easter." So in Lent, we don't count the Sundays as being part of Lent.

Do you view every Sunday as an Easter? Do you cheerfully respond "He is risen indeed!" with a voice full of exclamation points?

Probably not. We all have grumble Sundays when we grumble more than rejoice about our opportunity to worship. To be honest, there may be some Easters when we don't really show the true happiness that only God gives through His risen Son, Jesus, our Savior. We sin, even on Easter.

But Jesus died for Easter sins, Sunday sins, and all-days-of-the-week sins. He rose on Easter, giving us forgiveness and life.

Try this. Write an Easter note to yourself and place it near your church shoes, your Bible, or something else you see on Sundays. Remember that we can celebrate Easter every Sunday and every day of the year.

He is risen! Happy Easter!

Journal: What is your favorite Easter hymn? Look at the words and write about the message. (Does it have any exclamation points?)

Pray: Dear God, thank You for forgiveness and life and love. I am so happy to share the wonderful news: He is risen! Amen. L. C.

Birthday

Psalm 100:1–4

God Said So

When you were born, your family was happy and very busy. You were needy and had to be held, fed, and kept warm. Your parents gladly did this because they loved you. You were a gift from God!

Each year, we celebrate the day we were born. We thank God for giving us life. The Creator of all gave us eyes to see His beautiful world, ears to hear birds and other animals, legs to run and play, and a mind to learn. But sin affects our senses and skills. Then God supplies us with unique ways to see, hear, or get around. And no matter if we wear glasses or need a wheelchair, we are still His.

The God who made us still takes care of us. Year after year, He gives us food and clothing. Day after day, He provides shelter and spiritual blessings. Does sin also affect these gifts? It does, but then God supplies for our needs through the generosity of others. That's what happens when we are His.

God gave His only Son to be our Savior from sin. Because of Jesus, we have a new life that never ends. He also gave us His Holy Spirit in Baptism so that we have faith in our Lord and Savior Jesus Christ. He continues to provide the forgiveness of sins each day.

Being "His" means more than we can imagine. So when you celebrate your birthday, "give thanks to Him; bless His name!" (Psalm 100:4).

Journal: With your parents' help, plan to celebrate your Baptism birthday. Jot down some ideas in your journal.

Pray: Dear God, thank You that I am Yours and You are mine. Thank You for life now and forever. Thank You for all Your goodness and mercy. In Jesus' name I pray. Amen. C. O.

Happy Birthday!

Today was not a good day, Kalisha thought as she got off the bus. Jasmine is mad at me, I goofed on the math test, and I fell down in gym. Kalisha kept thinking about her day as she trudged up the driveway.

She walked into her house, hung up her jacket, and plopped her backpack onto the floor. Then she smelled something delicious—**chocolate cake!**

Kalisha followed her nose to the kitchen. Whoa! What was this? There was a beautiful chocolate birthday cake with pink icing and one big candle. Did I forget somebody's birthday? she wondered.

"Happy birthday, Kalisha," Mom said.

"Thanks, but I think you're mixed up," Kalisha said. "We already celebrated my birthday a month ago."

Mom laughed. "My memory isn't that bad," she said. "Last month we celebrated when you became a part of the Jackson family. Today we're celebrating the day you became a part of God's family. This is your Baptism birthday."

Kalisha asked, "Is it really that important?"

"It's the most important day in your life," Mom said. "It's the day you became God's child. As God's child, your sins are forgiven through Jesus' death. Someday, you will go to heaven and live forever with Jesus and all believers. It is definitely a day worth celebrating."

"Remembering my Baptism makes even a bad day seem good," Kalisha said.

"You got it, girl," Mom said as she added the final touches.

Journal: Ask your parents about your Baptism. Find out if there are pictures of the day or maybe a baptismal candle. Write about why your Baptism is so important.

Pray: Dear God, thank You for making me Your child. As I splash with water, remind me of Your Baptism blessings: forgiveness, life, and salvation. In Jesus' name I pray. Amen. J. D.

Contributors

Aaron Grube

Angie Bierlein Watt

Annette Schumacher

Ashley Bayless

Beverly J. Soyk

Bret Taylor

Carol Albrecht

Carolyn C. Sims

Carrie Kober

Cheryl Ehlers

Cheryl Honoree

Christine Lawton

Christine Ross

Christine Weerts

Craig Otto

Cynthia Schilf

Dale Pritchard

Dawn Napier

Deanne Schussler

Dennis Goff

Diane Grebing

Donna Streufert

Doreen Moyo

Doris Schuchard

Dot Nuechterlein

Edward Grube

Eileen Ritter

Elizabeth Friedrich

Emily Barz

Eunice Graham

Gail Marsh

Gail Pawlitz

Glenda Schrock

Gretchen Gebhardt

Hal Whelply

Heath Lewis

Jacqueline Loontjer

James Gimbel

James Hahn

Jane Heitman

Jasmine Duerr

Jeanette Dall

Jeanne Dicke

Jennifer AlLee

Joel Hoffschneider

Jonathan Schkade

Judy Williams

Julie Hadler

Julie Riddle

Julie Stiegemeyer

Kari Vo

Karin Semler

Kathy Johnson

Kim D. Marxhausen

Kristin Genther

Kristine Moulds

Lacy Marsh

Lawrence Eatherton

Lindsey Eggold

Lisa M. Clark

Lisa Ellwein

Lisa Hahn

Lonie Eatherton

Loreene Bell

Lori Doyle

Malinda Walz

Mary A. Krallmann

Mary Jane Gruett

Michael Parris

Michele Pickel

Michelle Bauman

Nicole Dreyer

Pat List

Philip Lang

Rebecca Spitzack

Renee Gibbs

Rosie Adle

Ruth Geisler

Ruth Maschke

Scott Rauch

Stephen Sandfort

Stephenie Hovland

Steven Teske

Sue Schulz

Susan Hammand

Susan Voss

Suzanne Ramsey

Tim Weseman

Trevor Sutton

Valerie Schultz